Terrys of Cork

1180-1644

Merchant Gentry

with selected material on descendants

Terrys of Cork 1180-1644 Merchant Gentry

with selected material on descendants

Kevin Terry

Phillimore

Alanna L. Terry

1983-1998

a beautiful daughter

2013

Published by
PHILLIMORE & CO. LTD
Andover, Hampshire, England
www.phillimore.co.uk

ISBN 978-1-86077-746-2 (Limp Edition)
ISBN 978-1-86077-748-6 (Cased Edition)

Contents

List of Illustrations

Acknowledgements

Thanks to the following for permission to use images: National Archives, Kew, 'Oath of the citizens of Cork, 1498'; Linda Blicher Brestgaard, Denmark, Tomas Terry Theatre; Rothe House and Garden, Kilkenny, Rothe House; The State Library, New South Wales, Roger Therry; Dr Kenneth Nicholls for Figs. 1.4 and 4.1; Gerry Horan O.S.A., for Fig. 7.4; John Williams for Fig. 10.1. Thanks to Damien Burke, Irish Jesuit Archives for providing information on Fr Francis Tyrry, S.J. Other acknowledgements are provided in the text. I wish to thank Deirdre, Aoife, and Kevin, my wife, daughter and son, for assisting me with French and Spanish translations and with genealogical charts. Others who have provided useful information are noted in the footnotes. To these and the many others who provided information, assistance and encouragement, I give my wholehearted thanks.

Preface

It must have been in the early days of national school at the age of four or five that I became aware of, and thought about, different surnames. Mine was Terry. Why was it not Murphy or Barry or O'Connell or some other such surname? Terry was not a common surname, it was different.

Forty years later, while working with Limerick Corporation, and living in Limerick, I learned of some historical connections that the Terrys had with Limerick. This was new to me, as I was generally aware of the association of Terrys with Cork and particularly the City of Cork in an historical sense. Who were these Limerick Terrys? This, I believe, is what aroused my interest in the family history of the Terrys.

For more years than I care to recollect, I have amassed much data on Terrys from various sources. In 2005, I wrote, with selected chapters by others, a book on the Terrys of Cork from 1600 to 2000. This book is a companion to that publication and covers the period 1180-1644. There is some overlap between both. Selected material on descendants is provided. Where there is conflicting information in the 2005 publication and this book, take it that this text has the correct information. In this text, I have taken the opportunity to correct known errors from the 2005 publication.

Throughout the book, several variations of the spelling of the surname Terry are used. I have used the form of spelling as I found it in the various references and documents. The most common variations are, apart from the present-day standard form of spelling: Therry, Tirry and Tyrry.

Any errors in the book are unintentional.

Introduction

The Cork merchant family, the subject matter of this book, is Terry. The surname Terry is not a very common name in Ireland; apart from Waterford, its highest incidence is in Cork. It is of Norman origin and, in former times, Terry families played a significant part in the affairs of Cork City. Of all the urban settlements in Ireland, it was only in Cork that Terrys played a significant part in civic affairs. The period covered is medieval and early modern times, from the arrival to Ireland of the Anglo-Normans in 1169 to the expulsion of the Irish from Cork City in 1644. There are also a number of chapters following this period on descendants. The purpose of this part of the book is to cover additional information to that provided in the 2005 publication. In this regard, particular reference will be given to the settlement patterns of Terrys in Cork, between 1644 and 1900.

Ch. 1 of the book deals with the background, context and early period while Ch. 2 covers aspects of settlement of a hereditary clerical family in the medieval period.

Chapters 3 to 7 inclusive cover a period from 1420 to 1644. This time period saw significant change in the outcome of English involvement in Ireland. This varied from a near collapse of English rule in Ireland, at the early stage, to its substantial recovery, and a very difficult situation for the Gaelic and 'Old English', in 1644.

While Cork City was ruled initially by the original Anglo-Norman settlers, and the surrounding countryside by various Anglo-Norman lords, it was cut off for much of the time from Dublin and London. The city was an outpost of the King of England, but largely self-administered. It was in this setting that the Terrys and about a dozen other families, predominantly of Anglo-Norman descent, worked and prospered. Chapters 3 to 7 of this book look at how the Terrys, as merchant gentry, gained this position of prominence, how they maintained it and ultimately how they lost it. Their place and role is examined with reference to social, economic, religious and civic perspectives. In the context of a social perspective, their place in Cork, their status, and the families they married into is examined and an approximation of the number of Terry families is provided. Some evidence of female Terry participation as educators and tutors is extant. In terms of the economic role they played, their role as merchants and traders is examined.

There is also evidence of their involvement in finance, through the provision of mortgages and indirectly in the minting of money. They were landlords in their own right, in both urban and rural Cork, and the settlement pattern of their land holdings is examined. Terrys played a significant religious role, albeit a changing one, and this is reviewed. Finally, it is in their civil role, predominantly in the local context of Cork City, that their significance, as a family grouping, is evidenced. There were also, I will demonstrate, 'the King's men'.

Much information, perhaps of a repetitive nature, is provided on Terrys in this period. This is taken from both primary and secondary sources. The primary sources available include Terry deeds, spanning the entire period of the subject of this book, Terry wills, from the 15th century on, the results of various surveys carried out in the 17th century. In addition, calendars of state and papal records provided a useful source of information. To put this information into context, various local histories of Cork are used. For a wider perspective, national and European histories, for the period, are used. Military and shipping records provided useful relevant information. Compiling and making sense of some of the local material was somewhat tedious, because of the use of archaic placenames and much of the information being written in Latin. However, setting it down, I consider beneficial, because it was drawn from diverse sources, and because of the context in which I examined the information, I was able to correct some obvious misinterpretations, or mistakes, that otherwise would have gone unnoticed.

Ch. 3 covers the initial steps to urban élite, from the initial period, about 1420, when one Philip Terry was bailiff for the city, and a very limited role by the Terrys in the city, to one where they had a strong foothold by the end of the century.

Ch. 4 examines the geographical and historical context of Tudor Cork, and the following chapter examines Terrys as merchant gentry in the same period. This is done by examining their role from social, economic, political and religious perspectives.

Ch. 6 examines the geographical and historical context of Cork City from 1600-44. Ch. 7, titled 'the nation of the Terries', covers the same period. In this period the Terrys were most influential, but it was also on the political and religious fronts a very turbulent period. The position of the 'Old English', the constitutional struggle, and the outbreak of civil war in county Cork, are examined. Again the role and position of Terrys are examined, up to the period when the Catholics were thrown out of Cork City and the civil authority in the city was abolished.

Following this and after the Cromwellian Plantation, their influence and numbers were greatly reduced. Some families continued in Cork, but it would seem with less wealth and status. Others immigrated to the continent of Europe, to such countries as France and Spain, and later further afield. Selected material on settlement patterns from 1644 is covered in the remainder of the book. Linkages between Terry families in the more recent period with those of four hundred years ago and earlier are established. Some attention is focused on the settlement of Terrys in other countries. This is done when the ancestors originated in Cork.

Chapters, 8 to 11 inclusive cover: Confiscation and Restoration, Terrys in the period of the Penal Laws, the 19th century and Terrys in 1900.

The next chapters of the book cover Terrys of Cork origin, who settled in other countries – France, Spain, Latin America, England, Australia and North America.

The French, Spanish and Latin American immigrants were from the 17th century onwards, and these were interconnected. Those that went to England, Australia and North America were predominantly from the 19th century onwards. These were from a more diverse range of Terry families.

The final chapter deals with conclusions from the examination undertaken in the book.

I

Background, Context and Early Period

In this chapter some background information and context for the subject matter of this book is provided. Firstly, the origin of the surname Terry in Cork is examined. Some information on the establishment and early period of an Anglo-Norman Colony is then provided under four headings,

- rural and urban settlement,
- the pattern of town organisation,
- town and country gentry, and
- endowments to and land ownership of church establishments

Finally, before examining the settlement pattern of Terrys in Cork, in the 14th century, an overview of the contraction of the Anglo-Norman colony in a local historical context is provided.

Origin of the Surname Terry in Cork

Before looking at the Terry surname in Cork, I will briefly consider the origin of Irish surnames. This information is taken from *Irish Pedigrees or The Origin and Stem of the Irish Nation* by John O'Hart.[1]

In ancient times there were no surnames. In order, however, to preserve more correctly the history and genealogy of the different tribes, the monarch Brian Boru, who ascended the throne A.D. 1001, made an ordinance that every family and clan in Ireland should adopt a particular surname. O'Hart states that, according to Connellan, some of the Danish settlers in Ireland took Irish surnames, and that the Goulds, Coppingers, Skiddys, Terrys and Trants in Cork were among these. O'Hart later goes on to state that the Coppinger, Goulds, Galways, Skiddys, and Terrys (considered by O'Brien and others to be of Danish descent) were, in former times, very numerous and powerful families in Cork.

In a directory of surnames, by Hanks and Hodges, the Terry surname is considered as follows:[2]

1. English: from the common Norman personal name, T(h)erry (OF Thierri), composed of the Gmc elements **þeudo* – people, race + *ric* power. Theodoric was the name of the Ostrogothic leader (*c*.454-526) who invaded Italy in 488 and established his capital at Ravenna in 493. His name was often taken as a derivative of Greek *Theodores*

(see Theodore). Hodgkin gives a slightly different explanation.[3] This (Theodoric, born 454) form of the name became current so early; it is referred to in the letters of Sidonius and the annals of Prosper. The true form of the name, which is fairly represented by the Theuderichus of the Byzantine historians, is Thiuda/reiks, and signifies 'the people/ruler'.

2. Irish: Anglicised form of Gael. *MacToirdhealbhaigh*; see McTerrelly and Curley.
3. Provençal: Occupational name for a potter, from OProv *terrin* earthenware vase (a dim of *terre* earth, L *terra*).

Reaney, in the *Origin of English Surnames*, indicates that, 'Terry, a common name both on the Continent and in England', is of French origin, OG *Theudoric*, OFr *Thierri, Terri.* Many of the ME bearers of this name were Flemish or German merchants, frequently described as *Teutonicus, Alemannus,* or *Flandrensis.*'[4]

MacLysaght states that 'Terry has been a notable name in the county and city of Cork since the 13th century.'[5]

The normal form of Terry in Irish was Tuiridh, this being a phonetic rendering of the Anglo-Norman Terri.[6]

O'Hart in the second edition of his *Irish Pedigrees*, published in 1880, in dealing with the Kinsela family refers to MacTorleice, son of Tirlach. The former is anglicised as MacTirlogh, MacTerence, MacTerry, and Terrie.

What then of the question, 'Are the Terrys of Cork of Danish descent?' In correspondence I had with the Centre for Viking and Medieval Studies, of the University of Oslo, and with the Institut for Navneforskning of Copenhagen, in 1999, it emerged that the surname Terry when occurring in the British Isles is generally considered to be a name introduced by the Normans, Old French *Thierri,* going back to Continental Germanic *Theodoric*. James Terry, Athlone Herald to King James II, states that Tyrry was so named by Theodorus, a certain noble German. A son of Tyrry, named William, accompanied William the Conqueror to England in 1067.[7]

O' Connell, in her book *The Last Colonel of The Irish Brigade*, states that the Terrys, or Therrys, of Castle Terry (North Cork), are of French origin, and claim descent from Thierri II, King of Orleans, Burgundy, and Metz (587-613).[8] His great-grand uncle was Theodoric I, whom Hodgkin states was probably named after Theodoric (454-526), the Ostrogothic leader, referred to earlier. Bryan O' Connor's Terry Genealogy of 1753 begins with Thierry the first King of France. This must be Theodoric I. O'Connor, further expanding on the Terry genealogy, moves to Hastings and the Tyrrells in Ireland.[9] O' Connor considered that the Terrys of Cork descended from the Tyrells of Castleknock. The Irish branch of this family established itself in Cork at an early period.

In Wagner's *Pedigree and Progress*, it is stated that the family of Fitz Ailwin, which gave London its first Mayor in 1192, was of English origin, descending, probably, from Ailwin Horne, a thane of Edward the Confessor.[10] This book goes on to state that a Professor Douglas established the fact that a probable member of this family (and certainly an Englishman), Thierry of Barrow, son of Deorman, married (*c.*1140) a Norman lady, Maud, who was akin to Earl Gilbert Strongbow of the great Norman family of Clare, descended from the Dukes of Normandy. Other evidence suggests that it was Deorman's great-grandson Theoderic, who married Matilda, a relation of the first Earl of Pembroke.[11] Thierry's daughter married a William Blemund, and of two children one was called Thierri.

Nightingale discusses the origin of the name Theoderic, and states that it was probably a German name, unusual in England, and its most conspicuous holder at the time of Domesday Book was the goldsmith of Edward the Confessor to whom numismatists trace the German influence in his later coinage and seal. Theoderic the goldsmith continued to hold land, after the Conquest, as one of the King's ministri.[12] Nightingale shows that this family were moneyers over a number of generations and were royal servants. It seems that this family was of Anglo-Saxon descent.

Tierry, Count of Flanders came with his army or sent an army to England in 1066 to help William the Conqueror to defeat the English.[13]

Fig. 1.1 *Map of Ireland.*

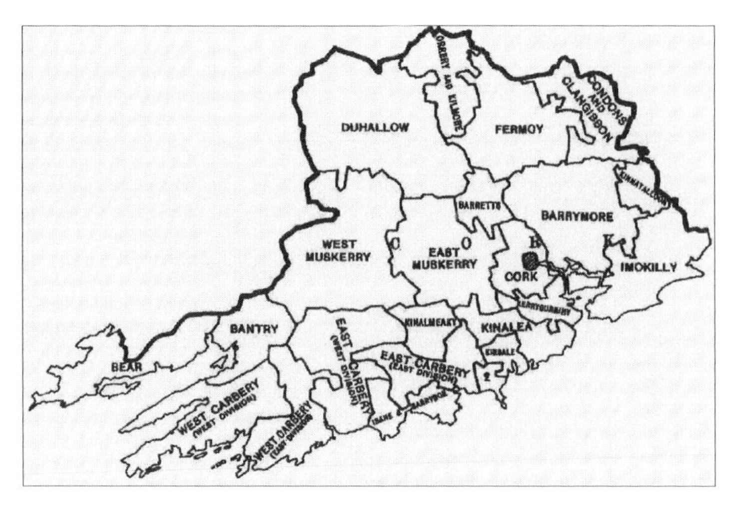

Fig. 1.2 *Baronies of Cork. (Source: O.S.I., Ireland.)*

A distribution of the Terry surname in England from data in the 1891 census indicates the highest occurrence, at 1475, in Kent.

In Evelyn Bolster's *History of the Diocese of Cork*, a Brother Tierri is a witness to a charter relating to Cork from the Register of the Abbey of St Thomas.[14] A Brother Thericus is a witness on a grant of land in Cork to the Church of St Nicholas, Exeter. In looking at the other witnesses named in these grants, it would seem that Brother Tierri and Brother Thericus are one and the same person. The period of these grants was 1172-82. Brother Tierri, also referred to as Canon Tierri, was a witness to several grants in Cork and, where he is, it is stated that 'this is the acquisition of Brother Tierri'. In the genealogy of 1690, earlier referred to, James Terry states that a descendant of William, son of Tyrry, named John, arrived in Ireland in 1170 with Robert Fitz Stephen, and established himself in Cork.

Incidence and Distribution of Terrys in Ireland

The primary focus of this book is on those Terrys who resided in Cork over a 500- year period from 1177 to 1644. In addition, selected material on descendants of these Terrys in Cork, Ireland and the rest of the world from 1644 to 2000 is provided. Fig. 1.1 is a map of Ireland, showing the counties of Ireland which are mentioned throughout the book. Cork is the biggest county and is located in the southern part of the island. The baronies of Cork are shown in Fig. 1.2.

One of the baronies where the Terrys had a number of strongholds in medieval times was Barrymore. Following the Norman Invasion, when the De Barrys had secured a firm grip on the land, the tenure of land underwent a change in the district around Barryscourt Castle.[15] The old tribal system was swept away and Lord Barry granted the different ploughlands to landlords, mostly of Norman stock: Terrys, Newtons, Galways, De Clavilles, Hodnetts, and minor branches of the Barry family. These landlords collected rents from their Irish tenants and paid a head rent to Lord Barry.

At an early date the Terrys held land at Old Abbey in the manor of Inishkenny, south of Ballincollig.[16]

In 1249, a James Tyrrye obtained land and property in the City from John Wynchedon.[17]

Terry Family Arms

This book does not specifically look at heraldry. The arms generally associated with the Terrys of Cork are those shown in Fig. 1.3.

Arms: On a blue field a silver bar between three gold crosses above which is a gold bar with a red half-lion.

Crest: The top half of a red lion holding a gold shield or a shield with a cross. These are the arms of the Terrys or Tyrrys of Baghyoghis, County Cork.[18] A variation is the top half of a red lion holding a shield with a blue human face ornamented and rimmed in gold. These are the arms of the Terrys of Cork and Spain.[19]

The King of Arms of all Ireland certified, in 1789, that these arms were the property of Don Ramon Terry of Spain, descended from William Terry of Co. Cork. On a visit to the Terry Bodega in El Puerto de Santa Maria, Andalusia, in 2001, I saw this coat of arms on a wine barrel of one Guillermo Terry, dated 1748, with the following slight change; instead of the human face within the shield of the crest, was a cross.

Fig. 1.3 *Coat of Arms: Ramon Terry, Malaga (Source: Genealogical Office, National Library of Ireland)*

In a note in the *Cork Historical and Archaeological Journal* in 1903, J. F. Fuller refers to these arms and states that on the will of one James Terry, of Essex, there is a seal quite perfect, and corresponding to these arms. James Terry mentions his nephew of Ballindangin, near Mitchelstown, and Fuller states that two facts seem plain; namely, the connection between the English and Irish branches, and that the family was an Essex one.

The will of David Tyrry Fitz Edmonde, 1570, gives an inventory of his goods, these including 'a good standing cupp duble gilte, a pice and a tastor marked under David's mark and armes'.

There is a footnote in the *Topographer and Genealogist*, 1858, edited by Richard Caulfield, referring to a seal of Alderman Dominick Terrye, in 1633. The shield has a chevron between three escallops, and above the shield 'HM'. This does not necessarily mean that these were Terry arms, as it was not unusual then to seal with maternal arms.

The Establishment and Early Period of an Anglo-Norman Colony

In terms of my understanding of the efforts of the 'Anglo-Normans' in Cork, to establish a viable colony, from the time of their arrival to the beginning of the 14th century, David Carpenter's book, *The Struggle for Mastery*, which deals with the history of Britain between 1066 and 1284, encapsulates many of the facets I wish to cover in this and subsequent chapters.[20] Some of the initial questions to ask, in the context of the arrival of Terrys, as part of the Anglo-Normans, to Ireland, is when did the they come, in what capacity, and to where. In examining how the Terrys fitted in at an early stage it is useful to examine the context in terms of:

- rural and urban settlement
- pattern of town organisation
- town and country gentry
- endowments to and land ownership of church establishments

RURAL AND URBAN SETTLEMENT

While the evidence for the first period of the Norman colony in Ireland is limited, with the reign of Edward I records become comparatively abundant, and they make it plain that, seen in its proper perspective, the Norman settlement of Ireland was no mere military occupation supported by the settlement of English and French burgesses in a few towns, but a part of that great movement of peasant colonisation which dominates so much of the economic history of Europe from the 11th to the 14th centuries, arising out of what can only have been a spontaneous growth of population, and slackening as that growth slackens with the troubles of the 14th century.[21] By the end of the 13th century, in many areas settlers of English descent formed at least half the population, and sometimes considerably more. In parts of Cork, as well as in other counties, there had been a relatively heavy immigration.[22]

The main innovation that the Anglo-Normans brought to Ireland was the English variety of feudalism including the medieval estate or manorial system.[23] In Ireland the settlement pattern of the manor was more dispersed than was the case in England. The manorial system was so effective that a surplus of food was created, which made possible the foundation of many new towns.

John Terry, junior, brought a case against John Terry, senior, of Olethan, where he was disposed of a freehold interest in land. Rob, Patric and Hugh son of John are mentioned in the writ. In the same Calendar, a Ric Terry occurs in 1297, and an Edm Terry occurs as a recognitor, in Cork, in connection with Barrys and land at Culdargan and Cullyrther. Desiderata (Désirée), widow of John Tyrry, claimed her dower in two carucates in Inchecolyn (Ballintirry) against Richard Fitz Richard de Barry in a plea of 27 Edward I. [24] In an Inquisition on the extent of the land holding of Thomas de Clare, in the vill of Youghal, in 1288, one Philip Tyrry is mentioned.[25] One Philip fitz William had five carucates of land, about 600 acres, in Ardagh parish, as a free tenant.[26] In the same Roll, the name Roger le Tery occurs. The name John Terry of Clonteyd also occurs in this Roll, where he made a payment for robbery and other trespasses.[27] From Terry deeds in the Sarsfield papers, a John Terry son of Roger, son of William, son of William, son of Maurice, resided near Cork City in the 13th century.[28]

THE PATTERN OF TOWN ORGANISATION

The most important privilege, secured by towns, and also the hardest to get, was that of accounting directly to the exchequer for the town's farm, the annual payment due to the king. This was nearly always linked to the right to choose the official who would do the accounting. In effect this emancipated the town from the authority of the sheriff and secured self-government under the king.[29]

The charter of Henry III, in 1241-2, granted these and other extensive privileges to the city of Cork.[30] This charter is fairly comprehensive in the amount of freedom conferred on the city. In fact, the citizens possessed extensive privileges in the administration of justice, not enjoyed today by any of our modern cities. Overall, the community was in a very independent position, enjoying an existence comparable in many ways with that of the Italian Republics. They were far less restrictive than the boroughs of England whose activities were often circumvented by the proximity of the central authority. The reason is not hard to find. For hundreds of years afterwards, they were used as the means for extending and maintaining the influence of the conquerors.[31]

From Carpenter's chapter on 'Structures and Society', how towns were organised is described.[32]

The privileges of self-government did not come cheap and townsmen had banded together to buy them. Such associations had various names, and the great law book *Glanvill* (*c.*1189) treated the two most usual, 'commune' and 'gild merchant', as virtually interchangeable. Some of the town charters were actually granted to the 'gild merchant', or gave the townsmen the right to form one. It was only the members of these associations, however described, who enjoyed the privileges conferred in the charters, and were technically burgesses. Their position was exclusive. 'Nobody not a member of the gild shall carry out their trade in the towns,' ran Henry II's charter to Oxford. There was no room here for labourers, artisans (including in some towns weavers), and women. Moreover, although all householders probably qualified as burgesses, when it came to government a series of complex checks and balances usually kept control in the hands of a wealth élite, something that became very clear from a study of the rulers of York and Newcastle upon Tyne in the 13th century.

In London, 70 per cent of the aldermen who held office before 1263 belonged to 16 interrelated families, most of them established in London since the early 12th century. The wealth of London's élite, like that of York and Newcastle upon Tyne, came from property, from trade, and from luxury crafts, notably goldsmithing. In London exporting wool and importing wine were fundamental activities.

The rulers of London, York and Newcastle upon Tyne were typical among urban élites in acquiring property in the country as well as the town. It was often from the country that their forebears had come.[33]

There is extensive evidence of Terrys in London and Kent in the 12th century.[34] Terrys traded for several centuries in or around Cheapside, London. They exhibited the characteristic of having property in the countryside as well.

Some early references to Terrys in Ireland are from a roll of the citizens of Dublin, possibly belonging to the first generation of the conquest, which has two Terrys, out of a total of some 1,600 names, Terri de Rettour and Rogerus filius terri.[35] The Dublin Guild Merchants of 1256-7 contain the names: Terricus de nouo foro and Terricus Pyivn.[36] The 1,600 names referred to include goldsmiths, tailors, shoemakers, weavers, mercers, cordwainers, tanners, saddlers, loriners, smiths, carpenters, masons, fishermen, bakers, vintners, butchers, and millers.[37] This list contains at least 27 people from London and 11 people from Cork.

Carpenter's description of how some English towns were initially established and developed could equally apply to Cork. In the city of Cork, Terrys became one of the leading merchant gentry families, the only urban settlement in Ireland where they achieved this status. In the context of their role in Cork, when did they arrive and what status did they have in the period after their arrival?

Finally, in the context of this book, a brief explanation on the formation of parishes, as administrative boundaries, is provided. Although no detailed map evidence survives from the Middle Ages, there are many medieval inquisitions and deeds, which clearly show that villages, open fields and scattered strip holdings were of fundamental importance in the rural economy. It is clear that it was the Normans who first undertook the task of organising the countryside into parishes, and in the south and east of the country there is a close correspondence between the extent of secular manors and the new parochial boundaries. These medieval parishes have evolved, often through many amalgamations, into the present-day civil parishes and may correspond closely with the ecclesiastical parishes of the Church of Ireland. The contemporary outlines of Roman Catholic parishes, however, derive from an 18th-century reorganisation and diverge appreciably from the medieval patterns. The parishes are smaller divisions within the City and the Baronies. These can cross over the city or barony boundary.

Town and Country Gentry

The political role of the country gentry in the 1260s, and especially of the knights who were its leaders, was as striking as that of London. Knights fought in armies, held local office as sheriffs, and at the national level appeared as representatives of the shires in parliament. The power of gentry families derived in varying degrees from their property, military prowess, and tenure of local office. They might be independent of great lords or profit from their service. Many such families sustained their power over generations. Central to the survival and success of these families was the way their principal properties were kept intact down the generations.[38] Carpenter expands on this.

The structure of the family and the way it handled property were fundamental to the working of society. We have already discussed the view that the Norman Conquest accelerated the transition from clan to lineage, from the extended to the dynastic family, so that property, instead of being divided widely on death, descended through primogeniture – that is, to the eldest son. Certainly such was the case with the chief properties of large numbers of families in the 12th and 13th centuries. The sense of lineage thus created was often emphasised by the use of the same selection of first names and the adoption of a surname either derived from an ancestor, as with the fitz Ellises, or from a place, usually the family's principal property.[39]

While generally stable, changes were occurring in the structure of society in significant ways. Families like the fitz Ellises were part of what historians often called 'the gentry', that group of men found in each county who were lords of one or a few main properties and were active in local affairs.[40] The thegns were the gentry of late Anglo-Saxon England and the county knights the gentry of the early 13th century. In the course of this century, however, the nature of knighthood altered radically, laying the foundations for the gentry of the later Middle Ages, one stratified into knights, esquires and gentlemen. At the same time the gentry were becoming involved far more intensively than before in litigation and local government, and were also operating within changing frameworks of magnate power.[41] The gentry began to staff the juries on which the new common law procedures depended, monopolised the old office of the sheriff, and filled the plethora of new offices called into being by royal government, acting as coroners, escheators, keepers of the peace, assessors and collectors of taxation, justices of assize and gaol delivery, and so on.[42] Terrys in Cork very much fitted into this category in the 16th and 17th centuries. But what of their role following the establishment of an Anglo-Norman colony in Cork? One Stephen de Turri was appointed one of the king's bailiffs in Ireland in 1228.[43] For a number of years from 1293 on, Nicholas Terry was collector in Kilkenny.[44] A William Tyrry is mentioned in a Roll of receipt, in 1285, in connection with a pledge in Waterford.[45] Fourteen years later, William, son of Philip, and Philip Tyrry gave pledges in connection with land in Waterford.[46]

In the later Middle Ages the gentry largely monopolised local office. Carpenter states that the extent to which they achieved 'self-government at the king's command' depended on the local power of the great lords.[47] In some regions throughout the medieval period – regions which varied according to the rise and fall of families and the changing structures of great estates – that power was limited, and the gentry could make their own political decisions and create their own local order or chaos. Yet there were equally times and places where great lords were dominant. Alongside the ties of families and neighbourhood, the power of lordship was often fundamental to the workings of local society.

An aspect of lord/tenant relationship, in the 13th century was where great lords sought particularly to retain men whom the king appointed to local office, thus nullifying the threat to themselves implicit in such employment.[48]

Endowments to and Land Ownership of Church Establishments

A brother Tierri is associated with a number of early charters relating to Cork, where endowments where made by the early Anglo-Normans in Ireland to church establishments.[49] These grants are fully dealt with in the next chapter.

In relation to local churches, often it was the local lord who built and endowed the church around which the parish was formed. He appointed the cleric, the rector, who ruled it. As a result the right of appointment (the advowson) was in diverse hands: king, baron, knight, bishop or monastery, the last because it was with advowsons that many monasteries were endowed.[50] A striking feature of the Irish clergy in the latter Middle Ages was the strongly hereditary character of the profession and this can be paralleled from other outlying parts of Europe.[51] The custom of hereditary succession – understanding the term to mean succession by election within the family, in the Irish manner, and not primogeniture succession from father to son – and a married clergy had of course been two of the 'abuses' of the Irish church most strongly attacked by the 12th-century reformers.

A connection between London and Cork, around 1200, is evidenced from the presence of the bishop of Cork at Westminster, in 1203, for the profession of obedience of the bishop-elect of St David's.[52]

In 1344, one Nicholas Tyrry, of the diocese of Cloyne, a student for 13 years in civil and canon law, was granted a canonry of Dublin with a reservation of a prebend.[53]

LOCAL HISTORICAL CONTEXT IN THE 14TH CENTURY

In the year 1300, the western half of County Cork was ruled by various MacCarthy princes and their clients, with the remainder of the county ruled by an efficient county administration, conforming to the normal practice of England itself and responsible to the administration in Dublin and in the last resort to the king of England himself.[54] This administration was a royal one, depending on the king's officials and not on local lords. While the latter enjoyed massive resources in land and retainers, and in the ever-multiplying members of their lineages,

Fig. 1.4 *Cantreds of part of Co. Cork, c.1300. (Courtesy: Dr Kenneth Nicholls.)*

their political and judicial authority was, in strict legal theory, minimal if non-existent. By European standards, the centralisation of authority and justice, which to those historians reared in the English tradition seems the normal system, was quite exceptional.[55]

This section outlines the contraction of the Anglo-Norman colony and examines, to the extent that records are available, the settlement pattern of Terrys in this period. Fig. 1.4 shows the cantreds of Cork County, *c.*1300, where there is evidence of Terry family settlement.[56] This Figure shows Barry's cantred of O Lethan encompassing Shandon and adjoining Cork City on its south-western boundary. The influence of the Barry family, in this period, in County Cork, can be gleaned from the fact that they were the frequent holders of the office of sheriff in the county in the 14th century. They held this office more frequently than any other family, including the Fitzgerald and Roche families. In the 15th century, the Barrys played the dominant role. For 44 years for which records exist, for this century, they held the office for 35 of these.[57] Their proximity to Cork City and the inner harbour must be an indicator of some influence in the affairs of the city in this period. However, a different grouping, of merchants and traders, dominated the affairs of the city. There were no Barry mayors of the city.

Contraction of the Anglo-Norman Colony

The 14th century saw a reverse in the prosperity that Cork City enjoyed in the 13th century. In 1315-7 a series of disastrous harvests and consequent famine heralded the onset of climatic change with cooler, cloudier and wetter conditions becoming general for the remainder of the Middle Ages. That encouraged a shift from intensive grain cultivation under the manorial system towards less intensive pastoral farming. Yet climate change was simply one of a series of challenges, which threatened the very survival of the English colony in and around Cork in the 14th century. Worsening political instability exacerbated enormously the natural catastrophes visited upon the region.[58] There is little documentary evidence for the trades and crafts which flourished in Cork in this period, but it seems likely that they were similar to those which were found in other Irish and European cities of the same period. The documentary evidence for Cork contains many references to mills, both within and without the walls of Cork; many of these mills were associated with ecclesiastical foundations. As a port city, the main imports would have been wine, cloth and spices, while the principal exports would have been wool, grain, beer and other agricultural produce from the countryside surrounding the city.

The prosperity of the city continued to decline during the Gaelic and Gaelicised Anglo-Norman resurgence of the mid-14th century and Cork requested exemptions from its annual fee farm payment to the Crown during this period.[59] This view is in contrast to the more up-beat description of commerce in Cork around this time by Green.[60] The city suffered a devastating blow with the arrival of the Black Death in 1349. It is likely that, of its 2,000 inhabitants, between 25 per cent and 35 per cent perished in the Black Death. It was further impoverished by the need to defend itself from attack by the native population outside the city and was severely damaged by a serious fire in or around 1354.

This period of relative decline in the fortunes of the city continued well into the 15th century. Archaeological investigations have also offered evidence of Cork's difficulties at this time. Though there is evidence of voluminous pottery imports from many quarters until the mid-14th century, the imports ceased from about 1350 on. The gap in the pottery record between 1350 and 1450 is a silent testimony to the decline in population, decrease in demand and disruption in trade that happened in the wake of the plague.[61]

The history of the English lordship of Ireland in the 14th century was one of increasing fragmentation, both political and economic. This, however, was accompanied by major changes in the structure of the Anglo-Irish nobility and landholding as lesser lords, in Munster primarily the earls of Desmond and Ormond, made determined efforts to expand their territories and to promote themselves to the first rank.[62] Power passed more and more from royal to seigniorial hands.

The charter granted to Cork City in 1318 strikingly illustrates the degree of disruption and upheaval, which the colony was already experiencing by the early 14th century. It provided that normally on election, the mayor of Cork was to be permitted to take his oath of office before his predecessor rather than in the exchequer in Dublin. The king allowed this because of the risk to the security of the mayor in travelling to Dublin.[63]

It would appear therefore, that as the 14th century progressed, the political vacuum created by the retreat of royal authority in Ireland was filled for the most part by the great territorial magnates whose role increasingly changed from one of destabilising the polity of the Irish lordship to that of constituting in their own regions new centres of power and stability.[64] Some landowners – such as the Tirrys and Sarsfields from Barrymore, the Meades from Kerrycurrihy, the Roches of Dunderrow near Kinsale, and the Whites of Killaminoge near Innishannon – while retaining ownership of their estates went to live within the city walls to escape the onerous exactions imposed by the greater lords and the depredations of the swarms of men of war who roamed the countryside.[65] The effect of the decline of royal authority can be seen in the decline of royal revenue, from about £6,000 in 1300, to less than £1,000 towards the end of the century.[66]

The English Crown was very anxious to support Cork as a bastion of English authority in southern Ireland. To help alleviate the financial straits which Cork's corporation found itself in with the onset of economic decline the English Crown regularly remitted the annual fee-farm rent due from the citizens. Probably the single most important means by which the English Crown supported the city of Cork in the later Middle Ages, apart from its charters granting urban autonomy, was the designation of Cork – together with Dublin and Drogheda – as a 'stable' town in 1326. This meant that those three towns, and none other in Ireland, enjoyed the right to hold the 'stable' or market for hides, wool and woolfells.[67]

SETTLEMENT PATTERN OF TERRYS IN THE 14TH CENTURY

In 1301, a William Terry returned the accounts for the mayor and bailiffs of Dublin to the Treasurer of Ireland.[68] John Tirry, Adam Tirry and William Fitz Philip Tirry are mentioned in connection with payments from Cork. A

Stephen Terry and William, his son, are referred to in the period 1305-1307 in the Justiciary Rolls, and Maurice Tirry and Stephen Tirry are also mentioned.[69] In an inquisition taken at Cashel a William son of Terry is mentioned. A Maurice Tirry of Cork is referred to in 1307. A dispute was heard before the Justiciar, John Wogan, in Dublin, in 1308, between Stephen Terry and Philip Maunsel, tenant. This dispute was about property and land in Morathbiran, Co Tipperary.[70] Stephen is referred to as the kinsman and heir of Walter Terry. This case was heard previously, in 1305, before the bishop of Meath. In crown court cases in Cork in 1311, John, son of Robert Tyrry was charged and acquitted of burglary in Cork.[71] In crown court cases in Cork in 1313, a John Terry (also spelt Torry and Torre) was a jury member, as were Robert Terry, Stephen Torry, and Maurice Torry.[72] A David Torre was charged and acquitted in Cork, in 1313, with receiving stolen goods.[73]

One account states that one David Terry was mayor of Cork in 1321.[74] This may be incorrect, as the more widely used list of mayors does not indicate this. A David Terry was mayor two hundred years later, in 1521.

The first Tyrry deed, in the Sarsfield Papers, refers to a grant by Rus fil John de Bradleye of 18 acres, in Kilcully parish, and other goods to John, son of Roger, son of William, son of William, son of Maurice.[75] This deed is undated, but an approximation of the period may be obtained from a reference to a Thomas Bradley as bailiff of Cork in 1313.[76] The full text of the deed is:

> May present and future persons know that I Richard son of John de Bradleye have given, granted, and by my present charter [confirmed] to John son of Roger son of William son of William son of Maurice, for a certain sum of money which he has paid me in advance, 18 acres of land with its appurtenances, which lie in the tenement of Kyslekan in Coulroch, that is to say, between the embankment of Rathneuke, which is the same tenement on the north, and the land of Thomas Bernard, on the south, withwise, and extends in length from the King's highway which leads towards Doconia on the east to the water of Currachdiron on the west. To have and to hold to the said John and his heirs and assigns from me and my heirs and assigns, freely, quietly etc together with common pasture anywhere in my lands etc. Paying yearly two silver pennies.[77]

An inquisition, held in Cork in 1344, concerns a quarrel that arose between various Barrys over tenancy of land around Rathcormac. Adam de Barry, of Rathcormac, did not wish to be a tenant of a David de Barry or to attend his court. David distrained against him for default and so Adam gathered a band of men together to wage war against David and all his people throughout the county of Cork. Oliver Tirry and Nicholas Fitz Adam Tirry were part of this band. They beat up the sheriff of Castlellethan, and killed Philip son of Nicholas Malenfaunt. They burned Laghare near Castlellethan and robbed and stole from the friars of Carmel. They were welcomed by Maurice, son of Thomas the Earl of Desmond, who let them ride about armed throughout county Cork and elsewhere.[78] Adam fitz William de Barry of Rathcormac, sued David in Dublin for the entire Barry inheritance.[79] In another inquisition at Youghal, in the same year Oliver Tirry's name appears again. With others he was indicted for robbery and murder. It would seem that he had the protection of Maurice son of Thomas the Earl of Desmond.[80] One of the places mentioned in this inquisition is Ardagh, in the barony of Inchiquin. The earl had the manor of Inchiquin taken from the king's hands, after it had been declared to be the king's, following the death of Giles de Badelismer.

In 1355, Henry Whyte granted property to Peter Fitz Thomas (presumably Tyrry) in the parish of Killaspugmullane.[81] The full text of the grant is:

> May present [and future] persons know that I, Henry son of Adam le Whyte, have given, granted etc jointly to Peter son of Thomas le … one acre of land and appurtenances in Kyllaspukmallan near Coghestown as assigned to me and described by these metes and bounds … to hold as of fee … These witnesses; Henry …, Miles le White, David le Botiller. Given on Monday after … in the 23rd year of the reign over England of King Edward the third since the Conquest and the 14th over France.[82]

2

Aspects of Settlement of an Hereditary Clerical Family in the Medieval Period

The early Norman knights who settled in Ireland granted land and other commodities to church establishments. There were some 34 grants to the abbey of St Thomas the Martyr in Dublin of land, fishery rights, alms and other income sources in Cork. In the case of four of these grants, the grants state that they were purchased or were the property of one Brother Tierri. In one of the four grants he is referred to as a canon. It is only with reference to Cork that he is mentioned in the grants to the church of St Thomas. These grants were made in the 1170s and 1180s. This Brother Tierri was also a witness to two grants in Cork to St Nicholas's Priory of Exeter. In one of these grants, Miles de Cogan makes a grant of land in the south suburbs of Cork City to the church. In the other, the grant was from Roger de Caunteton of the churches in Corkbeg, and possibly Inch, to St Nicholas's Priory. These grants were made in the years 1177-82.

Brooks states that Tierri was probably a monk of St Thomas' Abbey.[1] It is only in grants made in the city and county of Cork that Tierri's name appears. This would seem to indicate that he resided in Cork. One of the grants relates to Spike Island. Some 260 years later, the Barrys granted its neighbouring island in Cork harbour, Haulbowline Island, to Edmund Terry. This perhaps indicates that the Terrys were residing in this area for a considerable time. Similarly, in relation to the grant of the church in Castlemartyr, evidence from Chartae Tyrannae indicates that Terrys resided in the adjoining area of Mogeely in the 15th century.[2]

The location of the granted lands, which were purchased by brother Tierri, were: Dungarvan in Cork City, Spike Island and Castlemartyr. From documentary sources, it would appear that the case could be made, that in some way, these purchases of Tierri are connected with land ownership by Terrys and Terry clergy in subsequent centuries close to these original purchases.

In Cork City several laneways were named after Terrys in the 17th century. In Cobh, the townland of Ballyleary, it is suggested, was in previous times known as Ballinterry.[3] From the 15th century there is evidence of Terrys holding land in Cobh, including Haulbowline Island. Similarly, in neighbouring Carrigtohill lies the townland of Terry's Land a location of Terry clergy and where they held property. Near Castlemartyr, there are one or two townlands that would appear to be named after Terrys. Here there were also clerical and land ownership connections from an early date. Also near Rathcormac, we have the townland of Ballinterry. In former times there were Terry archdeacon priests here.

The objective of this article is to propose that, from the documentary evidence available, there is a discernible link between some of the original grants to the church of St Thomas the Martyr and the Terry family in terms of location of land ownership, placenames and their being members of the clergy for a number of subsequent centuries. The land ownership is in Cork City and some specified locations in east Cork.

THE CHARTERS

CHARTER 238. THE CHARTER OF MILES DE COGAN[4]

Milo de Cogan [Miles of Cogan] sends greetings to all loyal men of the King of England, both present and future, that is to say, French, English, Welsh and Irish:

> Know that I have given and granted, and by this my charter confirmed, on behalf of the lord king of England and of John his son, and on my behalf, as a king's justice, to God and the precious Saint Thomas the martyr, the fourth part of a [fish]pool under the bridge of Dungarvan, that is to say on the north side of Corcha, and a tenth/tithe of the same pool, as much as belongs to me to give, in perpetual alms for the lord king of England and John his son, and their heirs.

With these witnesses: Richard de Cogan, Roger the steward, Richard de Pincheni, William de Bridesal, William Fitzgeoffrey, Luke de Londoniis, Roger de Oxenford, Stephen the clerk, who wrote this charter – This is the property of brother Tierri.

CHARTER 239. THE CHARTER OF MILES DE COGAN

Miles de Cogan sends greetings to all his liegemen of the king of England, both present and future, French, English, Welsh and Irish:

> Know that I have given and granted, and by this my charter, confirmed, on the part of the Lord King of England, and of John, his son, and on my part, as a justice of the King, to God and St Thomas, the precious martyr, the land purchase, which the brother Terri bought of Walter de Leministre, for the service of God and St Thomas, namely a burgage and outhouses and an oven, which the aforesaid Walter held, with all appurtenances, freely and quietly and honourably in fee and inheritance, to be held of the Lord King of England, and of John his son, and their heirs, with all privileges, except the free service of the King of England.

With these witness: Richard de Cogan, Richard de Pincheni, William de Bridesale, William son of Geoffrey, Roger de Chirchehille, Roger of Oxford, and Stephen, the clerk, who wrote this charter. This concerns the purchase of brother Terri.

CHARTER 241. THE CHARTER OF MILES DE COGAN

Milo de Cogan sends greeting to all his lords and men, French, English, Welsh and Irish:

> Know that I have given and granted, and by this my charter confirmed, all the alms which my men have given and will give on behalf of our Lord the King of England, and of John his son, that is to say: from my land, which is within the district of Corc, to the most precious St Thomas, in churches, in tithes, in towns, in markets, in lands, in meadows, in pastures, in woods, in waters, in fisheries, in mills, in ponds, in pannage, and in all places, freely and peacefully and dutifully, and in free alms to the holy church, to the aforesaid most holy martyr Thomas, for Henry, King of England, our lord, and John his son, and for the souls of their ancestors, and for me, and the souls of my ancestors, in perpetual alms.

With these witnesses: Richard de Cogan, Richard son of Godbert, Geoffrey de Cogan, Luke de Londiniis, Richard de Pincheni, William de Brideshale, William Fitzgeoffrey, and Engelram, who wrote this charter, and many others. This is the property of brother Terri.

Charter 258. The Charter of Reimundi Mangunel

> May all the sons of holy mother church, that is to say, both present and future, know that I Reimundus Mangunel have given and granted, and by this my charter confirmed, to God and St Mary and the precious martyr, St Thomas, the mother church of Ynespic, with the tithes and oblations and profits of the whole of the aforesaid island, which by right belong to the holy church. And likewise I have given to the aforesaid martyr, St Thomas, the church of Kairultan, with the tithes and oblations and profits which by right belong to the holy church, in perpetual alms, for me and my wife, and for my and her successors, and for our souls and for the souls of our ancestors.

With these witnesses: Robert Fitzstephen, Milo de Cogan, Ralph son of Robert, Robert des Auters, Thomas des Auters, Stephen the parson of Holy Trinity, who wrote this charter, and many others. This is the property of Tierri, the canon.[5]

From these four charters it emerges that Tierri, the canon, purchased property in Dungarvan (Cork City), Spike Island and Castlemartyr. Norman knights granted the property to the Abbey of St Thomas the Martyr. It is only for Cork that Tierri's name appears on the charters to the Abbey. These locations occur again in land transactions involving Terrys in the 15th century. Some of these transactions are now considered.

In a subsequent confirmation grant by Matthew, Bishop of Cloyne, of churches, including the one at Caherultan, the grant states that it is to the church of St Thomas in Dublin and the friars serving God there.[6]

Land Ownership

In 1440, there was a grant from William Savage, chaplain, to Sir William Tyrry, chaplain, of lands in Keapagh, Stontoistowne, Speristown and Ballymoilyn, in the lordship of Castlelleghan (in all probability this is Castlelyons), Tybtotistown, in the burgage of Carrigtohill for life, remainder to William oge Tyrry and the heirs male of his body, then to John Tyrry, brother of William oge, then to Edmund Tyrry, citizen of Cork, and the right heirs of the said Sir William Tyrry; to hold of the chief lords of the fee, by the services due and customary. As the granter's seal was unknown to many, he has caused John Skyddy, Mayor of Cork, to affix the seal of his office.[7]

An Edmund Tyrry was involved in several land transactions in Cork City, and its suburbs, in the mid-15th century. In 1438, William Gowlis conveyed to Edmund Tyrry and his wife Katherine a messuage in Downgarwan in the suburb of Cork and, in the same year, he purchased the adjoining property from William Wynchedon.[8] A Phūm Tyrry had the power of attorney for the first transaction. Two years later he purchased a further property in the same area. There is a landgable roll extant for Cork City for this period.[9] In this roll, Edmund has three properties. Although estimates of the date of this roll vary, it would seem to date from the time of the early years of acquisitions of property in Cork City by Edmund Tyrry. In the list, which appears to be in the order that the houses are situated along a street, the house of John Kiere is mentioned, followed by two properties belonging to Edmund Tyrry, and finally the house of William Fitz Robert White. This is exactly as described in Tyrry deeds. In 1440, Edmund was granted all the land and mills in Shandon then held by William Tynan. He also obtained in this year a messuage in Dungarvan from Alisia Brachagh and two messuages in Shandon from Robert Bernard.[10]

Not only was this Edmund, described as a citizen of Cork, purchasing land and property in the City and suburbs; he also acquired Haulbowline Island in the harbour from William Barry in 1442.[11] The Mayor and commonalty granted Edmund three messuages one of which was called Paradise, presumably Paradise Tower, in the same year. In this grant the name Philip, the son of Robert Terry, is mentioned. He seems also to have lived in Cork City. On 30 June 1446, a mortgage was executed by William Fitz Nicholas Staunton to Edmund Tyrry, citizen and merchant of Cork, for six marks (in addition to 12 marks already paid) of his weirs in Cork harbour. Tyrry is to enjoy the above weirs rent free, in return for the cancelling of a bond of 20 pounds of silver which the above William, Philip (his brother), and Patrick Fitz Simon Staunton have passed to him.[12] In 1451 Edmund obtained a small parcel of land in Shandon, and in the following year obtained a messuage from Richard Stone in Dungarvan. In 1454 William Burdeny granted to Edmund, who is described as a burgess and merchant of Cork, of his tenement in the suburb of Cork. An adjoining house is called 'stonehouse'.[13]

Edmund Tyrry's will was executed in 1454.[14] Edmund orders that his body be buried in the Church of St Peter's, in the suburbs of Cork. He owed money to a Gilbert Smith of Bristol. Edmund has a son David. At the time of his death, he had ownership or interest in 11 houses in the City, and also land, gardens and mills in Shandon, Haulbowline Island and weirs in Cork Harbour.

In 1503, James Wache, Chaplain, granted to Philip Fitz Thomas Tyrry all the lands which he had of the feoffment of the said Philip, in the lordship of Belachochyll, Ardnichwlyn, Balyychorrygeny, Balyychochlayn, Balydawpadryg, Balynamony, Balynaraha, Balyyglassayn, and Balynacaylly in the lordship of Kynealtalyn, with the advowson of the church of Ardnichwlyn, to Philip and his heirs male of his body, then to Edmund Fitz David Tyrry.[15] This grant was sealed with the seal of the Mayor of Cork, Edmond Gowlle.[16] These lands were in Gortroe parish and Mogeely parish, with the church being in Gortroe parish.

Sometime later, in 1520, a deed was executed wherein the Lord John Barrymore, son of John Barry, Lord of Olyehayn and Oryry, grants to Edmund

Tyrry, citizen of Cork, all his rights in the same land, namely in the lordship of Belachochyll, Ardicolyn, Ballycherrygeny, Balyychgehlayn, Ballydawpatryd, Balynamoney, Balyintley, Balynaraha, Balyyglassayn and Balynacoilly in the lordship of Kynealtalwn, with the advowson of the church of Ardcolyn. David Tyrry, mayor of Cork, witnessed this deed.[17] Some of these townlands are in the parish of Gortroe, near Rathcormac, and some are near Mogeely. In all, there was some 2,000 acres of land involved in the transaction.

Placenames

To reinforce the Terry connection with these locations at an early period, some placenames with Terry or possible Terry connections are now considered.

Of the medieval laneways in Cork, several were named after Terrys.[18] These were:

David Thirry's Lane,
Robert Tirry's Lane,
James Tirry's Lane,
David Tirry's Lane,
Thirry's (Richard) Lane,
Dominick Tirry's Lane,
David Terry fitz-Stephen's Lane, and
William Tirry fitz-Patrick's Lane.[19]

The townland of Knockane, parish of Killeagh, is referred to in the Down Survey map of this parish, as Carrigarran & Knockmcteyrry & Carrygenery.[20] Part of the townland Gortnagappul, parish of Killeagh, is referred to in the Down Survey map as Gortnacaple & Ballym chērry.

There was on the Great Island (near Ringmeen) in 1634, some adjacent land called Ballinterry that identified by Dr Caulfield with Midleton Park. It is possible here that Ballinterry meant the present Ballyleary, which name has been substituted for it.[21]

At the present time there is a townland called Terry's Land in the parish of Carrigtohill, and a townland called Ballinterry in the parish of Gortroe, near Rathcormac. Power puts forward the possibility that the official name 'Ballinterry', in the parish of Gortroe, is derived from David and Edmund Tyrry, Archdeacons of Cloyne, 1520 and 1521 respectively.[22] Part of the townland of Ballinterry was also called Gortroe.

The Clergy

In the following, consideration is given to the continuing role of Terrys as members of the clergy in the early medieval period.

In 1344, one Nicholas Tyrry, of the diocese of Cloyne, a student for 13 years in civil and canon law, was granted a canonry of Dublin with a reservation of a prebend.[23]

There is further evidence of a number of Terry priests in Cork in the following century.

In 1440 a grant from William Savage, chaplain, to Sir William Tyrry, chaplain, was already referred to. This was for lands in Keapagh, Stontoistowne, Speristown and Ballymoilyn, in the lordship of Castlelleghan, Tybtotistown, in the burgage of Carrigtohill for life, remainder to William oge Tyrry and the heirs male of his body, then to John Tyrry, brother of William oge, then to Edmund Tyrry, citizen of Cork, remainder to the heirs of the said Sir William Tyrry, chaplain.[24]

In the diocese of Cork, in Little Island parish, Thomas Terry was parish priest in 1441. Concerning Thomas, what follows is an extract from a Papal Registrar, for the year 1441:

> To the abbots of Tracton and Gill Abbey, Cork, and the official of Cork. Mandate – the pope having being informed by Johne Walsche, dean of Cork, bachelor of canon law, that Thomas Tyrri, rector of the parish church of Little Island in the diocese of Cork, has remained for several years under a sentence of excommunication pronounced by authority of the ordinary and, although publicly proclaimed excommunicate, has celebrated masses and other divine offices, and has committed perjury and fornication – if John will accuse Thomas before them etc. as usual, to summon Thomas, and if they find the above or enough thereof to be true, to deprive Thomas and in the event to collate and assign the said rectory, of the patronage of laymen and value not exceeding 6 mark sterling, provided that the said patrons assent, to John; whether it become void by such deprivation, or be void by the free resignation of the said Thomas, or in any other way, and notwithstanding that John holds the said deanery, which is a major elective dignity with cure, for the performance of whose burdens the dean is bound to keep with him two priests, and whose value does not exceed 12 marks sterling. The pope hereby dispenses John to receive the said rectory and hold it for life with the said deanery, and to resign both, simply or for exchange, as often as he pleases, notwithstanding his late constitution to the contrary.[25]

In 1444-5 a mandate was directed to the abbot of Tracton, to assign to William Skiddi the precentorship of Cork, whether it be void as stated, or by the death or resignation of John Tyrri.[26]

The diocese of Cloyne had the following parish priests,

In Carrigtohill parish,
William Terry, in the year 1450,
John Terry, between the years 1459 and 1464. This John was the son of his immediate predecessor, William, and of an unmarried woman.[27]
In Rathcormac parish,
John Terry, *c.*1458.[28] This was the same John as held Carigtohill.

In 1459, this John Terry had a bond for the rectory of Templeroan als Templetrine. Two years later he was to have canonry of Cork and prebend of Caherlag and rectory of Ballintubrid if two other priests are deprived of these prebends.[29] This indicates not only the Terry association with the Anglo-Norman church, but also an association with Terry strongholds in terms of land ownership, notably Carrigtwohill and Rathcormac. Also Templinrine is close to the parish of Clontead, near Kinsale. There is a reference to a Terry from this locale in 1292.

In 1461, a mandate to the abbot of Midleton, that the fruits and rent from the rectory church of Rathbarri, in the diocese of Cloyne, belonging to the Augustinian monastery of All Saints, Dublin, be granted to John Terry for life.[30]

In 1464-5 there was a mandate to the dean of Cloyne to assign the parish church of Karygthuatal, vacant by the death of John Terry, who was on his way to Rome. The Pope specially dispenses John Sawache to receive the vicarage, notwithstanding the defect of illegitimacy, as the son of a priest and an unmarried woman.[31]

These grants indicate that at this time, priests owned land in their own name, and that this ownership could be passed by hereditary succession. Hereditary succession can mean succession by election within the family, in the Irish manner, and not primogeniture succession from father to son.[32] However, the land in and around Carrigtohill that Sir William Tyrry received was to pass to William oge. This would appear to imply that William oge was the son of Sir William. Also, John Terry the parish priest of Carrigtohill was the son of his predecessor William Terry.

As previously referred to, there is evidence of the Terrys holding the advowson of the church of Ardnichwlyn at the beginning of the 16th century.[33] In relation to local churches, it was often the local lord who built and endowed the church around which the parish was formed. He appointed the cleric (the rector) who ruled it. As a result the right of appointment (the advowson) was in diverse hands: king, baron, knight, bishop or monastery – the last because it was with advowsons that many monasteries were endowed.[34]

The role played as clergymen and in the church by Terrys in the 16th century, is outlined in Ch. 5.

In conclusion, it would appear that the presence and activities of one Canon Tierri, in 1177-82, with a number of specific locations in Cork, may indicate a link with Terry involvement in, or close to, these places; as land owners, in the context of placenames and also as members of the clergy. This involvement spanned a number of centuries.

3

1420-1500 Initial Step to an Urban Elite

In this chapter the geographical context of the 15th century is examined first, followed by an examination of the historical context. Following this, all known records referring to Terrys are set down. These are from 1420 onwards. There is evidence of their involvement in church and civic affairs. From 1438, records show that one Edmund Tyrry was engaged in several land and property transactions in the city and harbour areas. In the mid-century their involvement appears quite limited, but, by the end of the century, there is clear evidence that they were a leading family grouping in the city.

Geographical Context

The whole 15th century was a period of strife and discord. There was war everywhere, north and south and west, on the borders of the Pale and within it – wars between rival candidates for the chieftaincy of their clans, wars between neighbouring chiefs and combinations of these, wars between the Anglo-Irish lords themselves, wars of aggression and of spoliation, wars of retaliation and revenge.[1]

In looking at this period in a geographical sense one can distinguish between English districts and Gaelic Ireland. The situation and economy of the English districts were determined by a number of factors, of which the geography of the earlier Anglo-Norman settlement probably remained the most important. The settlers had aimed to acquire profitable land, especially good arable, and intensive occupation had not normally occurred above the 400-foot contour line, or in boggy lowlands.[2] In general, settlement in the south and east of the country was more intensive than in the north and the west. However, resulting from reduced population after the plague and encroachment by Gaelic chiefs, by the close of the 14th century, mixed farming in the traditional English manner was concentrated in the Pale, south Wexford, Kilkenny and Tipperary, with isolated agricultural borough communities in Carlow, Cork, Waterford and Limerick.[3] Much of the land that had been painstakingly developed reverted to pastureland or even waste land.[4] Another feature of the English districts was the large number of towns. Even in the exceedingly difficult circumstances of this period, many of the towns managed to survive and, with the revival of trade in the later 15th and early 16th centuries, some of them, particularly the port towns, managed to generate a modest prosperity.[5]

In Gaelic Ireland, the economy was predominantly a pastoral one. Large areas were still covered by scrubby forest, lakes and undrained bogs.[6] After the Gaelic revival and decay of areas previously ruled by the English in the 14th century the only towns of importance that survived and continued their municipal organisation would be about twenty, of which Dublin, Waterford, Drogheda and Wexford, Cork, Limerick, Dungarvan, Kilkenny and Galway were chief. The worst period for the towns was from about 1400-60; it improved under aristocratic Home Rule, and many of them, such as Clonmel, Kilkenny, New Ross, Limerick, Cork, were glad to put themselves under the patronage of the great earls of Ormond and Desmond and other magnates who now ruled Ireland. But for all that, while the 'March English' and even many in the pale adopted Irish speech and culture, the towns remained the only strongholds of Englishness.[7]

From estimates given earlier, and those for *c.*1600, the population of the city in the 15th century would have been about eight hundred.

At different periods in the 15th century, coins were minted officially and unofficially in Cork. Minting enterprises, of native Irish and English colonists, were halted by statutes of Henry VI in 1447 and 1456, while Edward VI established the principle that money in Ireland should always be kept at a lower value than English currency.[8] This struck a blow at Ireland's foreign commerce since foreign merchants would not bring their merchandise to a country where money was light and bad. A new national coinage was struck in 1459 and the old coins were condemned. Alongside the mint in Dublin the old mint towns of Cork, Limerick and Waterford produced coins from 1465.[9] In 1472 the parliament was to pass legislation against moneyers in the city of Cork and towns in Cork, who made false coins without authority.[10]

Considerable trade from the coastal towns, to Europe, took place in the 15th century. This was extensively in the hands of a merchant class in places like Cork City. The profits to be derived from foreign trade were very large, especially when compared with the relative poverty of Ireland in general. Their size was reflected in the prosperity of the trading towns, which although small by European standards were well built and contained many fine houses.[11]

Green describes the relations between town traders and the Irish people in surrounding districts. This account could well describe how Terrys and other merchant gentry families prospered from the mid-15th century.

The closest relations were gradually established between the town traders and the Irish people, through whose labour alone they existed. Merchants bought up the surrounding estates, or took them on mortgage, and tied the tenants to furnish to them alone all their wares. They evaded the laws against dealing with the Irish by employing agents to traffic in the country, and through two centuries complaints were sent to England of the great abuse of the merchants of the haven towns, who 'in amity with the Irish rebels' sent servants and factors called 'laxmen' or 'grey merchants' through all the Irish countries, to buy up Irish wares.

Every December, when ships from France and Spain arrived, their wines were carried in little barrels on horse-back through the Irish countries, by dealers who brought back corn of the old grain or of the new harvest, and horses and beeves then in best condition from the great men and large farmers, and from the cottages stores of woollen and linen cloth and yarn.[12]

HISTORICAL CONTEXT

The collapse of King Richard's settlement of Ireland and the Lancastrian usurpation in England meant that the early years of the 15th century witnessed a new phase in the development of Ireland. The forces of separatism, already at work since early in the history of the lordship, now took over, and everywhere independent lords pursued their own ways, often through exploiting Irish customary rights exercised by captains of nations and the like. In 1402-3 the bishop of Cloyne tried to protect himself and his tenants from Anglo-Irish levying Irish exactions locally, by entering into agreements with three of the leading magnates in his diocese.[13] Even the towns, later to be called 'the sheet anchors of the state', became more autonomous in this new age.[14] Judges ceased to be appointed for either Munster or Connacht soon after 1400.[15]

In this period, the earls of Desmond controlled an earldom that was estimated to contain several hundred thousand acres spread over five counties. The earldom probably affected the lives, both directly and indirectly, of a majority of the population of Munster, whether they were tenants or servants of the earl, inhabitants of towns, with which the earl traded, or potential allies or opponents.[16]

The new alignments of lordships in Ireland, the blurring of distinction between Gael and Anglo-Irish, and the increased autonomy of the lords in the localities, made the government as a force in Irish politics less important that it had been in the 14th century. In any case, it was less effective because it was financially starved and was in no condition to undertake ambitious schemes of renewal.[17] There was conflict between the Irish and the Anglo-Irish. In Munster, for example, in 1430, Desmond and the MacCarthys were at war. The expansion of the area of west Cork, dominated by the MacCarthys, towards the city continued after the decline of royal authority, with Blarney Castle being built sometime in the mid-15th century.[18] The Irish chiefs, at times, exacted a Black Rent from the Anglo-Irish. Cork made an annual payment of £40 to MacCarthy.[19] At the opening of the 15th century, Cork still retained links with the Dublin administration, although these were becoming increasingly tenuous. From the mid-15th century there is evidence of a revival in Cork's economic fortunes. This may have been facilitated by greater political order in the Cork harbour region as the Lords Barry extended their sway over Great Island and over Shandon, the earls of Desmond (who already dominated Imokilly) extended their sway over Kerrycurrihy to the south of the city, while the MacCarthys of Muskerry extended their lordship to the western approaches to the city (taking possession of Blarney Castle *c.*1480).[20] That degree of political consolidation may have been conducive to more intensive agriculture over much of the city's immediate hinterland and, at the same time, may also have helped in safeguarding maritime traffic passing through the harbour, to and from the city.

TERRYS 1420-1500

There is evidence of a number of Terry priests in Cork in this century. These are dealt with in Ch. 2.

From 1425 on Terrys were prominent among the list of bailiffs for the city in the 15th century.[21] These were:

Year	Name	Year	Name
1425	David	1475	Petter
1427	David	1482	James
1431	Philip	1487	Richard
1432	Philip	1488	Petter
1438	John	1489	Richard
1451	David	1490	Petter
1452	David	1492	Richard
1455	John	1493	David
1463	Joseph	1494	Edmond and Robert
1468	Samuel	1495	Richard

Table 3.1 *Terry bailiffs in the 15th century.*

There is a deed, recited twice, for the year 1420, witnessed by Philip Tyrry, one of the two bailiffs for Cork City.[22] This deed related to the advowson of Glanmire. In 1432 Royal authority constituted a Philip Tirry, presumably the same person, one of the Coroners of the City of Cork.[23]

One Edmund Tyrry was involved in several land transactions in Cork City, and the suburbs, in the mid-15th century. Selected details on these are provided in Ch. 2. From the records available, it would appear that Edmund, who died in 1454, was the first significant Tyrry merchant in the city, and from him an increasing number of, and more influential, Tyrry merchants and traders prospered in the city for the following two centuries.

The Landgable Roll of Cork City lists 170 properties.[24] If the population of the city was in the order of eight hundred people at this time, this would imply a household size of slightly less than five. It would also tend to indicate that the Landgable Roll listed more-or-less all the houses in the City. Edmund Tyrry, the only Terry recorded, presumably lived in one of the three houses he owned as recorded, and had tenants, who may or may not have been Terry families in the other two houses. Then the number of Terry families in the City in the mid-15th century was three or less.

There are a number of grants of property and land to David Fitz Edmund Tyrry in the 1460-70s.[25]

In 1462 there is a grant of land to David, from Maurice Kyery. In 1466, Thomas Shnyane, from Downralle in Fermoy, granted to David, citizen of Cork, all privileges pertaining to land, mills and marshes in Shandon near Cork. A further grant in 1468 of rights relating to mills in Shandon is made by John Fitz William Tynan. David's father Edmund received a similar grant from John's father 28 years earlier. In 1469, David was granted a parcel of land in Shandon by David Walshe.[26] There is a grant, in 1474, from John Fitz Patrick Forres, citizen of Cork, to David of all his lands, tenements, rents, and services, which he held in the parish of Kilcorihine. There is a power of attorney to John Nywtone.

David Tyrry's will is executed in 1479.[27] He bequeathed property to his sons. To his son Rowland, one messuage in Downgarvan, suburbs of Cork, in which John Niger dwells, to his son, Richard, the rent which he had in Bewere

Fig. 3.1 *Oath of the citizens of Cork, 1498. (Source: National Archives, Kew.)*

(Carrigaline) in the lordship of Kerycurthy. To James, his 'younger' son, one hill which he has near Clonbeg, and to whom he also bequeaths all orchards and gardens near the church of Shandon. Amongst his debtors were, Cormac, son and heir of MacCarthy, Dermot, son of Cormac, and John de Barry, chief of his clan. Catherine Roche was David's wife.

In 1482, a cargo containing goods belonging to William Tyrry, of Cork, merchant, on the ship *John of Cork*, embarked at Bridgwater, south west of England, from Cork.[28] Around this time also, one William Tirry, son of Sir William Tirrey, Co Cork, married the daughter of JohnFitzThomas FitzGerald, self-styled Earl of Desmond.

The King issued a general pardon to Robert Stackpoole and David Tyrry in 1488.[29]

The Oath of the citizens of Cork in 1498 contains 45 names, Fig. 3.1.[30] The Terry names on this document, from C.J.F. McCarthy's note, are:

Edward Tyrry William Tyrry
Robert Tyrry Richard Tyrry
Philip Tyrry Edward the son of Piers Tyrry
Oliver Tyrry Roland Tyrry.

Presumably, the Roland and Richard are two sons of David Fitz Edmund Tyrry who died in 1479. On the assumption that the population of the city was approximately the same as 50 years earlier, and a correlation between the number of Terry families from the signatories and the total population, then there was a significant increase in Terry families living in the city by this time.

Also in 1499, a patent was granted by the King, to William Tirry, Edmund, son of David Tirry, citizens of Cork and to two other citizens of Cork, receivers and collectors of customs, fee-farms and taxes of Cork, and also to superintend and govern the city.[31]

4
Geographical and Historical Context in the 16th Century

Geographical Context

Lennon states that for most people in early 16th-century Ireland the world was narrowly confined to locality.[1] They drew their concepts of space and time from direct experience of the environment. Nature, pristine and primeval, framed the lives of a great number of the inhabitants, although forest clearances, bog reclamations and nucleated villages had brought some adaptation of geography for settlement during the medieval centuries. For all, in whatever location in the island, or age group or station in society, high mortality rates cut ties of family and friendship with sad regularity. The implacable forces of famine and disease were frequent influences upon life spans. In 1500 the taming of the physical environment and the overcoming of its attendant perils were scarcely dreamed of. As other maritime countries in Europe embarked upon overseas explorations, Ireland was itself a land for discovery and eventual colonisation by newcomers. The plantation estate and the purpose-built town of the early 17th century entailed the shaping of the countryside and the harvesting of its resources in a way, which was inconceivable one hundred years earlier. Even further in the future lay the breakthroughs in agriculture and science, which was to affect fundamentally the recurrence of plague and famine.

Towns and cities, with their hinterlands, played an important role in this period. Although perhaps not as numerous or as large as in the earlier Anglo-Norman period, urban centres are seen to have had well-ordered polities, clusters of wealthy families which profited from trade and rents, thriving spiritual institutions, and the dynamism to draw into their nexus through markets and fairs the people and produce of the vicinities.[2] Close to the heart of most substantial towns was the merchant guild with its strict rules for trade, expressive ritual and powerful personnel who were interchangeable with the ruling city councillors.

The growth of Irish medieval towns had been fostered by royal and aristocratic grants, but in 1500 most major urban centres aspired to self-government, with varying degrees of success.[3] The old Viking ports of Drogheda, Dublin, Wexford, Waterford, Cork and Limerick, along with Galway, had developed quasi-autonomous powers after three centuries of royal beneficence in the form of charters and statutory regulations. The main aims of the royal or seigniorial benefactors of urban settlements were to support trade through establishing settled market centres and fairs and to advance manufacture and crafts. Administrative and judicial institutions complemented economic ones.

In Europe, Duplessis categorises workers into three broad strands, on the basis of degree of autonomy, at this time.[4] These were independent artisans, artisans employed in 'putting-out' and dependent wage earners.[5] Independent artisans were often guild masters, who had charge of the production process from the purchase of raw materials to the sale of the commodity, whether to another artisan for further manufacture, to a merchant, or to the final consumer. English provincial capitals were vital nodes on the transport and commercial network. Through them flowed most of the produce of their own large hinterlands, and most of the incoming trade from other areas and abroad as well. Some were centres of specialised functions; for example, York for pewter and gold products.[6] In sharp contrast to England the great difficulties of travel in Ireland, both natural and man-made, hindered internal trade. Irish towns looked to the continent and England rather than to one another. Also, Ireland at this time was very short of 'artificers' except around Waterford.[7] Society was little commercialised and this meant that specialised production of craft items for a wider market was very limited. The role of the craftsman was a lowly one. To put it another way, the division of functions was not as marked between Irish towns as English; each town had to provide a wide range of services for its hinterland. In a backward and overwhelmingly rural country, the specialist economic function of the towns was to provide a commercial drive to the economy.[8] In addition, society was organised around consumption rather than capital investment. For Cork, the inference that its trade in the Tudor period was probably very modest in scale finds confirmation in the very scant archaeological record in Cork City.[9] Even at modest levels, for those engaged in it, it provided them with a comfortable living.[10] Cork, at this time, would have handled significantly less trade from Bristol than Waterford; about three per cent of Irish trade with Cork and 58 per cent with Waterford. Wexford and Youghal had three per cent and four per cent respectively.[11] There would have been some trade with Spain, as is evidenced from the will, 1582, of Richard Terry, who had nine hides in Spain, in the custody of David Carruill.[12] Tirry's inventory also referred to 'a piece of Turkey grogron containing fifteen yards and a half worth', presumably transhipped via Spain. The inventory of goods attached to the will of David Tirry, 1570, listed Spanish wine and 'a new Flanders table cloth'.

Trade in towns was affected by the political changes and disturbances in the countryside. These changes made inland communication as difficult and dangerous between Cork and other towns as it had been in the 14th century.[13]

The small ruling groups of patricians in the major boroughs by 1500 comprised affluent merchant families. As the Crown devolved more and more governing powers to the corporations, these leading citizens were best positioned to benefit politically and economically.[14] In the two largest cities, Dublin and Waterford, with perhaps the widest trading networks, the number of families achieving elevated civic office over a two- to three-generational span was comparatively high; up to 30 or 40 in the 16th and early 17th centuries, indicating a fair degree of openness of the ruling coteries. By contrast, the smaller cities – Galway, Drogheda, Limerick, Cork and Kilkenny – were dominated by élites of 12 to 15 families. The clannishness of Anglo-Norman families was also present in Cork City.[15] In all cases, however, the men and women of the patriciates were

Fig. 4.1 *Lordships of part of Co. Cork. (Courtesy: Dr Kenneth Nicholls.)*

closely linked through intermarriage. In Cork the top three families held just over half of the mayoralties during the reigns of Elizabeth and James. Tirrys, who held the mayoralty 13 times in this period, headed this.[16]

This was another noticeable difference between England and Ireland; in England there was a much higher degree of population mobility between town and country, with a continual change in names dominating civic life in the towns. In Ireland, the closed nature of municipal life fostered the growth and continuation of small, powerful élites.[17]

Fig. 4.1 shows the lordship of that part of Cork, from about 1570, where there is evidence of Terrys.[18]

Sheehan states that it is impossible to separate social structure and political order in early modern Irish towns; the latter was a function of the former and the personnel of both were largely interchangeable.[20] They were governed by a merchant oligarchy, dominating trade through the guild merchant and politics through its monopoly of urban office. Sheehan goes on to state that the fundamental reason for this control can be traced to the political, and to a lesser extent economic, isolation of the urban areas from their hinterlands

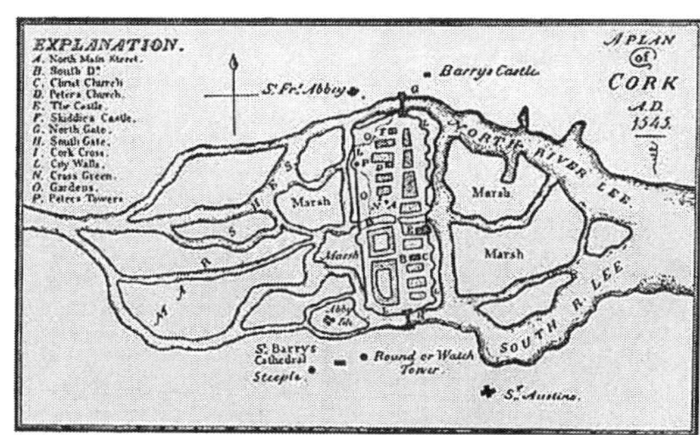

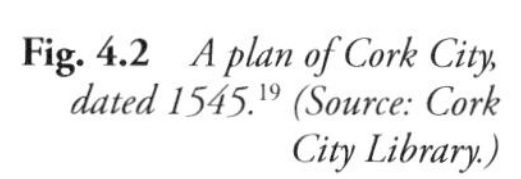
Fig. 4.2 *A plan of Cork City, dated 1545.*[19] *(Source: Cork City Library.)*

during the later Middle Ages. This restricted immigration and encouraged the growth of a strong sense of community identity. With a small and probably stable population kept low by the periodic outbreaks of disease, such as the plagues of 1535-6, 1540, and 1574-7, and the constant intermarriage between the chief families of the town, there was little chance for outsiders to break the stranglehold of the few. Based on holders of the Mayoralty between 1558 and 1625, Sheehan ranks Tirrys first, followed by Galloways and Roches.

The accumulated wealth of the merchants not only provided scope for overseas trading ventures and advancing of loans, but also allowed for investment in leases and land in the neighbouring countryside. County seats of successful municipal families dotted the hinterlands of Dublin, Drogheda and, to a lesser extent, Waterford.[21] By about 1600, the value of trading activity in the main ports was: Dublin – £80,000 per annum, mainly with England; Waterford – £30,000 per annum, mainly with Spain and Bristol; Galway and Cork – £20,000 per annum, mainly with Spain.[22]

Determinants of Europe's industrial advance in the 16th century were population growth, demand for supplies in Spanish possessions in the New World, increased urbanisation in Europe, and increased income of workers.[23] Europe's population grew from 61 million in 1500 to 78 million a century later. In Ireland, the population grew from about one million to 1.4 million in the same period.[24] This population growth was not evenly spread across the country. The southern part of Munster seems to have a much lower population density in the late 16th century, if not earlier. Depopulation following the Desmond rebellion was at least partly responsible. In the case of Ireland, a second dynamic for change was the redistribution of landed resources and property rights between natives and newcomers, commencing from 1550 onwards. A third dynamic for change, as viewed by Gillespie, was a shift from a redistributive economy to a market economy over the course of the century.[25]

An aspect of land ownership around Cork in the late 16th century can be gleaned from a situation in 1553 where a William Sarsfield got extensive land around Cork from one James Sarsfield. William, captain of his nation, continued as a merchant.[26] The truth seems to be that at that time, in consequence of the exactions of the great territorial lords, land was productive of little wealth to its owners. Sir Henry Sidney came to Cork in 1575, whither he tells us there came to him many ruined relics of the ancient English inhabitants of this province, as the Arundels, Rochfords, Barretts, flemings, Lombards, Ferries (Terries?), and many others whose ancestors were able and did live like gentlemen and knights some of them, 'and now all in misery, either banished from their own or oppressed upon their own'. In 1571, the mayor and brethren of Cork petitioned the Queen for the return of the earl of Desmond and his brother, Sir John, so they could aid the president and council and for the greater tranquillity of Her Majesty's impoverished subjects.[27] Sixteen people, including the mayor Maurice Roche, signed this. One of the signatories was Stephen Tirry, bailiff. In the 16th century, a system emerged, in Munster, where lords would take over lands whose owners proved unable to cultivated them or to pay his tribute, and disposed of them as his own, allowing the hereditary owners a quarter of the rent he received. A refinement of this system was that, by 1576, it had become usual for lords, for example, Barry and Roche in Cork, simply to take over, in lieu of his exactions, three quarters of every freeholder's land and set it to whatever tenant he willed.[28] Nicholls suggests that it must have been in consequence of this system that the Barrys mortgaged land from the Tirrys in Gortroe parish; lands that the Tirrys were hereditary owners of.

Historical Context

Henry VIII became king of England in 1509. He ruled until his death in 1547. Initially he was Lord of Ireland, but subsequently became King of Ireland as well. Edward VI succeeded and reigned for six years. Following Edward was Queen Mary. Elizabeth I, who reigned until 1603, succeeded her.[29] These, together with Henry VII, were the Tudor monarchs.

Edwards suggests that to reconstruct properly the political and social texture of an Irish local community during the 16th and early 17th centuries it is not enough simply to borrow from English historical models.[30] For example, Irish cities, such as Cork, had far more extensive privileges than their English equivalents. During the late medieval and early modern period most regions in Ireland were closely identified with the aristocratic lineages that ruled them.[31] Co. Cork was divided between the 'countries'[32] of the Barretts, Barrys, Courcys, Roches, Condons and, of increasing influence, the countries of MacCarthy Reagh, MacCarthy Muskerry and the Desmond Fitzgeralds.[33] In the absence of a strong central government these countries were the key component of political life. Until the late 1500s Ireland was primarily a land of lordships, a place of constantly shifting frontiers where, above all, politics was usually conducted locally. However, the 16th and early 17th centuries are regarded, by historians, as a period when central government expanded at the expense of regional lords.[34] Outlying cities, like Cork, had long called for the revival of royal authority in Ireland and hoped for greater political stability, law and order, and economic prosperity as a result.[35] Instead, the 16th century was punctuated by major rebellions which had devastating consequences for Cork's hinterland, and thus for the city's economic development.

In the context of English rule in Ireland at this time, at the head of the administration of the English lordship of Ireland was the chief governor who, in the absence of the king, represented him for his subjects in Ireland. For most of the first third of the 16th century the position was held by one of the three

Irish earldom families, that of Kildare.[36] From the 1490s the government of Ireland was carried on with the minimum expense for the new Tudor monarchy. Generally the Geraldine rule of the early decades of the century presided over a revival of Crown institutions in the lordships. In 1534, Silken Thomas, son of the then governor, Garret Oge, earl of Kildare, rebelled against the King. On the suppression of the rebellion several Fitzgeralds were executed in London. Aristocratic delegation was now out of favour as a mode of governing Ireland, and English-born viceroys were seen as the most acceptable heads of the Dublin administration, within the framework of more bureaucratic, London-controlled rule within a unitary state. The risks of the alienation of the Old English had to be managed, as well as the issue of royal ecclesiastical authority.[37] Tudor reconquest began, and the Anglo-Irish nation was effaced by a monarchy, that tolerated no opposition and had no sympathy with, or wish to understand, Irish or Anglo-Irish national distinctiveness.[38]

After 1534, English policy regarding Ireland began to envisage the necessity for a thorough conquest of Ireland to be secured by 'colonisation of new English settlers either on a local or national basis. Thereby Tudor conciliation in Ireland, the policy that marked the closing years of the reign of Henry VIII, gave way to Tudor conquest.[39] It has been argued that English thinking had evolved to the point that, inspired by the model of Imperial Spain and its treatment of the native Indian population of the Spanish colonies, there now existed in England a mature ideology of colonisation.[40]

The supplanting of papal royal authority over the Irish Church received formal public expression in the parliament of 1536-7. A Church of Ireland within the overall Anglican communion of Henry VIII emerged.[41] In the spring of 1539 commissions for the dissolving and leasing of monastic houses within the Crown's jurisdiction in Ireland were issued.[42] How far the country remained attached to Rome, simply because the break with Rome came from England, will always remain in dispute. The chief governor, Grey, was superficially successful, though his methods involved him in a quarrel with the Butlers, ending in 1541 in his own execution, ostensibly for treason but really for failure. However, the country was far from pacified or reconciled, and the progress of the religious Reformation was to render futile all hopes of a genuine settlement.[43] Henry VIII was made King of Ireland in 1541. In the decades following the death of Henry VIII there was a breakdown of consensus politics in Ireland. The result was pronounced discontinuity of policy, encouraging the growth of an articulate opposition movement which cut across traditional factional politics, undermined respect for the governorship, and threatened to unite Gaelic and Old English opinion against Tudor rule.

Of great significance for the city of Cork in the Tudor period was the stability, or otherwise, of the earldom of Desmond. The earldom dominated the region around Cork.[44] In the aftermath of the failure of the Kildare rebellion, the colonial élite in Ireland, and Cork, acquiesced to the juridical aspects of the Henrician reformation, even to the extent of endorsing them in the Irish parliament of 1536-7.[45] Jefferies suggests, based on examining Cork wills, that the Tudor reformations could well have succeeded.[46] An indication of the Earl of Desmond's influence in Cork can be obtained from a case, in 1548, that when the King's bailiff at Cork, Edmund Tyrry, had a dispute with some of the Barries about land, the earl of Desmond was appealed to. He took Tyrry to Lord Barrymore, desiring the latter to do him justice.[47] Unfortunately for Tyrry, matters did not work out too well for him. Barrymore took him to his court-baron, or 'parliament', and the case was partly heard and adjourned to a future day. On his return journey towards Cork, Tyrry was waylaid and murdered. However, arising from representations from the City, the murderers were turned in by Lord Barry, and executed.

By 1579 traditional consensus policies were near collapse and a political climate was emerging which was conductive to the spread of novel ideological forms of opposition.[48] In addition, the extension of English rule meant that earls such as Desmond were no longer able to count on the same level income from their under lords. Desmond was in fact in a difficult position. In 1568 commissioners valued his properties at less than IR£1,000 per annum.[49] With the revival of Crown government in Munster, feudal services customarily paid by neighbouring Old English and Gaelic landlords were increasingly withheld and Desmond's overlordship questioned. His response, a major demonstration of his power, drew him into conflict with the Queen. The consequence was the Desmond rebellion, its suppression, and the plantation of Munster. One account suggests that Terrys lost a considerable portion of their ancient possessions for siding with the Pope and taking up arms with 'their Kinsman', Gerald the Great Earl of Desmond against Queen Elizabeth.[50] This plantation was not fully successful. Cork City remained loyal to the crown during the plantation. An indication of the difficult position in Cork can be gleaned from the letter of one John Thickpenny, writing from Youghal in 1573, to Lord Deputy Fitzwilliam. He states that no man may pass by land to Cork, so he freighted a small bark to go there.[51]

Following this was the rise of Hugh O'Neill in the north, the nine years war and the defeat of the Irish at the Battle of Kinsale, in 1603. Again Cork City remained aloof and did not support O'Neill.

It is clear that the wealthy merchants of Cork, such as the Terrys, had resources at their disposal greatly in excess of what their rural counterparts had, when one compares the value of mortgages and financial transactions of these merchants with the wealth of the Kilkenny gentry in 1560.[52] Indeed, lords were frequently close to bankruptcy.[53] Another aspect of the power of the Cork merchants, during the course of the plantation of Munster, was their ability to challenge, under English common law, claims of those who were offered land. Arthur Robyns, who was granted land in the plantation, was constantly challenged both by the former owner, James FitzJohn Barry, a pardoned rebel but a former coiner of money, and by Edmund Tyrrey, a merchant of Cork, who claimed to have a mortgage on Barry's land, if he recover it from her Majesty.[54] Robyns was learning that the gentlemen and freeholders of Ireland were accustomed seldom or never to sell any land but to mortgage it, and that such acquisitions were as good as freeholds and fee simples for they are seldom or never redeemed. In this instance the operation of a mortgage procedure meant that Robyns had to confront the claims of a Cork merchant, Tyrrey, who was better able than Barry to challenge his claims under English common law.

By the end of the century, the cumulative effect of England's promotion of religious reformation and attempts at political reforms culminating in wars of conquest and much colonisation, profoundly alienated the citizens of Cork from the Tudors' administration in Ireland.[55] Jefferies suggests that the dramatic shift in favour of the catholic church towards the end of the 16th century did have a religious basis.[56] This dramatic shift can be traced with some precision, for Munster. Sir John Dowdall, governor of the fort of Duncannon in Waterford, summed up the transition from 'indifference' to recusancy was in 'about the year 1593 or a little before'.[57] It would appear that the strong support by the merchant gentry for the catholic church in Cork, then, occurred at a later date than in Dublin as put forward by Lennon.[58]

The effect of popular recusancy soon became apparent. The priests worked upon the people to withdraw from the protestant church, getting them to swear on oath that they would not attend its services. Local civic officials in Cork, who previously had co-operated with Bishop Lyon of Cork in enforcing attendance at church on Sundays, now refused such help, and they stopped going to church. Most importantly, the native clergy started to abandon their ministry. Such a move was hardly surprising when one examines the leading recusant families in Cork – Tirry, Coppinger, Marshall, Miagh – all names that were represented amongst the clergy serving the Church of Ireland in the late 1580s and 1590s.[59] A number of Terry priests functioned from this time on, one of them, William, would become a future bishop of Cork.

5
Terrys in Tudor Cork Social Perspective

Social Perspective

Many of the land transactions that the Terry's were involved in, were sealed and witnessed by some of the leaders of society in Cork, in this period. This must be taken as a reflection of the Terrys' own place in Cork. When in 1503, James Walsh, Chaplain, granted to Philip Fitz Thomas Tyrry lands in Gortroe parish and Mogeely parish, the grant was sealed with the seal of the Mayor of Cork, Edmond Gowlle.[1] Several deeds were executed directly between the Lords of Barrymore and the Terrys.[2] When, in 1521, Lord John Barrymore granted to David Tyrry of Cork and William Richard Barry, another citizen of Cork, the castle of Belvelly in the Great Island and a carucate of land in the wood of Hodyne called the half carucate of Ballynacrusy, this grant was witnessed by the Abbot of Choro,[3] and the Archdeacon of Cloyne, 'maðro' Edmund Tyrry.[4] They themselves were also witnesses to deeds executed between significant landowners. Patrick Tyrry was a witness to a conveyance, in 1590, by David Fitz James Barry, Lord Barrymore, Viscount of Buttevaunte, to Thomas Sarsfield of the city of Cork, alderman, of all his right and title to Sarsfield Courte and other nearby land.[5]

As merchants, traders and landowners, evidence exists of several examples of alliances with other merchants, traders and landowners.[6] The Terry's had the standing and wherewithal to challenge successfully in the courts leading land magnates, such as Lord Barrymore.[7]

In 1567, a decree was given to David Tirrye against Lord Barrymore, as follows,

> A complaint being made before the Queen's Commissioners by David Tirrye Fitz-Edmund of Corke, Merchant, that James, Viscount Barrymore detained from him the three parts of Ballynesperry for coyne and livery, his Lordship alleged that his Ancestors were seized of the said three parts, as of their ancient inheritance but the plaintiff producing ancient evidences, made by his Lordship's ancestors to his ancestors, showing how the said lands were by them given frank and free, without any kind of impositions of the country, save 2 shillings by the year of his Lordship and suit of his Court of Carrigetwohill, the Commissioners adjudged and recorded that he should enjoy the said lands free.[8]

The decree also provided that it was open to Lord Barrymore to come before the Mayor and Recorder of Cork with a better case, within a couple of months. When Barrymore did not do this, the decree was confirmed and effective from 27 September 1567. They were also able to engage the best attorneys to defend their interests. This can be observed when in 1588, Patrick Tyrry of Cork, gent, son and heir of William lately deceased, and William Tyrry Fitz William, Patrick's brother, engaged their attorney, a Dublin-based attorney, in connection with property near Cork.[9] Presumably, the Dublin based attorney was better able than a local man to represent their interests. Terrys themselves acted as agents for others, including Irish chiefs. In 1588, Cormac McDermott McCarthy, in a petition to Burghley, sent his agent Robert Terry to make his suit to her Majesty to pass him a new grant of the manor of Blarney with a release of all conditions.[10] As Green pointed out, the most trusted mediators from the English to the Irish were the merchants of the boroughs.[11]

Again, William Fitz William Tyrry, of Cork, petitioned the Queen's Commissioners complaining of a trespass committed by James Fitz Morish upon his lands in Kerricurihie. In 1584, William's title to these lands was affirmed.[12]

In 1585, an injunction was granted to maintain William Tyrry of Cork in possession of the fourth sheaf of corn growing on the lands in Ballyorbane and Kiellvirry in Kerrycurrihy, Co. Cork.[13] In the following year the Vice President and Council of Munster to Mr Christopher Sampson, commanding William Fitz William Terry of Cork, Alderman, to be maintained in possession of the same lands, comprising two townlands, his title having being confirmed.

Terrys acted as jury members in major inquisitions. A James Tyrry was a jury member in an inquisition into the land of James Barret of Ballincollig in 1568.[14] Clement and Thomas Tyrry were witnesses to arbitration in connection with fishing rights at Blackrock in 1538.[15]

There is also evidence of disputes of a commercial nature between the merchant families of Cork. These often arose after someone died and concerned title to property or payment of debts. One case was David Tirry fitzEdmond of Corke, gent, v. Anstace Walter (late wife of the suppliant's grandfather David Tirry fitzEdmond), David Tirry (uncle to suppliant) and Andrew Walter, re houses in Cork.[16]

In this period, the Terry families of Cork City were one of about 12 families where records show that they held significant sway in the city and had at the same time strongholds in the surrounding hinterland. These families intermarried.

In the Sarsfield papers, there is a reference to 'notes drawn out of my brother Tyrries and Christopher Skyddys writings of the moore of Grinkittene'.[17] These are abstracts of eight deeds, 1366-1534. This indicates the linkages between these three families. Another indication of the connection, through marriage with the Sarsfield family, comes from an instrument, dated 1524, where one Oliver Tyrry, gent, and his wife Elena Sarsfield are mentioned.[18]

A link between the Cogans and Terrys from *c.*1540 comes from the marriage of William Tyrry to Ellen, daughter of Robert Goggan, alias (the) Goggan.[19] Also around this time, the Terrys received land, west of Cork Harbour, from the Cogans. It is reasonable to deduce that there was some connection between the grant of land to William and his marriage to Ellen Cogan. Ellen's great-grandson, Patrick Tyrry, appears to have claimed land in her name in 1596.[20]

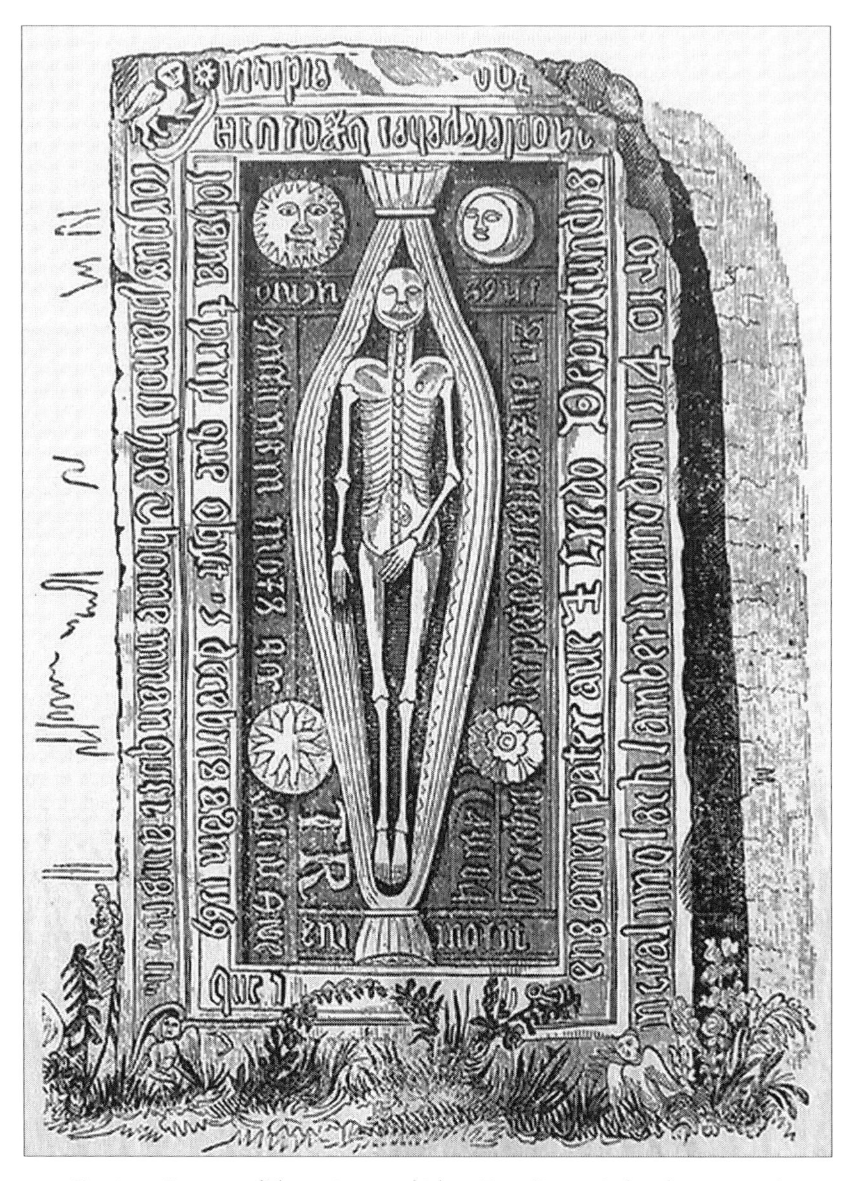

Fig. 5.1 *Gravestone of Thomas Ronan and Johana Tyrry. (Source: Cork Archives Institute.)*

Evidence of a link with another merchant family of Cork, this time of Irish origin, is in the gravestone of Thomas Ronan, one time Mayor of Cork who died in 1554 and his wife Johana Tyrry, which is now in the vestibule of Christ Church Centre. This is shown on Fig. 5.1.

The name Johana Tyrry is inscribed on the left-hand side of the headstone. Presumably these are the same people; Johannam Tyrry and Thomas Ronayn are mentioned in a deed in 1523.[21] The will of David Fitz Edmonde Tyrry, executed in March 1570, refers to his son's wife Anastas Walter, showing a connection between the Terrys and Walters, another prominent Cork family. A Dominick

Terry, born *c.*1540, was married to Martha Haly of Cork.[22] An Oliver Tyrry of Ballynory in Co. Cork had a son David, who died in 1599.[23] This David was married to Catherine Myagh, who died in 1612.

These intermarriages continued throughout the Tudor period. An Edmund Tirry, born 1535, of Cork, who married Catherine Galway, had five sons: William, born 1574 and future bishop of Cork, Robert, Dominick, George, and David as well as a daughter, Joan.[24] Joan (1567-1625) married Dominic Sarsfield, who was knighted by James I and became a chief justice of the Crown and the premier baronet of Ireland. The above mentioned Catherine Galway is referred to in the will of Richard Tyrry Fitz Adam, who referred to his daughter, Ellyne and committed her to the tuition of Catherine. The will of Richard also highlighted a Terry/Roche marriage connection. The will of one Christopher Galway refers to his brother Edmund Tyrry, and he makes bequests to him. A Peirs Gold was married to Johanna Tirrie.[25]

As well as intermarriage with other merchant families, there is some evidence of family ties with some of the major landlords in the county, such as the Roches, who were also a prominent merchant family in Cork City and the Fitzgeralds. There do not appear to be strong family ties with the Barrys, even though most of the Terry rural land holdings were in Barry's territory, i.e. the barony of Barrymore. One account states that a William Terry, who was Mayor of Cork in 1574, was married to Elizabeth, sister of Gerald the Great, Earl of Desmond.[26]

Some evidence also exists for marriage into Irish families. In Patrick Heynne's will in 1521, he referred to his true friend, David Fitz Edmond Tyrry, executor of his will, and apparently married to Patrick's daughter.[27]

From the information that is available, there were at least 18 Terry families living in, or close to, Cork City in 1550. They represented at least five per cent of the city population at this time. These figures should be increased, if some allowance is made for families for which no records are extant.

Some evidence is available on the role of female Terrys. In the will (1582) of Richard Tyrry Fitz Adam, in referring to his daughter, Ellyne he committed her to the tuition of Catherine Galway, wife of Edmonde Tyrry, and Dominick Galway, until she came of age.[28]

In a deed from 1560, a James Roche is referred to as a tutor of David Fitz Edmund Tyrry. From a Cork deed, in 1560, there was a contention between David Fitz Edmund Tyrry and Patrick Coppinger, son and heir of Thomas Coppinger of Youghal. David's grandfather was James Roche.[29]

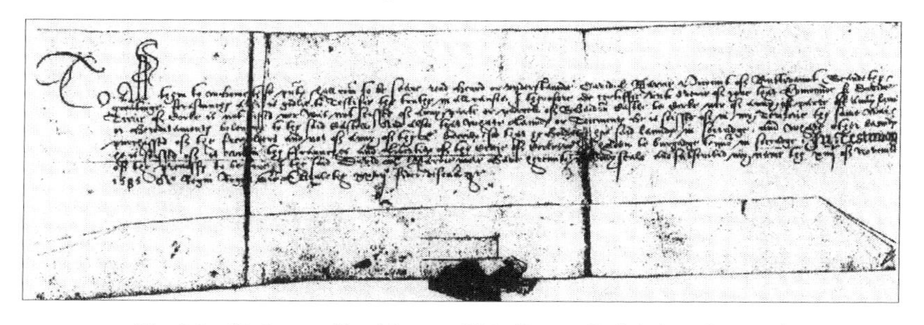

Fig. 5.2 *Testimony of Lord Barry – 1585. (Source: Cork Archives Institute.)*

Ship Name	Port	Destination	Date	Commodity
Fraunses	Bristol	from Ireland	6/10/1503	salmon, herring, hake and mantles
Lenard	Waterford	to Ireland	20/10/1503	saffron
Franses	Bristol	to Ireland	24/10/1503	beer
Franses	Bristol	to Ireland	7/11/1503	pilores tinct
Mare Cooke	unknown	from Ireland	20/11/1503	sheep skins, herring and mantles
Lenard	Waterford	from Ireland	16/12/1503	salmon, hides and herring
Mare Towre	unknown	from Lisbon	22/12/1503	Wine, wax and marmalade
Franses	Bristol	from Ireland	2/1/1504	Hides, herring, mantles, wax and hake
Jhes us bonavunture	unknown	from Bordeaux	16/1/1504	wine
Gabriell	Bristol	from Andalusia	16/1/1504	wine
Michaell	Bristol	from Andalusia	16/1/1504	Wine and dactul
Mare	Penmarch	from Bordeaux	17/1/1504	wine
Marget	Bristol	to Bordeaux	25/1/1504	cloth of assize and hake
Mare Belhous	unknown	from Algarve	22/2/1504	fruit
Trinite	Milford	from Ireland	26/2/1504	hides
James	Waterford	from Ireland	1/3/1504	wax
Trinite	Combe	from Algarve	1/3/1504	wine and fruit
Trinite	Cork	from Ireland	2/3/1504	herring and hake
Lenard	Waterford	from Ireland	15/3/1504	salmon, hake, herring, mantles, hides & wax
Trinite	Cork	to Ireland	19/3/1504	pilores tinct
Lenard	Waterford	to Ireland	28/3/1504	pilores tinct
Marget	Bristol	from Bordeaux	11/4/1504	woad
Marget	Chepstow	from Chepstow	18/4/1504	wine
Katren	Bristol	from Ireland	30/4/1504	hides, lamb and sheep skins
Gelian Bonaventur	unknown	from Spain	30/5/1504	iron
Mawdlen	Waterford	from Ireland	25/6/1504	lamb and sheep skins
John	Cork	from Ireland	18/7/1504	sheep skins and mantles
Sondaie	Waterford	from Ireland	23/7/1504	sheep and lamb skins
John	Cork	to Ireland	3/8/1504	worked orchil and pilores tinct
Fraunses	Bristol	to Algarve	9/8/1504	cloth of assize
Katren	Bristol	from Ireland	12/8/1504	salmon and sheep skins
Katren	Bristol	to Ireland	23/8/1504	pilores tinct
Marget	Bristol	to Bordeaux	5/9/1504	cloth of assize
Mare	St David's	from Ireland	17/9/1504	salmon, sheep skins and wax
Lenard	Waterford	from Ireland	22/9/1504	salmon and herring

Table 5.1 *Trading activity of William Tirrie, 1503-4.*

In 1585, 'David Lord Barrie Viscount Buttivaunt certified that Edmonde fitz David Tirrie of Cork is not seissed of any parte of Shandon Castle nor lands of said Castle, also that what lands he is seissed of in my territory the same was purchased of the freeholders and not any of the Lords Barries, so he holds said land in soccadge, and what other lands he is seissed of within the liberties of Cork which is holden by burgadge tenor in soccadge'.[30] This deed is shown on Fig. 5.2.

This David Lord Barry was in dispute with a Francis Galway about land sold to Galway by Dominick Tirry in Cobh and 'Monslstowne'.[31] Again David Lord Barry was, with a number of others including Patrick Terrie, in dispute with Morric Ronayne of Cork concerning land in Cobh, namely Ballencrushy, Ballincurragg and Mon Ivollen.

ECONOMIC ROLE

The economic role in Cork, played by Terrys in the Tudor period, in terms of their entrepreneurial and trading activities, financial activities and in their capacity as landlords is now considered.

ENTREPRENEURIAL AND TRADING ACTIVITIES

James and Patrick Tirrie exported produce from Cork in 1504. William Tirrie engaged in extensive trading activity from the ports of Waterford and Cork in this period. Data for the period, October 1503 to September 1504, for William Tirrie is provided in Table 5.1.[32] The accounts from Bristol show that for this accounting year, William engaged in either exporting or importing commodities on 36 separate ship arrivals or departures, with a total value of exports on those accounts of £183 sterling and a total value of imports of 374 sterling.

In the years 1516-7, Oliver, William Robert, Edmond and Nicholas Tirry were exporting from Cork to Bristol commodities such as mantles, skins, wool and herring, and importing commodities such as wine, silk, cloth and saffron.[33] Some of the Terry imports were unloaded at Kinsale and Waterford, in addition to Cork. Some of the exports went to Carmarthan, Wales and Penmarch, France, in addition to Bristol. David Terry, of Cork, chartered the ship *Francoyse* in 1517, to import 46 tonnes of wine from Bordeaux. Various commodities, mantles and fish paid for this.[34] In January 1518, a contract was concluded for a ship, *Marie-Jacques*, of Cork, of which William Barry was master, to ship 15 tuns, one pipe of wine from Bordeaux on the account of two Cork merchants, David Roche and William Tierry, and a merchant of Bordeaux, J. de Pedetroye.[35]

In 1526, a merchant, Tege Tyrry, exported produce from Waterford to Bristol. In the same year Robert and Walter Tyrry imported clothe and silk from Bristol.[36] In the years 1543 and 1546, the merchant Christopher Tyrry was importing and exporting commodities from both Cork and Waterford.[37] In 1546 one Richard Kyrry was both the master and merchant of the ship *John* exporting both skins and hops from Waterford to Bristol.[38] Another indication of the Cork City Terrys' involvement in trade can be obtained from Admiralty Examinations.[39] A Cork City merchant, Edmund Tyrry, was engaged in extensive shipping activity in the 1580s. In 1583 he petitioned the Privy Council, as he lost £500 worth

Fig. 5.3 *Cork Deed Edmund Tyrry and Thomas Skyddy – 1584. (Source: Cork Archives Institute.)*

of goods, due to an act of piracy off the coast of Cornwall.[40] At the same time he asked for a licence to transport corn to Ireland. In a similar petition to the Queen, he refers to losses at two locations off the coast and asks for a licence to transport 600 qrs yearly for four years to Ireland. He petitioned Burghley to do this free of custom because of his great losses due to pirates. Other petitions by Edmund Tyrry, requested a licence to import wheat to Ireland, between 200 and 300 qrs, without custom. In 1585, there was a mention of a bark laden with Flemish goods belonging to Edmond Tirrye of Cork, Merchant. The will of one Richard Terry, proven, 1582, referred to nine hides he had in Spain.[41]

In the will of David Fitz Edmonde Tyrry executed in March 1570, he referred to his ownership of a mill.[42]

Two years later the will of another Richard, this time Richard Tyrry Fitz Adam, was executed. He asked to be buried with his ancestors in Christ Church. He refers to his uncle, Nicholas Tyrry and Nicholas' daughter, Johane. Also receiving bequests were his aunt, Anastace Tyrry, her son, Dominick, and her daughters, Catherine and Genett Roche. Anastace's husband was Patrick Tyrry. They also had other sons named, James, John and Clemente. To John Fitz Christopher a sum of money and all his sheepfell, paying for them at cost price, in the discretion of Edmonde Tyrry and Dominick Galway. To Genet Tyrry Fitz Christopher a sum of money. Richard appointed his cousins, Edmunde Tyrry Fitz Edmunde, Nicholas Tyrry, and Dominick Galway, executors of his will. In the inventory of his goods was merchandise, which indicated that he possibly had a drapery and shoe making business. He had some hides in Spain, and Turkish cloth, indicating trading activity with Spain. From the pledges of gold rings etc. is an indication that they were used to transact trade and to obtain money. He had pledges with Edmonde Tyrry and Patricke Tyrry. From the will of Christopher Galway, 1582, it would appear that Nicholas Tyrry and Edmond Tyrry were brothers and that Edmond was from Carriggns, near Cork.[43]

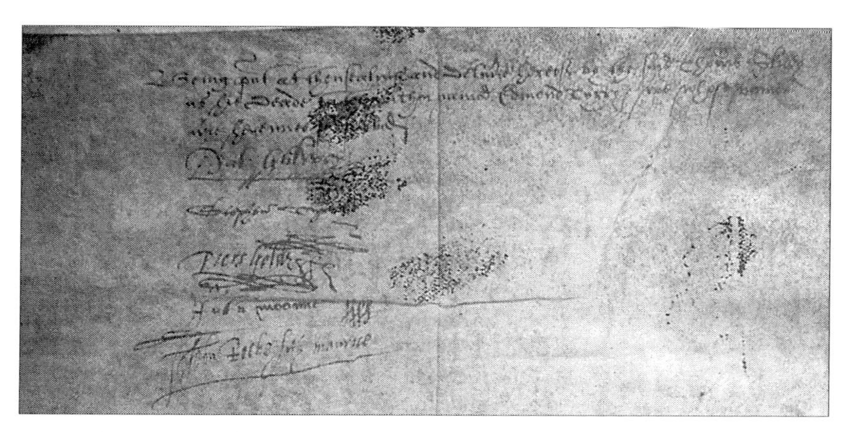

Fig. 5.4 *Signatories of Cork Deed Edmund Tyrry and Thomas Skyddy – 1584. (Source: Cork Archives Institute.)*

In 1582, one Mychelle Bluett, a merchant of the town of Youghal, bound himself unto David Tyrry, gent, of Cork. The term of the apprenticeship was four years.[44]

Financial Activities

In 1584, from a Cork deed, Edmund Tyrry Fitz David Tirrie (Tyrry) is owed £1,000 sterling by Thomas Skiddy.[45] A copy of this deed is shown on Fig. 5.3 and the signatories on Fig. 5.4.[46]

In this year Patrick Galwie and Stephanne Tyrrie granted to Thomas Skidde:

> The castle called Skiddy Castell with all and singular etc. in Downgarwan in the suburbs of the city of Cork, and the principal messuage of the said Thomas with the Kilehouse situated in longitude from the Queen's Street …

as well as other property in the suburb and elsewhere. Skiddy was not long in possession of the property, for in the same year he mortgaged to Edmond Tirry, Skiddy's Castle with its cellars, chambers, etc., together with the tenement held by Richard Walsh, and Skiddy's principal messuage and the kyle house situated in Dungarvan for £278.[47] In the following year Tirry leased the property back to Skiddy.

Land Ownership

Terrys were involved in extensive land and property transactions throughout the Tudor period. Listed in Table 5.2 are some 44 such transactions.[48] This involvement was in land and property in the city and its suburbs, around the harbour of Cork, from Kinsale to Youghal on or close to the coast and inland as far as Rathcormac. Clearly what had begun in the mid-15th century, continued uninterrupted throughout the 16th century. Of interest in this is that, from the sources researched, and displayed in the Table, there is no reference to the Terrys of Castleterry, near Mitchelstown, and to the Terrys of West Waterford. One deduction from this is that both Mitchelstown and West Waterford were outside the limit of the city/hinterland sphere of interaction in the Tudor period. What is also of significance is that over and over again, throughout the 16th century, the same families owned land and property in the city and countryside. This would indicate to me a more open interaction between town and country, than would generally be considered in the context of a 'walled' city in medieval times. However, inland travel must still have been difficult, as was evidenced from the clear preference in each cargo, coming from the continent, to offload its produce at a number of ports, e.g. Kinsale, Cork and Youghal, rather than all the cargo at one port, with inland distribution to the other towns.

It would not make for very easy reading to go into the detail of each land or property transaction indicated in Table 5.2. It is relevant to the research topic to give details of some of these transactions, and of others.

The very first transaction referred to is when, in 1503, James Wache, Chaplain, granted to Philip Fitz Thomas Tyrry lands in the parishes of Gortroe and Mogeely. Details of this and a subsequent transaction is provided in Ch. 2.

David Terry, Cork Mayor in 1521, and William Richard Barry, also of Cork City, were granted, by Lord Barrymore in 1521, Bevelly Castle, Cobh, and nearby land.[49] The land amounted to a carucate of land in the wood of Hodyne called the half carucate of Ballynacrusy. Witnesses to this grant include the Abbot of Choro,[50] and the Archdeacon of Cloyne, 'maðro' Edmund Tyrry.[51]

In 1525, Anastatia Johannis, relict of Edmund Tyrry, citizen of Cork, granted to her eldest son, David Tyrry, her tenement and messuage in Youghal, a certain messuage of her father fitz Johis Phillip junior, burger of Youghal. A witness to this grant was Dominick Tyrry, vicar of the Holy Trinity church, Cork. Dominick, later rector of Shandon church, was appointed bishop of Cork and Cloyne in 1536.[52]

Thomas Coppinger, son of Thomas Coppinger. burger of Youghal, in 1526, granted to David Tyrry a piece of ground in Dungarvan, in the suburbs of Cork. In the same year, Christopher Lawallyn, granted to David Fitz Edmond Tyrry property in Dungarvan, Shandon, including mills, weirs and fishing rights in the city of Cork. In the same year there was a separate deed of transfer, relating to a tenement in Dungarvan. The witnesses to this deed included William Tyrry, burger of Cork, John Skiddy, mayor, and George Tyrry.

In 1528, Edmund Roche granted to Richard Tyrry Fitz Patrick land in Kilvourihumulan in Kerycourihie.[53] George Tyrry was a witness to this deed. In a deed in 1528, David son and heir of James William Junior Tyrry of Carrigtohill, granted to David Fitz Edmund Tyrry, citizen of Cork, a caricature of land in Ballinsperry, Carrigtohill. A witness to this deed was Edmund Tyrry, vicar of Carrigtohill.

In 1539, Philip Gogan, a nephew and heir of William Gogan conveyed to Richard Tyrry, citizen of Cork, land in Bally an Monwylyg in Kerrycurrihy.[54] In a further deed, Richard is referred to as a citizen and merchant of Cork. In 1540, a conveyance was executed whereby David Gangcaughe, son and heir of Thomas Cogane McShiarie, son of Miles Cogane, granted and conveyed to William, son of Patrick Fitz William Terrie, a messuage and lands in Kilvourrye (Kilmoney?) and in Ballyurbane (Ballyorban), near Kilvourie, with the appurtenances in Kierrcourihye, Co. Cork; to hold forever.[55] The mayor of Cork sealed the

Year	Grantor	Grantee	Location
1503	James Walsh	Philip Fitz Thomas Tyrry	Gortroe, Mogeely
1506		Edmund Tyrry	Shandon
1506	Philip Sarsfield	Oliver Tyrry	Cork City
1513	Edmund Tyrry	David Cregh	Cork City
1514	David Myagh	Edmund Tyrry	Shandon
1517	Richard Lavallyn	David Fitz Edmund Tyrry	Cork City
1520	Lord Barrymore	Edmund Tyrry	Gortroe, Mogeely
1520	Richard Lavallyn		Shandon
1520	Patrick Heynne	David Tyrry	Suburbs of Cork
1521	Lord Barrymore	David Tyrry & William Barry	Cobh
1521	Richard Lavallyn	David Fitz Edmund Tyrry	Shandon
1521	Richard Lavallyn	David Fitz Edmund Tyrry	Cork City
1525	Anastatia Johannis	David Tyrry	Youghal
1525	Richard Lavallyn	David Fitz Edmund Tyrry	Shandon
1526	Thomas Coppinger	David Tyrry	Cork City
1526	Christopher Lawallyn	David Fitz Edmund Tyrry	Cork City, Shandon
1527	Richard Lavallyn	David Fitz Edmund Tyrry	Cork City
1528	Edmund Roche	Richard Tyrry Fitz Patrick	Marmullane
1528	James William Junior Tyrry	David Fitz Edmund Tyrry	Carrigtwohill
1529	John Walsh	David Fitz Edmund	Shandon
1539	Philip Cogan	Richard Tyrry	Mansfieldstown
1540	David Gangcaughe	William, son of Patrick Fitz William Terrie	Kilmoney, Carrigaline
1541	Milo Roche	Richard Tyrry	Marmullane
1551	John Wynchedone	Edmund Goolde and James Tyrrye	Cork
1559/60	Patrick Fitz David Tyrry	David Fitz Edmund Tyrry	Cork City
1566		David Tyrry	Youghal
1569	Michael Faggan	David Tyrry	Cork City
1570	David Fitz Edmonde Tyrry	Edmonde Tyrry	Cork City, Shandon, Youghal, Carrigtohill
1570	David Fitz Edmond Tyrry	George Gallway	Cork City
1575	James Tyrry	Christopher Tyrry	Cork City, Shandon
1576	James Tyrry	Dominick Roche	Cork City
1578	Patrick fitz Davy Tyrry	James Brown fitz Andrew	Cork City
Pre-1582	Christopher Galway	Nicholas Tyrry	East Cork
1582	Christopher Galway	Edmond Tyrry	North suburbs
1582	William Tyrry	Edmund White	Cork
1584	Patrick Galwie, Stephanne Tyrrie	Thomas Skidde	Cork City
1584	Thomas Skidde	Edmond Tirry	Cork City
1585	Thomas Sarsfield	John Tyrry Fitz Christopher	Templeusque, Glanmire, Kinsale, Shandon
1587	Thomas Sarsfield	Patrick Tirry Fitz Francis	Cork City, Shandon, Blackrock
1587	Stephen Tyrry	William Roche	Douglas
1588	David O'Kyericke	Edmund Tyrrie Fitz David	Shandon
1589	Edmund Tyrrye	Richard O' Henie	Cork City
1592	Edmund Tyrry Fitz David, Robert Tyrry Fitz Oliver	William O Haghiery	Carrigaline
1595	Edmond Tirrie Fitz David	David Fitz David Tirrie	Carrigtwohill
1599		Oliver Tyrry	Kilnaglory

Table 5.2 *Land/property transactions.*

deed. In the parish of Marmullane, Edmond Roche, son and heir of Milo Roche, conveyed in 1541, to Richard Tyrry, son and heir of Patrick, the whole of his right in 'half the town of Kilvorihusham, in Kerycourihie'.[56] This is to the west of the Great Island, where a Patrick Tyrry operated a ferry some 70 years later. In 1542, this William and Richard FitzPatrick Terry, together with Donnell Terry, signed a declaration of innocence for Thomas Ronan, a former Mayor of Cork.[57]

An inventory of the property of the Hospitallers, in 1541, showed that they had one church roofed with tiles but which was ruinous and in decay; five acres called the 'Masters feelde', three small parks containing one acre, an acre of arable land in Gortnaclogh and seven gardens all occupied by Richard Newgent and Clement and Nicholas Tyrre of Cork.[58]

In 1559 or 1560, Patrick Fitz David Tyrry of Cork grants to David Fitz Edmund Tyrry, his brother's son, a house in his messuage in Dungarvan the suburb of Cork, inhabited by Richard O' Carroll, Anastasia Tyrry wife of said Patrick.[59]

The will of David Fitz Edmonde Tyrry was executed in March 1570.[60] He desired to be buried in St Peter's Church, Cork. The bulk of his estate was left to his eldest son Edmonde. David's wife was Anastas Walter, and he had a brother Edmond. In the will he refers to his property in the city, Carrigtohill, Youghal, and in the north suburbs of the city, namely Clonbege. He also owned a mill. He also requested a specific sum of money be given to Nicholas Tyrry of Carrigtohill, to repay Andrew Galway a debt.

In 1570, David Fitz Edmund Tyrry granted to George Gallway a messuage in Dungarvan.[61] Adjoining this property was a property formerly owned by William Walshe of Youghal. A David Tyrry of Cork died in 1573.[62] David was the son of Edmond and he had a son Edmond.

In 1575, James Tyrry of the city of Cork, son and heir of Robert Tyrry, deceased, granted to his son Christopher Tyrry property in Cork City and land in Shandon.[63] Christopher Tyrry and William Tyrry are mentioned in the will of Stephen Galway.[64] The will, 1580, of Richard Tyrry, citizen of Cork, refers to four sons: Dominick, George, William and James. He bequeaths property and merchandise to them.[65]

In 1584, Edmund Tirrie son and heir of David Tirrie lately deceased granted to two Cork merchants of Skiddies Castle, land and premises in the city to hold to them for the use of the said David Tirrie and his heirs with various remainders to the Terrys.[66] A full translation of this deed is,[67]

> Edmond Tirry son and heir of David Tirry recently deceased, Cork, for various goods, exactions and national causes, gave and conceded to Richard Pounche and David Carrulle of Cork, merchants, all (my) messuages, castles, tenements, gardens, fisheries, and rents, mills, and all my inheritances inside and outside the city and county, and especially my principal messuage in Dungarvan suburb Cork, from the Queen's Street on the West to the walls of the city on the East, and extends in length from my messuage, which Anastasia Water holds for the term of her life, on the South, to the messuage of Patrick Tirry Fitz David on the North ... to the messuage of Andrew Skiddy on the South.

> The messuage held by Anastasia is now inhabited by John Goold Fitz Stephen, and another of Edmond held by Thomas Fitz John and Elena Barry, from the Queen's Street on the West to the walls on the east, from the messuage of James Ronane on the north to the tenement of Robert Tirry from the south, and also my messuage called 'le great messuage, with tavern, cellars, and other 'members' and buildings, and other premises in Dungarvan ...
>
> The messuage of George Goold, the messuage of William Roche, and my small castle called 'parandis' near the quay (le Klie) and my castle called Skyddy's Castle, and the principal messuage, recently of Thomas Skyddy, called captain of his nation, and two mills in Shandon, commonly called Archdeacon 'miles' (later written 'mills'), and my lands called Knockfrure near Cork, and Inisheynaghe, and messuages in the villa of Yeoghude, and my villas called Balynsgerye, Balianpadrig, Balyntley, in Barrymore, Mynynaghe, Baliriedor, Balynsgenye, and ferrigtowne, ville de Yeoghia (sic), Balinidonyeshe, Balisantadrig, Balyntley, Mynynadh, Balyriedi, Baynsperie, ferishetowne, insula mea (my island) called Inysheyingh, Knockfruye near Cork, and all the lands, tenements and rents, pertaining to the aforesaid Richard (Pounche) and David (Carrulle) for their use, to be held in fee by services according to customary law.'
>
> Edmond (Tirry) appended his seal, and signed at Cork, 4 October 26 Elizabeth, then 1584.
>
> Signed again on the reverse, Edmonde Tyrrye Fitz Davide, apparently to ensure that if he died with no male heirs, the indenture was to be of use to Edmond Tirrie Fitz Edmond, his uncle, and if he has no heirs, to the use of David Tirrie Fitz David, brother of the said feoffer, namely Edmond Tirry (Tirrie).

Caulfield provides the following additional information.[68] Remainder to Patrick Tirrie Fitz David. Remainder to David Tirrie Fitz Oliver. Remainder to Robert Tirrie Fitz Oliver, provided always that every of said Edmonde Tirrie Fitz David's daughters shall have a hundred marks marriage good on said lands.

In 1588, Patrick Tyrrye of Cork, merchant, and his wife Anstace Tyrry, claim the lands of Ballinckillick [Bballinkillick] and Knockaple.[69]

Political and Civic Role

Terrys provided mayors for the city on 15 separate occasions, and bailiffs on 30 separate occasions, in the 16th century. Their names are given in Table 5.3.[70]

An indication of the role played in these capacities can be gleaned from various deeds of this period. In 1533, in a document concerning John Barry and the castle in Shandon, bailiffs William and Walter Tyrry are mentioned. A Patrick Tyrry is also a witness to this document.[71] It would seem that William was the son of Patrick. In 1543, John Terry was one of the sheriffs of Cork.[72]

A David Tyrry, in a lease executed in 1569, was referred to as a former bailiff. The lease was executed between David and Michael Faggan, for property in Dungarvan.[73]

In a document, in 1533, concerning William Sarsfield of Dungarvan, Cork, the following Tyrrys are mentioned: David, Peter, Oliver, Edmund Peter and bailiffs William Patrick and Walter.[74]

In a dispute before James Redmond, arbitrator, in 1538, between James Sarsfield and Gerald Sarsfield, Clement Tyrry and John Tyrry are witnesses.[75] A David Tirry is mentioned in a Cork deed from 1538,[76] and Richard Tirry and

Year	Mayor	Bailiffs
1500		Richard
1505	William	
1508		Robert
1511	Edmond	Edmond
1514	Edmond fz David	
1515		Edmond
1519	Patrick fz William	
1520		David
1521	David fz Edmond	Nick & Robart
1522		Dominick
1525	William fz Patrick	
1527		Phillip
1529	Patrick	
1531		William and Walter
1534		Richard
1537		John
1538	William fz Patrick	
1539		Richard
1540	Richard fz Patrick	
1546		Edmond
1547		Edmond
1548		Christopher
1551	William fz Patrick	
1554	Richard fz Patrick	
1557		Patrick
1559		Francis
1569		William & David
1571		Stephen
1572		Robert
1574	William fz William	
1576		Edmond
1578		David fz Oliver
1583		Stephen
1584		Stephen
1585		Edmond
1586	Stephen	
1588	Edmond	Patrick
1591	David	
1592		Patrick fz Francis

Table 5.3 *Terry mayors and bailiffs of Cork City –16th century.*

Fig. 5.5 *Part of a side panel of a chest tomb of William Terry, Mayor of Cork. (Source: see footnote 80.)*

William Tirry are mentioned in a Cork deed from 1540.[77] In this year William Tyrry referred to as 'magister' was mayor, and Richard Tyrry was public notary.[78]

William Tyrry is named in a judgement in 1545.[79]

Fig. 5.5 depicts a stone carving, which was located in Christ Church.[80] This is a damaged side-panel of a chest tomb. The initials refer to William Terry and a Roche. MacCarthy states that the William was apparently a mayor.

The political role of Terrys enabled them to occupy other positions in which they could accumulate wealth. In a return for duty collected on the import of wine to Cork, for the six-month period ending March 1570, David Tirry, customer of Cork returned £452.[81] This was the third highest amount, after Dublin and Waterford. In 1572, David is referred to as the collector of Cork in money received by Sir John Perrot[82] since coming to Ireland.[83] Again, in the following year David Tirry gave money to Sir John Perrot. Here David is referred to as the collector of the impost at Cork.[84] In fact, David was appointed 'Customer' for Cork in 1569.[85]

In 1573, Richard Tirry and William Tirry are witnesses to a testimonial of the mayor, John Water.[86] Richard, William and Stephen Tirry are signatories to a letter by the mayor James Ronayne, in 1575, to Burghley, looking for money for the cess of soldiers in the city.[87]

One account states that this William, mayor in 1574, was married to Elizabeth, sister of Gerald the Great, Earl of Desmond.[88] This account also states that William was one of the 24 nobles and gentlemen of Munster who signed and published a manifesto in conjunction with the earl of Desmond, against the

Queen, in 1574, in which they bound themselves by an oath to defend the Catholic faith.

The will of James Andrew Fz Brown, in 1582, mentions Michell Tyrry and Patrick Fz David Tyrry.[89]

After the Desmond Wars in Munster, the delay in furthering the plantation allowed the Irish who had left the land to return. Among the names of the applicants was 'Tyrry'.

In 1585, Thomas Sarsfield of Cork, Alderman, for a sum of money, granted to John Tyrry Fitz Christopher Sarsfield Court, other land near Glanmire, a park near Kinsale, other land near Cork and Shandon Castle.[90] Presumably, this was a mortgage taken out by Thomas Sarsfield on his property.

Edmund was one of two agents for Cork City in 1582, and is the man who was described as well balanced and accounted of for his good life and behaviour.[91] In 1585, Edmund Tyrrye requested to be allowed as a retainer of Lord Burghley to inform of abuses in the county of Cork and in the province of Munster. A letter of Edmund's refers to the extortions tolerated in the province of Munster, and referring to the evils, which resulted from the sale of office.[92]

In 1587, the same Thomas Sarsfield granted to Patrick Tirry Fitz Francis a property in Cork City. John Tirry had property nearby. He also granted Patrick a kyll house within the city, a garden in Shandon called the great garden, another garden in Shandon, and the weir called Tullymore in the haven of Cork by Blackrock. To have to the said Patrick Tirry and his heirs for the use of Johan' Myagh Fitz Partick's wife during her life, and afterwards as shall be declared in my will.[93]

Religious Involvement

There exists a 16th-century rental roll of Cork, where there are references to Terry involvement in episcopal affairs.[94] These references are:

> George Tirry in Downgorne ijs and in Agglish iiijs,
> Edmund Tirrey and David Tirry FitzStephen;[95]
> Patrick Tirry.

In 1520, David Tyrry was archdeacon of Gortroe and Dysert, and Edmond Tyrry was archdeacon in the following year.[96] Edmond Tyrry was vicar of Carrigtohill in 1524 and as late as 1528.

The Act of Supremacy, 1534, made the King head of the Church. When the last pre-reformation bishop of Cork and Cloyne died two years later, Cork would seem to be the first Irish diocese filled by Henry VIII in his self-appointed role as supreme head of the church in his own dominions.[97] The King recommended Dominic Terry (Tirrey), rector of Shandon, for appointment, and he was duly appointed to Cork and Cloyne in 1536. The Archbishop of Cashel, Edmund Butler, and the bishops of Ross, Limerick and Emily consecrated him.[98] Dominick held the See in opposition to the Pope's nominee. Dominick received the profits of the See all of his time, and resided about twenty years. He was believed to be in favour of the religious changes then taking place.[99] In 1553 he was named in the patent for the investiture of Roland, Archbishop of Cashel, and in 1554 gave certain rents to the vicar choral. In 1555, the papal legate to Ireland, Cardinal Reginald Pole, absolved Bishop Tyrry of Cork and Cloyne for embracing the Henrician schism. Bolster described Tirrey as a timeserver, determined to maintain his preferment and to accommodate himself to the ecclesiastical novelties of his time.[100] A commission set up for each county, in 1556, to enquire about church goods, included, for county Cork, the Earl of Desmond, and bishop Tirrey among others.[101] Tyrry remained bishop of Cork until his death in the following year, but was never formally recognised as such in Rome, because the Pope's nominee as bishop was still alive.[102] Bishop Tirrey was undoubtedly a catholic.[103]

When in 1582, Dominick Sarsfield was admitted as rector of Little Island church, the admission was on the presentation of the parishioners of the Holy Trinity, Cork.[104] These parishioners, 40 in all, were headed by the mayor, Patrick Galway, bailiffs, James Creagh and Adam Goold, recorder, Andrew Skiddy, churchwardens, William Tirry and James Hore. Other Terrys named were Edmond Terry, David Tirry Fitz Oliver, Robert Tyrry, schoolmaster, and Patrick Tyrry. Nine years later, one Alexander Meagh or Mead was rector of Little Island and David Tirry was vicar. This David Tirry (Tyrry) was also vicar of Caherlag, Carrigtohill and Kilcurfin, Templebodan, Lackeen, and rector for Britway. Presumably this is the same vicar Tyrry referred to in the will of Christopher Galway in 1582.[105]

6

Geographical and Historical Context in the Early 17th Century

This chapter covers the years 1600 to 1644, which was a period of economic expansion in Cork, but also a period where new groupings of people became part of the settlement landscape in Cork, with consequent political and religious tensions. Up to 1644 civic administration, to which the Terrys where very closely connected, functioned in the city, although the situation for the Old English was becoming increasingly difficult. The geographical and historical context, of this period, is examined in this chapter. In the context of the geographical examination, the relationship between the city and the adjoining baronies was important. Cork harbour was a significant asset to the economy of the area. It played a part in linking settlement in the city with the baronies in addition to other areas in Ireland, Europe and beyond.

In a historical sense, in this period the Terrys fall into the category of 'Old English'. Significant change took place due to various conflicts and political upheaval. These are outlined in the context of the part played by a particular cultural unit of society in Cork, i.e. the Old English. This context is chosen because it provides a background for the settlement pattern of Terrys in Cork from 1600.

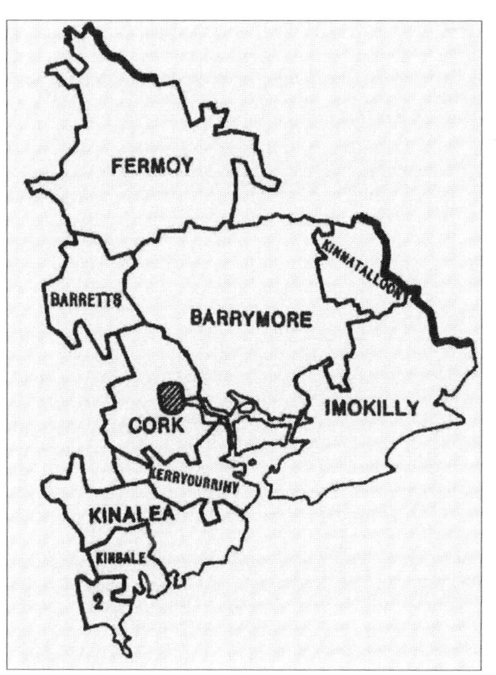

Fig. 6.1 *Cork Baronies associated with Terry settlement. (Source: Kevin Terry.)*

Geographical Context

Fig. 6.1 shows a barony map of part of county Cork. It should be remembered that in 1600 the baronies did not exist in this way.[1] A better representation is Fig. 4.1 in Ch. 4, showing the lordships in this part of Cork for 1570. That showed the baronies of Barrymore (Oliehain) and Kerrycurrihy bounded each other along the Lee valley, in the vicinity of Cork City, with Shandon being in the barony of Barrymore.[2]

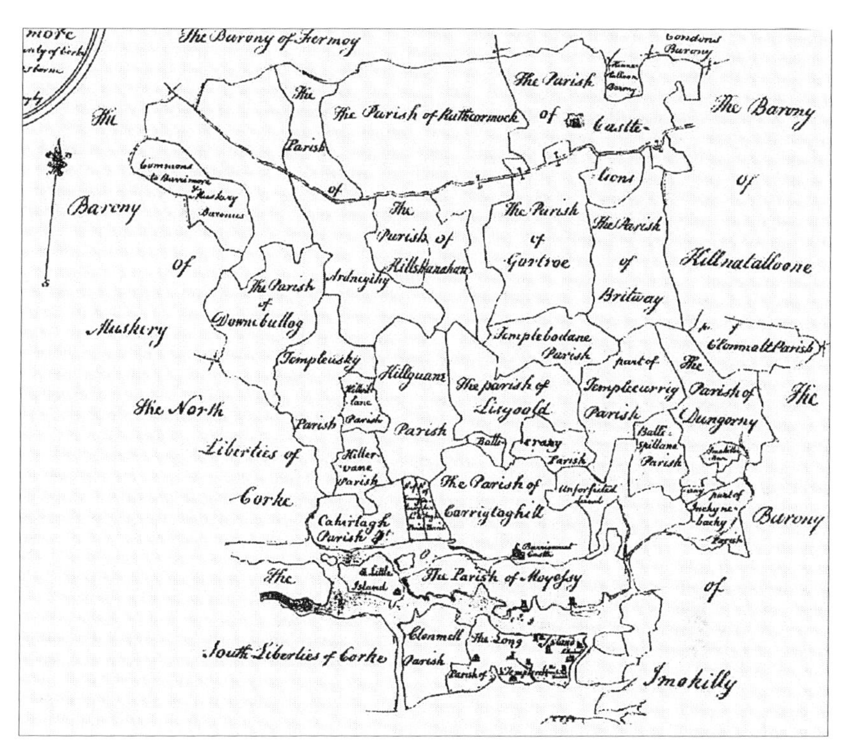

Fig. 6.2 *Shows the barony of Barrymore from the Down Survey maps. (Source: Boole Library, U.C.C.)*

The barony map is shown because it is more useful, from a current perspective, in understanding where Terrys resided. The baronies shown are where Terrys resided. Their strongholds were in the city and the barony of Barrymore. In relation to the barony of Barrymore, 'Lord Barry granted the different ploughlands to landlords, mostly of Norman stock, Terrys, Newtons.'[3] The name Ballinterry in Rathcormac may be derived from David and Edmund Tyrry, Archdeacons of Cloyne, 1520 and 1521, respectively. However Terrys are recorded here as early as 1300.[4]

Fig 6.2 shows the barony of Barrymore from the Down Survey maps. This map illustrates the various parishes of the Barony. Some of these associated with Terrys at this time would include Rathcormac, Gortroe, Carrigtohill, Clonmel and Templerobin parishes. Of interest in this map is that Little Island is shown as an island. In modern times it is not an island. In the 15th century, a Thomas Tyrri was a rector in the parish church of Little Island.

By the 16th century, the County was divided politically into a multitude of small but fundamentally autonomous lordships, ruled by both Gaelic and Anglo-Norman lords. In Cork the two major lords of Anglo-French stock were Barry and Roche. Neither of these admitted the superiority of the Geraldine lords of Desmond, who ruled over a considerable part of the County. The city of Cork appears to have looked to Barry and Roche as protectors against local lords. In the west of the County, MacCarthy lords ruled.[5]

While the focus here is Cork City and the Baronies of Cork, Barrymore and Imokilly and Terry settlements within this area, there were settlements of Terry families in many other baronies also, such as Barretts, Fermoy, and Kerrycurrihy. In

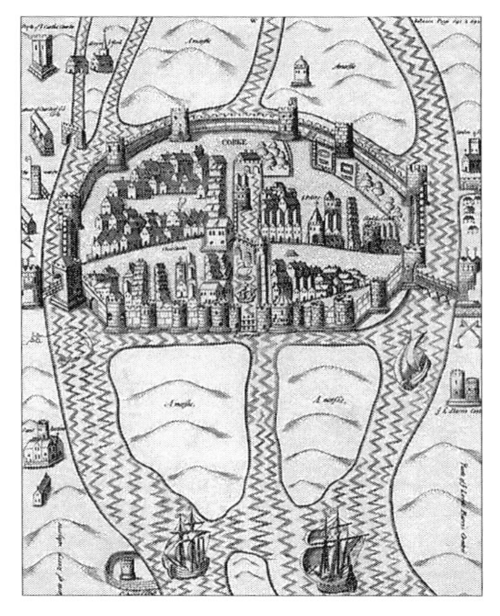

Fig. 6.3 *Cork City 1600.*

the parish of Ballydeloughy, barony of Fermoy, Castle Terry and Ballindangan are situated.[6] Castle Terry was the seat of a branch of the Terrys spelt 'Therrys', in former times.

A map for Cork City, Fig. 6.3, is from the period *c.*1600.[7] This is the *Pacanta Hibernia* map of Cork of 1587. This is an artistic presentation of Cork and not a map drawn to scale.

This map shows the city to be walled and bounded on all sides by channels of the River Lee. The city centred on what are now North Main Street and South Main Street, with laneways off these streets.[8] Marshes are indicated to the west and east of the City outside the city walls. The map indicates buildings closely packed together with some open space, and channels for ships to harbour within the city walls. The population of the city at this time would have been about 2,400.[9] Another estimate of the population in 1600 is about 2,900, with 6.5 people per household.[10] Eight laneways in the city named were names after Terrys.[11] These are named in Ch.2 and represents about 12 per cent of the 68 streets or lanes.

There was also a Therry's Castle in the city. This is said to have stood on one of the small lanes, which spread on either side of Main Street. The house and

Fig. 6.4 *Rothe House, Kilkenny. (Source: The Kilkenny Archaeological Society.)*

Fig. 6.5 *Location of Skiddy's Castle. (Source: Kevin Terry.)*

garden in Dominick Terry's Lane, North Main Street, is mentioned by John Windele, and this is probably what the 'Castle' was; a relatively small 'stone-house' of a wealthy citizen. There exists the possibility that Skiddy's Castle was meant here, since the Terry family seem to have occupied that building at times during the late 16th and early 17th centuries.[12] There are no stone houses from this period still standing in Cork City. Rothe House, Fig. 6.4, in Kilkenny city, a merchant's house built in the period 1594 to 1610, is perhaps an example of what some wealthy merchants of Cork lived in, in this period.

The location of Skiddy's Castle is on the left of the photograph on Fig. 6.5. The shop number 103 North Main Street occupied part of Skiddy's Castle. The lane between the two shops was once known as Skiddy's Castle Lane.

Historical Context

In examining the history of this period, the term 'Old English' frequently occurs. The term Old English, or Sean-Ghaill, was commonly used in the early 17th century to denote the descendants of those who had colonised Ireland from the period of the Norman invasion to approximately that of the Reformation. Later colonists, and their descendants, who were for the most part differentiated from their predecessors by the profession of forms of the Protestant religion, were distinguished by the term New English. The denotation of the term Old English did not necessarily rest upon exact historical criteria: in both urban and rural districts, the descendants of earlier invaders, the Danes, had mingled so closely with the newcomers as to become within very few generations indistinguishable from them, and assimilation also took place to some degree, almost exclusively within the towns, between Irish families and the colonists. Apart from the qualifications of the historical accuracy of the term Old English, which arose from occasional assimilation of extraneous elements, the term English itself was by no means strictly accurate, because the first settlers were, in fact, a heterogeneous gathering of Anglo-Normans, Welsh and Fleming, as well as English.[13]

THE SITUATION IN 1600

In 1600, there were three distinct groups in Ireland, Gaelic Irish, Old English and New English. The vast majority of Gaelic Irish were rurally based. Towns were not characteristic of Gaelic lordships, except for episcopal centres and the unusual exception of the O'Reillys' settlement at Cavan.[14] The towns existing in 1600 were often imposed on older foundations or sited at a port or estuary. Franchises and liberties were extensive by English standards. The freemen of these towns tended to be aristocratic merchants rather than craftsmen: Old English burgher families or local gentry who had migrated inside the walls. There were Gaelic merchant families too, e.g. Ronaynes of Cork. The nature of urbanised society was essentially defined against threats from outside.[15]

The 'Old English' combined loyalty to England with a Catholicism that, since the Reformation, no longer attracted English support. They also controlled one-third of Irish land at a time when political acceptability was becoming dependant on religious conformity.[16]

Of the twelve or so families who came to dominate the civic and commercial life of Cork City, the Tirrys were the most prominent in their allegiance to the Crown of England. While political loyalty to the Crown was a point of honour for the Tirrys and the other Old English citizens, religion was a different matter. The Tirry family was closely identified with the Roman Catholic Church, e.g. Blessed William Tirry, O.S.A. (1609-54).[17]

In Cork, in 1600, there were sporadic outbreaks of fighting between the Irish (McCarthys of West Cork) and the Old English. There was some settlement of New English south of the city in the Barony of Cork (then part of Kerrycurrihy). Barrymore was still very much under the control of the 'Old English' family, the Barrys, who supported the Queen and refused to side with the Irish leading up to the battle of Kinsale.[18] Following the defeat of the Irish at the Battle of Kinsale, the President of Munster, George Carew, rode roughshod over the liberties of the citizens of Cork by building a series of forts around the city, most notably at Haulbowline. This despite the city's claim that this was within its franchises and so a fort should not have been built without its permission. Haulbowline came into the ownership of Terrys in the middle of the 15th century.

In Imokilly, the Desmond Wars had some impact on the influence and power of the Fitzgeralds. However, they still had a dominant position in the Barony. Sir Walter Raleigh and the new English planters were given extensive grants of land around Youghal. For example, in February 1602, the Lord Deputy on his return to Dublin from Cork lodged with Sir John Fitz-Edmond Fitz-Gerald at Cloyne.[19]

PROTESTANT AND RECUSANT: THE CONSTITUTIONAL STRUGGLE, 1603-41

On Queen Elizabeth's death, James VI of Scotland became King James I of England. James was a son of the Catholic Mary Stuart. In expectation that he would show himself well disposed towards his mother's faith, the Irish recusants, i.e. those who refused the Oath of Supremacy of the King (or Queen) as Head of the Church, looked forward hopefully to his reign. It was among the Old English, and not among the natives, that this expectation was highest.[20]

This was the case in Cork City, where the delay in proclaiming the new King was intended to impress upon the new monarch the seriousness of the opposition of Catholics to the law compelling them to attend Protestant worship. This gave rise to the slogan 'Rebel Cork'. One of the ringleaders to the opposition was Edmund Tirry.[21]

Traditionally, the Old English had held themselves aloof from the conspiracies and rebellions of the Gaelic Irish. But during the first four decades of the 17th century their loyalty was placed under increasing strain. They were excluded, in theory, from local as well as central government; heavy fines were imposed on prominent citizens refusing to attend Protestant services and even their titles to land, like those of the Gaelic Irish, began to be questioned in courts that inevitably found for the Crown. For periods, the English establishment took a pragmatic view, and the evidence shows that Catholics still held positions in civil authorities.[22] The turning point came in 1640-1, when it seemed that the King, from whom the Old English had expected some favourable treatment, trading toleration for political and financial support, was about to lose power to a parliament that reflected much more closely the strong anti-Catholicism of ordinary Englishmen. Charles I himself blurred the question of loyalty by encouraging the army of the Gaelic Irish of Ulster as a reserve to be used against his English and Scottish enemies. In October 1641, the Ulster Irish rose in arms. They claimed they were defending the prerogative of the Crown against its enemies in Parliament and elsewhere. The Old English, after several weeks of hesitation, agreed to join them.[23] At this time, an indicator of the influence of the Old English can be obtained from the extent of their ownership of land in County Cork. In 1641, the Old English owned 23.9 per cent of the profitable land in County Cork.[24]

Outbreak of Civil War in County Cork in 1641

The Irish Rebellion broke out, during which there were sometimes five different parties in Ireland.

1st: The Royalists, headed by the Earl of Ormond.
2nd: The Parliamentarians, headed by different people at different times.
3rd: The Scots of the north.
4th: The party of the Supreme Council, with Preston and others at their head.
5th: The Nuncio's party led by Owen Roe and others.

In 1642, the Earl of Barrymore was with the Lord President of Munster at Ballyhoura Mountains to fight the rebels. There was some confusion as the rebels claimed to be working for the King. Youghal was at this time in the control of the New English, and the Earl of Cork, who obtained much of Sir Walter Raleigh's land, raised an army here. The Irish blockaded Cork City, with some Old English and Lord Roche, on the side of the Irish.

In September 1643, a cessation was agreed between the Marquis of Ormond on the King's side, and Lord Muskerry on the part of the Irish, this to continue for one year. The night before the truce was concluded, the Irish took up arms in the Baronies of Imokilly and Barrymore, killed all the English they could meet with, and plundered the County.[25]

In 1644, Inchiquin drove all the Irish out of Cork and Youghal. The civil authority in Cork ceased as a result and was not renewed for 11 years. This was the end of the domination by the Old English of civil affairs in Cork.

In 1641, Catholics owned 59 per cent of the profitable land in Ireland, while in the city of Cork, Old English families owned about two-thirds of the property.[26]

7

The Nation of the Terries, 1600-44

This Chapter, covering the period 1600-44, was the period when the Terrys were most influential in the affairs of Cork City since one of their members was bailiff in 1430. The Terry families in Cork in the early 1600s are identified and analysed for the following areas of Cork: the city, Rathcormac, Cobh, and Carrigtohill in the lordship of Oliehain, and Ballynora in the lordship of Kerrycurrihy. These two lordships subsequently became the baronies of Barrymore and Kerrycurrihy. Some other areas where Terrys also resided are commented on. The number and extent of Terrys in the city, and where in the county they resided, is examined. Also, their movement out of Cork to other parts of Ireland and to Spain is commented on. Examples of how power and positions were confined to a small élite number of families are provided, and how, by intermarriage within this group, they were able to maintain this position. Genealogical data is provided to assist in understanding some of the developments outlined. Some concluding remarks are made on the number of families in this period. Much of the material for this chapter derives from the Council Book of the Corporation of Cork, Sarsfield Papers, and Windle Manuscripts. The title of the chapter is taken from the will of one James Tyrry, in 1618, where he refers to 'the nation of the Terries'.

As in Ch. 5, this family grouping will be considered in terms of social perspective, their economic role in terms of merchant and trading activity, financial and land ownership. Also their role in political and civic affairs in the context of Cork, and their involvement in religion will be examined.

Social Perspective

In the years 1612-41, 16 Terrys were sworn freemen of Cork City.[1] These were:

John Tyrry fz Edmond, in 1612,
Domk Tyrry fz Patrick, in 1612,
William Tyrry fz James, in 1614,
William Tyrry fz Patrick, in 1616,
Richard Tyrry fz Patrick, in 1616,
Dominick Tirrie fz James, in 1618,
George Tyrry fz William, in 1620,
Patrick Tyrry fz Peeres, in 1622,
Peeres Tyrry fz Peeres, in 1622,

Richard Tyrry fz Peeres, in1626,
William Thirrie fz Domk, in 1636,
James Thirrie, fz Domk, in 1636,
John Tirrie fz David, in 1637,
William Tirrie fz David, in 1637,
David Tirrie fz David, in 1639,
Patrick Thyrry fz Patrick, in 1641.

These 16 were the sons of Councillors and the merchant classes. Looking for the occurrence of the father's Christian names, Patrick, James, William, Peeres, Dominick, and David, among the Mayors and Sheriffs of the City, in the early 1600s, the following are recorded.[2]

Fig. 7.1 *St Peter's Church, North Main Street. (Source: Kevin Terry.)*

Edmond FitzDavid Terry, mayor in 1604, married Margaret Skiddy, daughter of Thomas Skiddy, and Edmond FitzEdmond Terry, mayor in 1614, married Catherine Galway. Edmond and Catherine had five sons: William, Robert, Dominic, George and David as well as a daughter, Joan. She married Dominic Sarsfield, who was knighted by James I and became a Chief Justice of the Crown and Premier Baronet of Ireland.

In the will of William Sarsfield of Cork, Alderman, his wife Ellis Tirrie is mentioned.[3] The overseer of the will was his brother-in-law, David Tirrie Fitz Stephen. David's father, Stephen, was married to Anstace Gould.[4] A cousin Dominick Tirry is mentioned in the will. This will is a good example of the inter-relationship between the dozen or so Old English families in the City at this time. Goolds, Roches, Coppingers, Galways, Terrys as well as Ronaynes all get mentioned. Many of these are related through marriage to the William Sarsfield.

There is some evidence of a loosening of the ties that previously existed almost exclusively between the Old English families. George Teirry's, alderman, first wife was Joane Gould of Cork City while his second wife was Francis Evans, from Wells in England.[5] A Margaret Terry was married to a Mountgomery.[6] Dominick, mayor in 1611-2, married Catherine, daughter of Colonel Anthony Fielding, nephew to Sir William Fielding, Earl of Denbeigh.[7] One William Fitz Oliver Terry worked in probably a legal capacity for the Earl of Cork, Lord Boyle. In 1635, Boyle employed Terry to collect licensing money from the alehouse keepers in the county of Cork.[8] There is also a broadening of the geographical areas where the Terrys resided. Some of their members had settled in Limerick and Spain, and a David Tyrry fz David spent part of his time in Dublin, as agent for Cork.[9]

The will of one James Tyrry fz Edmond, 1618, refers to the 'nation of the Terries'.[10] Several are mentioned. He asked to be buried near the great altar of St Peter's Church, see Fig. 7.1.

He refers to his brother John Tirry, his wife Catherine Meade, his uncle David Tirry, his brother Stephen Tirry, who died some 18 years later, in 1636, his uncle James Tirry, and to the following:

> Edmund Tirry fitz Edmund,
> James Tirry fitz Patrick,
> Clement Tirry fitz Patrick,
> David fz James,
> William fz James, and
> Dominick fz James.[11]

There are no witnesses and no seal to this will.

There was an enquiry by Cork Corporation into the goods of William Tyrry fz James in 1628, after he had drowned himself.[12] In 1627, a King's Letter, Westminster, was issued ordering that David Terry (FitzEdmond) be made a baronet of Ireland 'in virtue of his services performed for the King and his other merit'. There is no record of the patent ever having been issued.[13]

A list of the ancient natives and inhabitants of the City of Cork (1652) contains 17 Terrys.[14]

William Tyrry fz Pa	John Tyrry fz John
George Tyrry[15]	Richard Tyrry fz Piers
Robert Tyrry fz Robert	James Tyrry fz Dominick
Dominick Tyrry fz Dominick	Francis Tyrry fz Dominick
Patrick Tyrry fz Patrick	Dominick Tyrry fz Patrick[16]
William Tyrry fz Oliver	Edmond Tyrry fz Wm
David Tyrry fz Stephen	Robert Tyrry fz Wm
Piers Tyrry	Richard Tyrry fz George[17]
Stephehen Tyrry fz George[18]	

Table 7.1.

From Ballinterry, Rathcormac, barony of Barrymore, a Richard Terry was baptised on 8 January 1600.[19] He married Helen Fitzgerald.[20] Their descendants moved successively to Limerick, France and Spain. Some of their descendants now live in the province of Andalusia, Spain. A son of Richard's, John, was baptised in St Peter's Church, Cork, in 1630,[21] and this John married Mary Ronan from Corkavaskin, Co. Clare.[22]

Economic Role

An indication of the extent of the wealth of some Terrys in the early 17th century can be obtained from examining the will of David Tyrry Fitz Edmond in 1570, and a deed executed in 1584, presumably by his son, Edmond Tirrie fitz David.[23] The father bequeathed the following property:

Stauntons-towne, Tybbots-towne, Speris-towne, a house in the city, a house in Youghal, a park called Clanbege, and a mill; in all possibly 600 acres of land, two houses and a mill.[24]

The son's grant included the following property: at least seven houses in Cork City and Youghal, two castles, including Skiddy's castle in the city, two mills, and seven townlands and an island, possibly 1,400 acres in total. The purpose of the legal document was to ensure that if Edmond died with no male heirs his property was to go to his uncle, Edmond Tirri fitzEdmond.[25] In 1584, Edmond FitzDavid had daughters, but no son. Subsequently, he had a son.[26]

Carrigtohill Church Tower, probably built in the late medieval period by the Terrys, is shown in Fig. 7.2.[27]

In the will of Patrick Lavallin, 1641, who was Mayor of Cork in 1638, and who owned about 6,000 acres of land in Cobh and other parts of the barony of Barrymore, his wife Anastasia (Terry) was to receive one third of his land. A more detailed examination will now be given of their entrepreneurial and trading activities, their role in finance, and their ownership of land.

Entrepreneurial and Trading Activities

In the Sarsfield papers, D.25, 961, there is a reference to a Deed of partnership between David Tyrry and Arthur Skyddy, merchants, at Cork, 30 March 1603.

Fig. 7.2 *Carrigtohill Church Tower. (Source: Kevin Terry.)*

A David Tyrre fitzStephen was Mayor of the Stable in 1618.[28] A David Tyrry fz David was Mayor of the Stable in 1620.[29] Other Terry merchants of the Stable at this time were Dominick, William and John Fitz Edmond.[30] In 1635, Edmund Tyrrie, alderman, was mayor of the stable.[31] Part of the Charter granted to the Corporation by King James I, in 1608, provided for the establishment of a Stable. In the charter, the names of those who were to constitute the 'Society of Merchants of the Stable' were specified, as was the Mayor.

A grant in the ninth year of the reign of James I, from the King to Patrick Terry, of Ballyleary within the Great Island, of a ferry over the river and port of Cork, from the cantred of Kyericurrihy, to the Great Island, forever.[32]

There was also a grant for a ferry over the river and port at Calloghrahagl, near the Great Island, viz., from the same, to the cantred of Imokilly.[33] This was really a regrant.[34] A Patrick Tyrry of Ballyleary, Cobh, died on 26 August 1623.[35] He had a son William Tyrry, and a daughter Anastasia, who married Patrick Lavallin Mayor of Cork, in 1638.[36] In the will of Patrick Lavallin, his wife was to receive one third of his extensive land holding.

In 1622, there was a lease by Patrick Tyrry to Philip Barry, Great Island, Cork, of boats and furniture.[37]

In 1615, the Earl of Cork, Boyle, paid Elizeus Skyddy for releasing his interest to Patrick Terry ffitz Wm in the particle of tithes in the Great Island, which he granted to the said Mr Terry and his wife, for both their lives at 40s per annum.[38]

Edmund Tyrry is recorded as owning a ship laden with wine from Bordeaux.[39] In 1607, the ship *Recovery of Bristol* was taken with its goods. These belonged to, among others, James Tirry, who was on the ship.[40] One Richard Terrye, a sailor, of Crookhaven, was a juror who decided a verdict on a murder charge, in 1614.[41]

One of David Terry's, mayor in 1614, descendants was Don Ramon Terry of Malaga, an officer in the service of the King of Spain. There is evidence of a number of different Terry families trading with and being resident in Spain throughout the 17th century and later.

In 1629, the will of John Terry Fitz Francis of Cork mentions his daughter Alson, his nephew Dominick, and his son and heir Francis.[42] A Dominick FitzJames Terry, a Cork merchant died in 1632. His sister was Janett. A Dominick Fitz James Terry was made a freeman of the City 14 years earlier.

In 1603 one Oliver Tyrry was operating as an attorney in Cork.[43] Twenty-five years later, one William Tirry fz Oliver is referred to as one of the attorneys of this Court.[44] In 1634, Stephen Terry, of the city of Cork, was admitted to Gray's Inn, London.[45] Among the leading Old English families of Cork City were to be found, as always, a network of London-trained lawyers: in 1625-41, 15 recusant youths from south Munster attended the Inns of Court in London.[46]

Financial Activities

Terrys were involved in lending money. In 1605, a David Roche from Kinsale gave a bond to David Tyrry fz David. The mortgage advance by Tyrry was redeemed by Roche.[47]

In 1606, a covenant was entered into between David Tyrry fz David and William Bradely of Dublin, where Tyrry gave £80 sterling, at Strongbow's tomb, in Christ Church, Dublin, for the wardship of lands of David Tirry fz Edmond.

Terrys were long closely associated with the Great Island, in the barony of Barrymore.[48]

In 1622-3, the Barrys of Ringmeen mortgaged to William Terry, of Cork, their part of Cuskinny and the lands of Ballycarwigg (Ballincurrig) and Ballyntertwing. These lands were subsequently forfeited.[49] This William was the son of Patrick Tyrry of Cork, merchant.[50] A William Terry lived in Cuskinny in the early 18th century, 90 years later. Terrys had strong connections with the townlands on the east of Cobh Island, owning them directly, as in the case of Ballyleary, jointly as in Passage and Belvelly Castle, and through marriage to a Lavellin, as in the case of Ringmeen. Haulbowline Island was also in the ownership of Terrys and they operated a ferry in the vicinity.

Land Ownership

Some documents relating to a David Tyrry of this period include: D.25, 942-60 Sarsfield Papers (Associated families); Leases, releases, mortgages relating to property at Holy Trinity, Half Road, and St Peter's, Shandon and other areas in the city and suburbs of Cork. Principal parties, David Tyrry, Edward Galway, Wm Skyddy, 1602-17.

Edmund Tyrry, Alderman, M.P., was part of a syndicate of land speculators which included Sir Thomas Roper, Patrick fitz Maurice Roch and Thomas Sarsfield, with Sir Dominick Sarsfield and his son William acting as assignees, in buying land in the barony of Duhallow in the early part of the 17th century.[51] Also a William (fitz-George) Terry of Cork bought 600 acres of land in Duhallow and had a financial interest in a further 950 acres. A Dominic Terry of Glanturke in the barony of Duhallow was involved in the 1641 rebellion.[52] Terrys were also buying land in Carbery, and they were also land owners in the baronies of Kinalea and Barretts. Ald. David Tirry, of Cork, also owned land in the barony of Duhallow.[53] One Dominick Terry had six ploughlands, about 2,500 acres, for the term of 21 years, in the barony of Kinalmeaky. This was part of land planted in the plantation of Munster.[54]

Blackrock Castle, the image of which is on the cover of this book, was granted to William Terry and heirs, in 1614, provided that 'it was handed back to the Corporation upon any specials cause of service' and it was also stated that Terry was 'to let the premises only to a freeman of Cork'.[55]

Other examples of Terry involvement in property in the City include David Fitz Edward [Edmund] Tirry and David Fitz James Tirry leasing property in St Peter's parish in 1615. Terrys were leasing land in and around the city on a large scale, and it would appear that some of these leases were to 'New English', Turner, Huelt, and Hawkins.

In 1618, a fee farm grant was made by the Corporation to Ald. John Thyrry of part of the East March lying northward of the way leading east to the *Old Custom House*, not then built. This now forms that part of the City between the North Channel and Paul Street.[56]

The Terrys had a long association with Carrigtohill, barony of Barrymore.[57] In 1623 and 1624, a number of transactions took place where the Earl of Cork, Lord Boyle, purchased from Edmond Terry fitz David from Carrigtohill of all his messuages, tenements, and land etc., these called Terries Lands, in Carrigtohill.[58]

In these references, John Terry of Carrigtohill, and Dominick Terry ffitz Edmond are mentioned. The transactions provided that Lord Boyle would pay rent for a number of years. In 1629 he still owed £80 sterling and had not received the ancient deeds of the property he purchased. The Earl of Cork's will made interesting reading on this subject:

> And whereas to prevent the coming of a great and powerful man into the town of Carrigtwohill ... that might be offensive and prove an unpleasing neighbour to the said late Earl of Barrymore, his son in law,' the Earl purchased several burgages and burgage lands, tenements and hereditanements from the Newtons and Terries 'who were ye ancient founders, inheritors, and freeholders thereof.[59]

From the Lismore papers, vol.IV is the following entry for September 1635:

> I (Earl of Cork) formerly paid unto Edmond Terry, of Carrigtwohill, for all the Terry messuages, lands, parks, and tenements in the town and fields of Carrigtwohill als Barriescourt the sum of £20 sterling; for him to Mrs Cade, widow and by his direction other £22, and now other £58, in all three payments of £100 sterling; for the fee simple of all his lands known by the name of Terries Lands, as well within and without the said town of Carrigtwohill, and upon his deed recovery return and yield up unto me all his ancient deeds and evidences, I made a lease of my whole purchase to his brother in law, Betau Mccvmegante, to his use for 21 years at xij pounds sterling per annum.[60]

A David Tyrry resided in Ballynora in the Barony of Cork.[61] His daughter Jane married Peter Goold fz Garrett of Cork and Douglas, who died in 1609.

Some of the Terry families of Cork owned property in Youghal and Kinsale.[62]

There is evidence that some Terrys also settled in Macroom, in1607-24.[63]

While Castleterry, in the parish of Ballydeloughy, barony of Fermoy, is referred to as the ancient seat of the Therry family, this family does not appear in the Terry deeds relating to the city and harbour area.[64] One William Terry, yeoman, was murdered near Mitchelstown in 1641.[65]

The Survey and Valuation of the City returned in 1663 gives a list of proprietors of property in 1641.[66] Terry names on this list are contained in Table 7.2.

In Table 7.2 there are at least 14 different Terry families. In 1641, Terrys were proprietors of 61 properties, in the city and suburbs.

The Civil Survey provides a house-to-house record of Cork City before the rebellion in 1641. The buildings within the city walls were houses, as opposed to cabins. Almost all were built of stone and slated.

POLITICAL AND CIVIC ROLE

A David Terry was Mayor in 1608 (David fz Stephen), 1614 (David Tyrry fz-David), and 1628 (David Tyrry Fitz-Edmond), and Dominick fz Edmond was Sheriff in 1611, and a Dominick was Sheriff again in 1634. A Patrick Tyrry was Mayor in 1613 (Fitz-William), and in 1617. A William Tirrie was Mayor in 1620 (Fitz-Richard), and Sheriff in 1630 (Fitz-George), and Sheriff in 1638.

An indication of the central role of Terrys in the political and administrative affairs of the City, and the strong position of the city merchants, can be gleaned from the following details taken from a publication by Richard Henchion on *Bishopstown, Wilton, and Glasheen*:

'1600 Edmond Terry, as agent for the city of Cork, wrote to Sir Robert Cecil requesting that the Liberties may be enlarged three or four times. At present the city had only one mile compass whereas Kinsale had even three or four. The lands within the three or four mile compass already belonged to the citizens of Cork. This had come about as a result of prosperous times for the

Area of City	Lane	Proprietor
South-West Quarter	New Street	James Tirry
	Mill Street	William Tirry
South-East Quarter	David Goold's Lane	Dominick Tirry
	Robert Tirry's Lane	Robert Tirry
North-East Quarter	David Thirry's and other's Lane	David Thirry
	David Tirry's Lane	David Tirry fitz Edmond
	Dominick Tirry's Lane	Dominick Tirry, David Tirry fitz James
	William Tirry fitz Patrick's Lane	William Tirry fitz Patrick, William Tirry, James Tirry, Patrick Tirry fitz Dominick
	James Tirry's Lane	James Tirry
	David Tirry fitz Stephen's Lane	David Tirry fitz Stephen
North-West Quarter	The Great Lane	David Tirry
	David Tirry's Lane	David Thirry fzStephen, David Thirry
	Thirry's Lane	Richard Thirry fitz George
	Skiddy's Lane	David Thirry fitz Edmond
	Back Lane	James Tirry fitz Dominick, James Tirry
	Mallow Street	David Thirry fitz Edmond
	Mallow Lane	David Thirry fitz Edmond
	Blarney Lane	David Tirry fitz Edmond, William Tirry, David Thirry
	Marker Green	Dominick Tirry
	Fair Lane	David Tirry fitz Edmond
	Church Lane	David Tirry
	Upon the Strand	James Thirry
The South suburbs	Bridge Street	William Thirry
	St Nicholas Low Street	Dominick Thirry fitz Edmond
Lands in the North Suburbs	Temple acre, 1 acre	James Thirry fitz Dominick
	Cloynebegg	James Thirry fitz Dominick
	West Gortiknockane, 2 acres	David Thirry fitz Edmond
	Knoppoge Andrew, 3 acres, Fair Hill, 4 acres, Skiddy's acre also called Cloghlea, 2 acres, Monenaheyny, 1 acre, and Parkykacky Begg, ½ an acre.	David Thirry fitz Edmond
St Brigetts Parish Lower in the South Suburbs	Stange and ½ Gortnacrushy, Boughaneboy, Bohernaslycrily, Bohernmanagh, Inshey, Bohernafrankagh, and Gortehoragh, comprising 4 acres	Wm Thirry fitzPatrick
	Carrigeens, 1 ½ acres	James Thirry
	Croughtynapeky, 2 acres	David Thirry
Land in the North Liberties	Keallogibegg, 1 acre	David Thirry fz Edmond
	Glankittane, 43 acres	Anstace Gold (alias) Thirry

Table 7.2 *Terry Proprietors Cork City 1641.*

city merchants and devastating times for rural dwellers. The latter, who were not able to protect themselves from the encroachment of soldiers, thieves and highwaymen, abandoned their isolated holdings and sold them to the city merchants who were only too eager to have an outlet for their surplus profits. To have the Liberties extended to include these properties would have been to their considerable advantage'.

The following deed is another example showing the Terry role and influence at this time:

'And whereas Edmond Tyrry, Maior of the Cittie of Cork, William Tyrry and Michell Galewey, 2 bailliffes of the same cittie and the commaltie of the said cittie hath given, graunted, bargained, and sold enfeoffed and confirmed vnto me the said John Coppinger, Geordge gold, Alderman, Edmond Moroghe, and David Tyrry fz. Stephen, all and singular the fishinge poolles and fishing places of bothe the northe and sowthe river of the said Cittie called the Kings powles, with the appurtenances, To haue and to hold the premises with the appurtenances vnto me the said John Coppinger, Geordge gold, Edmond Moroghe, and David Tyrry, our heires and assignes in comen and not jointe in mortgadge of towe hundreth poundes sterlinge currante money of England as by the same deede bearing date the 11 of October 1608'.[67]

Edmond FitzDavid Terry was Mayor in 1604, and in 1614 Edmond (fz Edmond) was Mayor.[68] The Terrys' political life was not an easy one. On the death of Queen Elizabeth, the citizens of Cork refused to proclaim her successor, James I and Terrys were involved in this refusal, it was proved against one of these Edmonds, and he was referred to as another rebel,

> that he advised the Mayor to take the key of Skiddy's castle from Mr Hughes the store-keeper, and place the ammunition in Dominick Galway's cellars, and that Hughes should not be suffered to come there without a sufficient guard, all of which the Mayor complied with.[69]

Some time later in the same month, April 1603, the Mayor

> appointed Gold and Terry captains over two companies, consisting of 100 men each ... who were billeted upon the citizens. They suffered no person to go to mass but such as swore to maintain their religion.

They carried out some actions against those who opposed the position of the Mayor. The King's representatives, the commissioners,

'finding no good was to be done by treaty, sent to Haulbowline for artillery, but the citizens having notice of their design, manned some boats under the command of William Terry to take the fort, or, if possible, to intercept the artillery; and in this attempt on the fort there were several killed on both sides; but the guns came safe to the commissioner's camp'.

Some Terrys were also involved in military affairs. There is mention in 1603 of a Captain William Terry.[70]

The following month, in May 1603, when the Lord Lieutenant arrived at Cork, the citizens were divided on whether or not to admit him.

'Mead the recorder strongly opposed his entrance, and drawing together the

Meads, Golds, Captain Terry, Lieutenant Murrough, Fagan, and an infinite number of mob, would have withstood his lordship's entrance had not alderman John Coppinger, alderman Walter Coppinger, alderman Terry, the Galways, Verdons, and Martels, opposed their designs'.[71]

It appears the Terrys had a foot in both camps. Lord Deputy Mountjoy was allowed to enter the City.

Edmond FitzDavid Tyrry died in November 1604.[72]

Dominick Tyrry fz Edmond was chosen coroner of the City in 1609.[73] He was mayor in the following year. A number of years earlier he was an undersheriff for the county of Cork. In 1616 he was the subsidy collector for County Cork.[74]

Of the freemen listed earlier, John, James and Peeres Terry do not appear on the list of Mayors or Sheriffs for this period.[75]

Other Terrys who were Mayors or Sheriffs during this period were:

George Tyrry Fitz-Edmond, Mayor in 1616; One George Terry of the city of Cork went surety for one of the sheriff's of Limerick county, Edmund Fitzgerald.[76] George was dead by 1637, while his brother Dominick was still living.[77]

Richard Tirry, Sheriff in 1632.

George Thirry FitzWilliam, Sheriff in 1644; this possibly was the same person that was admitted a freeman of the City 24 years earlier.

Robert Thyrry Fitz-Robert, Sheriff in 1644.[78] Between 1609 and 1612, his father, Robert Tyrry, was deputy clerk of the Crown in Munster to Sir Richard Archdeacon.[79]

These named Terrys were not the full extent of Terry families in Cork in this period. A James Tyrry fzPatrick was a Juror in 1610. There were also several others.[80]

The high number of people from the same family group or 'nation' holding civic offices can be attributed to the system of nominating and electing these people.[81]

In 1633, when the City Council adopted a new charter with 24 councillors, the following Terrys were councillors:

Dom Tirry, Ald.,
David Tirry fz David, Ald.,
William Tirry fz Richard, Ald., and
David Tirry fz Edmund, Ald.[82]

In 1610 a David Tyrry fz David was employed as agent for Dublin about the affairs of the city.[83] A David fz Edmond Tyrry was in Dublin, in January 1618, where he received a letter from the mayor of Cork, John Coppinger, concerning affairs of the city, and this David fz Edmond was agent for the city in London in 1630.[84] Also in the same year, David Tirry fz David, Ald., was appointed agent for Dublin, and in 1631-2 it was David Tirry fz Edmund again. A William Thirrie, Alderman, was one of the two overseers of the work in the City in 1635 and subsequent years.[85]

Both members returned to Parliament for Cork City in 1613 were Terrys. One was David Tyrry. He was the son of Stephen Tyrry. While it is stated that he was Mayor of Cork in 1608 and in 1614, Caulfield indicates that the Mayor in 1614 was David Fitz David Tyrry.[86] The David Terry, Mayor in 1608, was the son of William Terry. This David married Ellen, daughter of Sir Dominick Sarsfield, Viscount Kilmallock.[87] His children included Dominick and David. O'Connor states that this David was Mayor of Cork in 1614, not the same as indicated by Caulfield.[88] O'Connor goes on to state that David went to Limerick and married Ann, daughter of William O' Ronan, of Cratella [Cratloe], Co. Clare. A son Dominick was Sheriff of Limerick in 1631. The second member of Parliament for Cork City in 1613 was Edmund Tyrry, Ald.[89]

In 1641, an Edmund Tyrry from Clonturk [Kanturk] and William, son of Dominick Tyrry, of Ballymacsperry, Carrigtwohill, were on the list of attainders.[90]

A William Tirry, who lived in Iniscarra, then barony of Barretts and now barony of Muskerry, was a sub-sheriff for the County of Cork.[91] He had a brother, David, and a sister married to a Galway.

Religious Involvement

The Lord Justices for refusing to attend Divine Services in the reformed churches fined a David Fitz Stephen Tyrry £50 in 1606.[92] In the same year a John Tyrrie Fitz Francis was similarly fined.[93]

Edmund fitzDavid Tirry's son William was the future Bishop William Tirry of Cork and Cloyne. William was born in about 1573. He studied in Belgium and was consecrated bishop in 1623. His episcopacy was a difficult one. From an early date he had to go into hiding, from time to time. Exactly a year after his consecration, he wrote to the Nuncio in Brussels, stating that a violent persecution had broken out against religion, and against the clergy and bishops. It was directed in an especial manner against himself, and the magistrate was in search of him from house to house.[94] Bishop Tirry opened the first post-Reformation church in the diocese of Cork, in the northern suburbs of the city in 1624.[95] In 1630 he convened a diocesan synod for the reorganisation of his dioceses.[96] He had to leave Cork in 1644 when the Catholics were ejected. He participated in the deliberations of the Council at Kilkenny. Edmund's second son, Robert, married his cousin Joan Tirry. Robert and Joan had three sons, Robert, William, and Francis, and one daughter, Katherine.[97] William was also a priest and was hanged in Clonmel in 1654. Part of the genealogy of this family is shown in Fig. 7.3.

Blessed William Tirry was born, according to Fr Michael Hackett, O.S.A., in 1609, and probably baptised in Holy Trinity, now Christ Church, in South Main Street. William received his education for the priesthood on the Continent, and on his return to Cork, in 1638, became secretary to his Uncle, Bishop William Terry. William's connection with other Cork families can be seen from the following passage from Fr Hackett's book on Augustinians.

William Tirry's first cousin, William Sarsfield, Viscount Kilmallock, asked him to become his chaplain and to serve as tutor to his two sons, Dominick and David. It was a request he could hardly refuse. Apart from its primary purpose, it brought him into very close relationship with his cousin and family, and indirectly, as events were to prove, with a wider circle. Lord Kilmallock's wife was Joan Roche, sister of Maurice Roche, Viscount Fermoy. These Roches were also connected by marriage with another prominent county Cork family, the

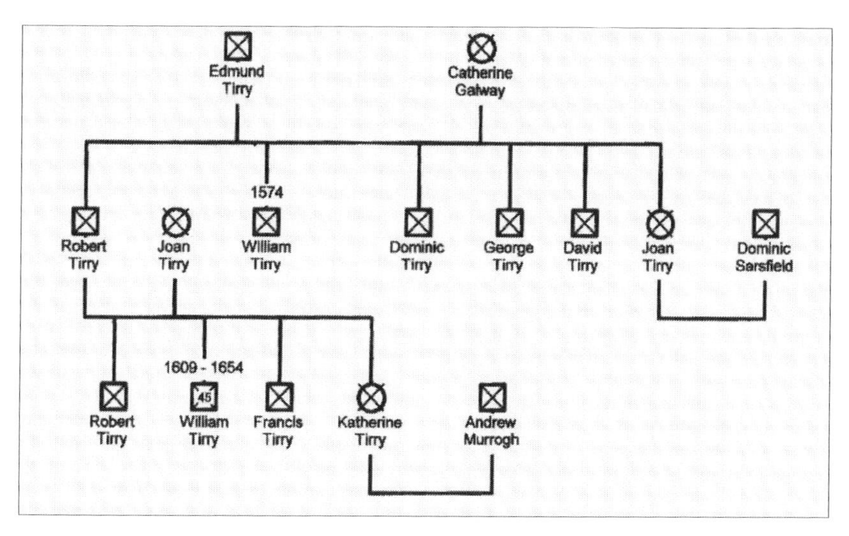

Fig. 7.3 *Children of Edmund Terry, Mayor of Cork.*

Barrys of Buttevant, one of whom David, Viscount Barrymore, had become earl in 1628. These three Catholic peers, Kilmallock, Fermoy, and Barrymore, especially Kilmallock, conducted themselves in a very different way during the Catholic rebellion that started on the night of 22 October 1641 in Ulster and spread to the province of Munster as well as the province of Leinster.

Kilmallock's wife Joan Roche also had a sister named Amy. Amy was the wife of John Everard of the prominent Everards of Fethard, county Tipperary. Several years later, when William was given an appointment in Fethard in 1643, Amy would call upon him to tutor her son Nicholas. His contact with Amy was to have far-reaching consequences for William during the Cromwellian persecution.

William was appointed to Fethard in 1643. He was arrested in 1654, and at his trial he acknowledged the power of government on temporal matters but 'in spiritual affairs wherein my soul is concerned I acknowledge the Pope of Rome and my own superiors to have greater power over me than yours'.

He was convicted and hanged in the same year. Pope John Paul II beatified William Tirry in 1993.

A Richard Tirry, son of Dominic Tirry and Ellen Gould, studied humanities for four years at Cork before going on to Salamaca where he was ordained about the year 1606.[98]

Another priest, Stephen Terry, a discalced Carmelite, was in Ireland in

Figure 7.4 *Blessed William Tirry. (From the Augustinian Abbey, Fethard.)*

this period. He was born in Cork in 1601, professed in Brussels in 1619, ordained in Louvain 1628, and was in Ireland between 1634 and 1653. He died in Parma in 1658.[99] Records exist of three other Terry priest from Cork in this period. In 1664 a marriage dispensation was issued for Andrew Morrogh and Genet Ronain by the Rev. Francis Tyrry S.J.[100] This priest born in Cork in 1610 was the son of Robert Tyrry and Elinor nee Sarsfield. He was educated in Belgium and France and was superior in Waterford and Cork. A David Terry, another Jesuit priest, lost his life in the siege of Limerick, in 1651.[101] He was the son of David Terry, mayor of Cork in 1614. The number of Terry priests, six, in this period, is an indication of the dramatic shift by the Old English to the Catholic Church towards the end of the 16th century.

At the same time, Terrys did business with the Protestant bishop where necessary. A Margaret Tyrry received a letter of administration form the Bishop of Cork and Ross in 1609.[102] In 1626, David Tyrry fz David, Ald., gave money to Bishop Boyle for the benefit of the bishop of Waterford and Lismore. This was a business transaction associated with land.[103] There is no evidence in Windele's work of financial support by the Terry merchants to Bishop William Tirry. Indeed, in dealing with Tirry and his successor, Bishop Robert Barry, Dickson states that despite their high family status and influential political connections, these leaders of south Munster Catholicism seem if anything to have become more alienated from the local sources of secular power than their peers in Leinster.[104]

David Tyrry fz Edmond and two other aldermen of the city were summoned before the Lord President in Mallow, in 1633, for the purpose of increasing the assistance to the pastors and vicars of Christ Church and St Peter's Church. No increase was forthcoming.[105]

TERRYS ELSEWHERE IN IRELAND

A fiant in the reign of Elizabeth I, 1600, mentions a Clement and Michael Terrie in connection with land in Co. Waterford.

One George Tirry, in the barony of Effa and Offa, made a deposition following the rising of 1641.[106]

One of the new settlers in Co. Donegal, on the plantation of Ulster in the reign of King James I, was an Arthur Terrie.[107] In 1612, Arthur Terry from Moyris, County Donegal, was a debtor to the stable town of Dublin.[108]

8

Confiscation and Restoration

From the time, in 1644, when the Catholics where thrown out of the city of Cork, things went from bad to worse for the merchant family of Terrys. Following the Cromwellian wars in Ireland less than 10 years later, and the widespread confiscation of land, the family lost out further. Now they lost property in both the city and county of Cork. On the restoration of the king in England in 1660 they recovered a small amount of what they had forfeited. Towards the end of the century their support for the short-lived reign of King James II resulted in Terrys losing out further.

After their initial expulsion from the city, some settled in the towns in the surrounding countryside. Others began to move abroad to France and Spain, where they already had trading links. A small number remained in the city, continuing their trading and civic roles. Some of these converted to Protestantism. Still other Terrys, at this time, lost their lives in wars and, arising from wars, in Ireland and on the continent.

Loss of land by Catholics

In Ireland, the years 1641-60 saw a revolution in land ownership. Virtually all Catholic landowners lost their estates. Many were dispossessed outright. Others, held to be guilty of lesser offences, received new grants of smaller amounts of land, in a group of western counties specifically set aside for the purpose. Some landowners in Cork were exempted from transplantation to Connacht, provided they settled in the baronies of Barrymore and Muskerry.[1] In 1641, Catholics owned 59 per cent of the profitable land in Ireland. By 1660, this had been reduced to eight or nine per cent, almost all of it in County Clare and parts of Connacht.[2] With the restoration of the monarchy in 1660, and the Act of Settlement, 1662, some Catholics got their land back.

The overall effect of the Acts of Settlement and Explanation was to increase the Catholic share of profitable land to around 20 per cent, more than twice what it had been at the end of the Cromwellian regime, but only a little over one-third of what it had been before 1641. What the Catholics had lost was divided between Old English Protestants and Cromwellian settlers.[3]

In 1656, all the Roman Catholic inhabitants were turned out of the City of Cork, and Protestant magistrates chosen for its government. In the City, in 1641, Old English families owned about two-thirds of the property, but by 1663-4 this portion had fallen to about 15 per cent.[4] In 1672, all

Roman Catholics were forbidden to enter Cork City or any walled town or fortification.

IMPACT ON THE TERRYS OF CORK

The impact of these changes for the merchant family of Terrys, in the city and baronies of the county, is considered now. The position of the Terrys immediately prior to the confiscation of their property is outlined in the previous chapter, together with the extent of their role in the City. Here consideration of the extent to which they lost their property, and were later restored to their property after the restoration of the monarchy, is provided. A brief account is given on how Terrys fared in the county of Cork.

In 1644, when the Irish were expelled from Cork City by the direction of Lord Inchiquin, the following Terrys were allowed to remain in the City: Ald. David Tirry, Robert Thyrry FitzRobert, William Tirry FitzOliver, and Domynicke Thyrry FitzPatricke.[5]

In addition aldermen's widows and sick persons were allowed to remain in the city.

The following Terrys were signatories for the representatives for Cork at the General Assembly of the Confederation in 1646: Robert Therrie, Dominick Terry, George Tyrry and David Tyrry.[6]

The Catholic families were expelled from the City on a number of occasions in the 1640s, so some must have returned for a period after the initial expulsion. In the confiscation of property, after the Cromwellian wars in Ireland, many Catholic families lost their property in Cork City and elsewhere. In various baronies in Cork, Terrys lost property, as indicated below:

Barrymore:	William Tirry fz George of Cork and William Tirry of Cork.
Barretts:	William Tirry, Dallingarry, George and Patrick Tirry of Cork, and William fz Oliver Tirry of Cork.
North Liberties of Cork:	Anstace Tirry.
Carbery:	James Terry.
Kinalea:	Robert Oge Tyrry.
Duhallow:	Dominick Tyrry.[7]

Some lost their lives, as is the case of Blessed William Tirry.[8]

OPTIONS OF RESETTLEMENT

Following their initial expulsion from the city, some of the ancient inhabitants settled in the surrounding towns. In the Cromwellian resettlement, some Catholic families in the City were given the option of settling in either the barony of Barrymore or the Barony of Muskerry rather than going to Connacht. Terry families settled in Macroom following their expulsion from Cork in the mid-17th century. There is evidence that some Terrys also settled here earlier, from 1607-24.[9] However, by 1800 the surname is not indicated as being associated with Macroom.

The Census of 1659 indicated that there were nine Terry families in Cork City and Liberties.[10] There were three tituladoes Terrys: John, Richard and Peirce. This is one half to one third the number of Terry families resident in Cork only 50 years earlier.

In Cork the number of Terry families who forfeited property in each of the baronies were:

Barrymore	2	Barretts	4
North Liberties of Cork (not a barony)	1	Carbery	1
Kinalea	1	Duhallow	1

In addition, a large number of Terry families in the City lost their property.

CONVERSION TO PROTESTANTISM

Mark McCarthy's Ph.D. thesis, 1977, on the historical geography of Cork's transformation from a late medieval town into an Atlantic port city, instances a number of Catholics who converted to Protestantism. These are in the parish books/accounts for Christ Church from 1664-8.

'Between 8/5/1665 and 8/5/1666 a sum of ¾ was paid to the churchwardens of the parish by Mr John Terry for burying his child. ... John Terry, a former Catholic, who converted to Protestantism, was listed as one of the tituladoes.

Of the 11 tituladoes recorded in the south west quarter of the city, Richard Terry was the only former Catholic, having converted to at a later stage.'

There are records of Holy Trinity (Christ Church) in the Representative Church Body Library in Dublin. These show that in 1665 John Terry was involved in distributing money to the poor. An 'Ells Terry' got money. In 1668 an Alice Terry got six shillings and eight pennies.

POSITION AFTER RESTORATION

The Civil Survey indicates that the following Terrys were restored to their property.

North-West Quarter of Cork:

Market Green, Dominick Tirry (possibly it was James Lombard that was restored here).
Mallow Street, David Tirry fitz Edmond,
Upon the Strand, James Thirry,

The South Suburbs of Cork City:

Wm Thirry. William Tyrry held land in the south liberties in 1674.[11]

Land in the North Suburbs of Cork City:

Fair Hill, 4 acres, David Tirry fitz Edmond,
Skiddies acre als Cloghlea, 2 acres, David Tirry fitz Edmond,
Parkykacky begg, ½ acre, David Tirry fitz Edmond,

Land in the North Liberties of Cork City:

Glankittane, 43 acres, Anstace Gold als Thirry.

However, these purported restorations should be qualified in that part of the Act of Explanation repealed the clause in the Act of Settlement empowering the King to restore 'innocent papists' to their houses in corporations.[12]

About five Terry families were restored to their property. In 1641, Terrys were proprietors of 61 properties, and after the restoration and settlement, they were proprietors of 18 properties. This represented about 20 per cent of what they previously owned.

In the inrolments of the decrees of innocents, the following Terrys are named: David fz Stephen, Anstace, Dominick, William, and William fz Patrick.[13]

After some Terrys were restored to their property, the total number of Terrys living in the City was less than half what it was 50 years earlier. Their influence on civil life was greatly reduced. However, a John Terry was Sheriff in 1672.[14] A Jonas Tirrie was a notary public and clerk of the stable around 1670.[15]

There is evidence of Terrys living in Cork City immediately after the period of restoration and settlement.[16]

A Richard Terry, city of Cork, a merchant is recorded as a creditor in the statute stable books for 1667. Ten years later a Richard Terry, a city of Cork maltster, is a creditor in the amount of £583, exactly the same amount as David Terry of Glancullane, Cork is a debtor.[17] This was in respect of a bond for the purchase of wool, leather and other merchandise.

THE COUNTY

Barony of Barrymore

In the will of Patrick Lavallin, 1641, who was Mayor of Cork in 1638, and who owned about 6,000 acres of land in Cobh and other parts of the barony of Barrymore, his wife Anastasia (Terry), was to receive one third of his land.

A David Terry of Ballyleary was a landlord in Cobh in 1652.[18]

In the Barony of Barrymore, a William Tirry Fitz George of Cork and a William Terry of Cork foDirfeited property.[19] One of these Williams lost 206 acres of land in Ballyleary, Cobh.

The attainders of 1642 include William, son of Dominick Tyrry of Ballymacsperry, Carrigtohill.[20]

The townland of Terry's Land was purchased by the Earl of Cork from the Terrys in the 1620s. From the Lismore papers, vol. IV is the following entry for September 1635 (see also the previous Chapter on Carrigtohill):

> I (Earl of Cork) formerly paid unto Edmond Terry, of Carrigtohill, for all the Terry messuages,[21] lands, parks, and tenements in the town and fields of Carrigtohill als Barriescourt the sum of £20 sterling; for him to Mrs Cade, widow and by his direction other £22, and now other £58, in all three payments of £100 sterling; for the fee simple of all his lands known by the name of Terries Lands, as well within and without the said town of Carrigtohill, and upon his deed recovery return and yield up unto me all his ancient deeds and evidences, I made a lease of my whole purchase to his brother in law, Betau Mccvmegante, to his use for 21 years at xij pounds sterling per annum.

Richard Terry from Rathcormac and his wife Helen Fitzgerald had a son, John, baptised in St Peter's Church, Cork in 1630.[22] This John married Mary Ronan from Corkavaskin, Co. Clare, and presumably moved to Limerick at some stage, as his children, James, William, Patrick and Stephen were baptised there in the 1660s.[23] James, was Athlone Herald to King James II, and lived in France after the defeat of James II, until his death in 1725. A Kathleen Murrough alias Tirry, widow, was the proprietor of 254 acres of land in Ballinterry, Parish of Gortroe, in 1641.

This townland adjoins Rathcormac. The land was disposed of to Andrew Murrough in 1663.[24] Andrew was the son of Kathleen (Catherine).[25] It would also seem that Andrew married a Catherine Terry, daughter of Francis Terry ('the great Terry's son'), and grand-daughter of Robert Terry of Lisinisky.[26]

From the Census of 1659, it would appear that there were fewer than six Terry families living in Barrymore, of which, three were Tituludoes names, William, Patrick, and Richard from Tinelassie, Cobh.

Barony of Imokilly

The name James Therry occurs in Cloyne in 1662. He was a tenant in a house owned, as claimed after the restoration, by Edmond Power of Shangarry.[27] Some other houses in Cloyne claimed by Power were let to Edmond Hoare, William Roch and Walter Gallway. These four surnames occur in the families of Cork City. Some of the ancient families of Cork City, after being expelled from the city in 1644, went to live in the barony of Imokilly. These included James Gallway FitzFrancis and Sir Robert Coppinger.[28]

This James Therry is the earliest record of Terrys in Cloyne that I have come across. It may well be the link for the many subsequent generations of Terrys from Cloyne parish with the ancient Terry family of Cork City. One of two people with the name James Terry may be the link. One was James Thirry fz Dominick, of Clonebegg in Shandon. He is a beneficiary of the will of David Tirry fz Edmonde in 1658, and this James was a proprietor of several properties in the city and suburbs in 1641 and as late as 1674. The other was James Tyrrie fitz John, of Sarsfield's Court, and nephew of the same David Tirry fz Edmonde.

One Francis Thirre was a witness to a Deed in June 1666, in which Martin Supple, of Ightermurrogh, granted to James Fitzgerald, of Glenane, certain lands. MacCotter suggests that Thirre may have been a tenant on the Supple lands here at that time.[29]

Barony of Cork

A deed from 1653 mentions a John Tirry fz Edmond of Sarsfield Court and James, his son and heir.[30]

Barony of Kinalea

In Lissiniskey, parish of Knockivilly, Robert Thirry and Francis Thirry, his son, were Tituladoes names in Pender's Census, 1659. In East Ballingary, parish of Bealefiard, William Thirry, Robert his son and Edmond Thirry were Tituladoes names.

Barony of Fermoy

A daughter of Robert Terry of Castle Terry, Katherine, married John Chinnery sometime before 1653.[31] In Mallow town, Domini Thirry was a Tituladoes name in Pender's Census, 1659.

TERRYS ELSEWHERE IN IRELAND

This Census shows no 'Tituladoes' Terrys in Waterford. Also, from this Census, it is clear that there were no clusters of Terry families in Waterford at that time, as was the case in Cork City.

Of the 16 counties where records exist with the names of people who forfeited land under the Cromwellian Settlement, Cork is the only county where the Terry name appears. The 16 counties were:

Cavan	Monaghan	Kildare	Fermanagh
Donegal	Wexford	Louth	Kilkenny
Kerry	Cork	Sligo	Mayo (part)
Longford	Dublin	Derry	Tyrone

Two records of Terry burials In Dublin are recorded for 1672 and 1674, Thomas and William.[32]

9

Terrys in the Period of the Penal Laws

In this Chapter, the incidence and distribution of Terrys is examined, first, for the period around 1700, and second, for the period *c.*1750. This is undertaken in the following way;

The period circa 1700

Terrys in Cork City.
Terrys, barony of Barrymore.
Terrys, barony of Imokilly.
Terrys, barony of Fermoy.
Terrys elsewhere in Ireland.

The period circa 1750

Terrys in Cork City.
- John Terry and Sarah Carden, Cork City.
- Information from the records of the Catholic parish of S. Mary's and St Anne's *c.*1750.
- Other Cork City Terrys.

Terrys, barony of Barrymore.
Terrys, barony of Imokilly.
- Terrys of Cloyne and Aghada.

Terrys, barony of Fermoy.
Terrys, barony of Orrery and Kilmore.
Terrys elsewhere in Ireland.

In examining Terrys in Cork for these two periods, attention will be given to their occupation, genealogical data, their place of residence, and their marriage patterns. These aspects will be commented on in the concluding section of the Chapter. The sources of information for this Chapter include various records of births, marriages and deaths, wills, deeds, the 1766 Census and other sources outlined at the end of the Chapter.

The Period *c.*1700

Terrys in Cork City

In this period, the names John and Richard appear in the records associated with Cork City on a number of occasions. John Terry signed vestry minutes of

Christ Church in 1686.[1] Transactions involving Richard Terry are also recorded. This Richard may be the maltster buried in Christ Church in 1684. His wife's name was Bridget, and he had sons Samuel, John, and Francis.[2]

A Richard Terry was one of the overseers of the will of Jane Chamption, 1686.[3] This is obviously a different Richard from the one who died a number of years earlier.

A deed executed in 1714 between Samuel Terry of Cork, merchant, and Joseph Enock, merchant, recounts that by a rent in 1696 John Boles of Inch, Co. Cork, leased to Samuel Terry a house bounded by Mill Street (Samuel Terry, his wife Hester, or Esther Hoare, and their son Richard).[4] Samuel, in the prerogative administration on his death, 1724, states that he was of Dublin.[5]

An administration bond list for wills of Cork includes John Terry Sr in 1700.[6]

Kings Inn's admission papers mention Edmond Therry, 2nd son of Robert, Cork, deceased, in 1703-4, and Richard Terry, clerk, 3 June 1715.[7] Edmond was admitted to the Middle Temple in 1703.[8] In 1697 one Edmond Therry married Ann French, daughter of George French, deceased, of Co. Cork.[9] In 1708 Edmond was resident in Dublin.[10]

In 1711, John Terry was Sheriff of Cork, and in 1719 was Mayor, and in 1678, a Richard Terry was Sheriff.[11] A Captain John Terry was one of a number of people assigned to collect money for the rebuilding of Christ Church, in 1716.[12] The Militia Commissioners for the City and the County of the City in 1727 included a Captain John Terry.[13]

In a deed in the Registry of Deeds, Dublin, dated 1721, a John Terry, merchant, is referred to as John Terry Snr, Ald., City of Cork, and John Terry Burgess, eldest son and heir.

The index of Cork and Ross wills 1595-1857, includes that of Oliver Terry, of Cork, 1722.[14] Oliver was a tailor in the city.[15]

Terrys, Barony of Barrymore

The Cork will of Patrick Tyrry, 1678, mentions his brother Richard Tyrry of Hodnett's Wood, Cobh, his brother David Tyrry and his sister Cate Tyrry. One of the witnesses to the will was William Tyrry.[16]

A David Thyrry, of Ardnageehy, died around 1710.[17] He was a Catholic, and together with Richard Wakeham, Protestant, gave the seventh part of his milk to the poor.[18] David had an Uncle Nicholas, a brother James, a sister Elizabeth who married Thomas Kissane, and a sister who married Charles Carty and children John and David.

A case was heard before the Irish Court of Chancery in 1711, between James, Earl of Barrymore and a number of individuals one of whom was Wm. Terry. The case involved land in Cobh.[19] There is a Cork will of William Terry of Cuskinny, Cobh, date of probate, 1715.[20]

Descendants of Terrys from Rathcormac were now resident in Cadiz and London. William Tyrry was a merchant of Cadiz and London, and some of his descendants still live in Andalusia.[21] Patrick and Stephen had distinguished military service for King Philip V of Spain, and descendants of Patrick also held prominent positions in Spain.

Terrys had ownership of a number of townlands in Cobh prior to the Cromwellian confiscations.

Fig. 9.1 *Down Survey Map, Barony of Imokilly. (Source: Boole Library, University College Cork.)*

Terrys, Barony of Imokilly

The barony as mapped for the Down Survey is shown in Fig. 9.1. The north direction of the map is at the top right-hand side of the Figure.

In this period, continuing indications of Terrys living in the parish of Cloyne occur. In reference C/12/1 of the records of the Church of Ireland Library, in the accounts for the period 1660-78 (these excluded the years 1664-5), there was no reference to the Terry surname. There is no evidence of them owning farmland when the first extant records show them living in Cloyne. The religious census of 1766 places them as living in the town of Cloyne. This is where James Therry, referred to in Ch. 6, was a tenant before 1662. For the baptism, in 1711, of Ml McGibbons an Ann Terry was one of the sponsors, in Cloyne Cathedral.

Here, in 1714, one R. Terry was a sponsor for the baptism of Joan Ahern, and Jane Thyrry was a sponsor of Ellen Elmer.[22] One year later, Joan Thyrry was sponsor again, this time to John Meagor.

A Richard Terry, son of Richard and Joan, was baptised in 1714.[23] Ann Terry married Morris Mullowny in 1724.

Terrys, Barony of Fermoy

Sir John Percival, progenitor of the Earls of Egmont, recorded in his diary for 16 March 1686, that the troopers 'being att Buttevant Fair this day took Will Tirry and his wife and brought them hither and I examined them'.[24] A Joanna MacCarthy, daughter of Donogh, of Spring House, Co Tipperary, married John Therry of Castleterry, sometime before the year 1700.[25] In the will of James

Therry of Mountnessing, Essex, in England, in 1723, mention is made of his nephew John Therry of Ballindangan.[26] James had a brother David living in Castleterry.[27] He had another brother John and sisters Margaret and Jane. Castle Terry was the seat of the Therrys. Apart from several distinguished clergymen, the family produced a number of successful men at law.

TERRYS ELSEWHERE IN IRELAND

A John Tyrry, of the City of Limerick, was a witness to the will of Morogh, Earl of Inchiquin, 1673.[28]

In deeds from the Registry of Deeds, transactions involving a William Terry, farmer, from Co. Carlow, are documented in around 1709. Also, from the Registry of Deeds, are references to a George Terry from Co. Clare. Many, if not all the Terrys in Co. Clare, at this time were descended from Terrys in Co. Cork, and would have moved to Clare from the early 17th century. Some of these Terrys resided for periods at Stone Hall, Thomond, see Fig 9.2.

Fig. 9.2 *Stone Hall, Thomond. (Source: The Journal of the Kilkenny and South-East of Ireland Archaeological Society, 1867.)*

A number of Terrys are recorded in Dublin from church records. Jane Terry daughter of Ignatius Terry and Katt Terry was baptised in 1723.[29] Ignatius was a merchant in Dublin and died in 1770. He was the son of William Terry of Cork and Mary Woulfe of Limerick. Jane married a Christopher Weldon of Dublin and she had brothers living in Spain.[30] A Doctor Patrick Terry and an Ignatius Terry, both of Co. Limerick, were witnesses to a will of Patrick Hayes of Co. Limerick in 1733. Both of these Terrys are nephews of the afore-mentioned Ignatius.

THE PERIOD *C*.1750

Terrys in Cork City

John Terry and Sarah Carden, Cork City

John Terry of Cork married Sarah Carden. They had the following children.[31]

John, b1728, d1785	Elizabeth, b1737
Henry, b1729, d1732	William, b1738
Jane, b1730, d1788	Barbara, b1740, d1813
Rebecca, b1731, d1732	Carden, b1742, d1821
Richard, b1732, d1734	George, b1743, George went to America
Samuel, b1733, d1734	Henry, b1744, d1820
Sarah, b1735, d1738	Edward, b1746, d1747
Ann, b1736	Paul, b1748

John, the father, is buried in Christ Church, 1751.[32] His name is marked on one of the vaults in the crypt shown in Fig. 9.3.

Fig. 9.3 *Vault of John Terry, 1751. (Source: Ciara Brett, City Archaeologist, Cork City Council.)*

As well as being one of the burgesses of the City, John Terry was a linen draper. His wife, Sarah, died in 1767. He was made a freeman of the City in 1728.[33] In genealogical notes from the National Library, it is stated that this John is of CastleTerry, Co. Limerick. However, it would appear that John was from Cork City, and was the son of Alderman John Terry who was Mayor in 1719 and who died in 1734.[34] These notes also state that his first son, John, was first married to the daughter of Mr Franklyn. This would also seem to be incorrect. His first wife was Sarah Nicholson, and she died in 1774.[35] The John Terry who married the daughter of Mr Franklyn more than likely resided in Cloyne.

The son, John, was made a freeman of Cork City in 1752.[36]

Of the several land deeds involving this family, is a deed dated 13 January 1752, between Sarah Terry, widow of John Terry of Cork, and John Terry, son of the said John Terry. Witnessed by George Terry of Cork, linen draper.[37] This George was presumably a brother of the John, deceased.[38]

Information from the records of the Catholic parish of St Mary's and St Anne's c.1750

The following parents had children baptised in the parish of St Mary's and St Anne's during this period.[39]

Parents	Children
Bartholomew Terry (Therry)/ Honora Sheehy	Michael, Thomas, Mary, Robert, Johanna, John, Hester, and James
Christopher Terry/Ellen Commane	Mary
James Terry/Catherine Sullivan	John
John Terry/Elizabeth F ... bs	James
John Terry/Ellen Murphy	Ellen
Michael Terry/Catherine Ambrose	William
Michael Terry/Honora Commone	Mary
Nicholas Terry/Johanna Walsh	Richard, Edward

Other Cork City Terrys

An Edmond Terry was made a freeman of Cork City in 1727.[40] An Edmond Therry was admitted to King's Inns in 1703, and an Edmond Terry, barrister, was admitted in 1734.[41] An Edmond Thyarry was witness to the will of Richard Fitzgerald of Midleton, in 1735.[42]

A Pat Terry was appointed one of the executors and guardians of the will of James Meade of Cork in 1731.[43]

A Richard Terry, Attorney Exchequer, was admitted to King's Inns in 1734.[44] He died in 1767.[45]

A Richard Terry was made freeman of Cork City in 1761.[46] He was the eldest son of Samuel Terry, merchant. This Samuel was married to Esther Hoare, sister of Joseph Hoare.[47] Richard had sisters, Mary and Sarah. Sarah resided in Dublin, and died about 1746. She was predeceased by her sister Mary.

John Terry, Sheriff of Cork, got land in Lackenroe, in 1739. A George Terry was admitted freeman of the City in 1740, having served Sheriff John Terry in 1739-40.[48] A George Terry died in 1771, and is buried in Christ Church.[49]

Joannem Terry married Hororam Leonard in St Peter and Paul's in 1772.

Mary Terry married John Mason, Royal Regiment Artillery, 1773.[50]

Terrys, Barony of Barrymore

A Patrick Terry of Cobh died *c.*1738.[51] In 1765, Martha, the daughter of Patrick Terry and Mary Reily, not his wife, from Cobh, was baptised. In 1770, a daughter of Patrick Terry of Cobh was buried. A Patrick Terry was a witness to the marriage of John Moore and Mary Creed in Cobh, 1775.[52]

An indented deed of mortgage between Patrick Terry of Cobh, Co Cork, farmer and Richard Herbert, City of Cork, Mariner, made in 1780 refers to an earlier lease in 1772 where Patrick Terry was referred to as a boatman and had a 31-year lease on a house.[53]

Two burials, side by side, in Ballinacurra burial ground are of Patrick Terry, born 1755, and John Tyrry, born 1759.[54]

At the time of death, both men were residing at Ballynaetach and Ballingaran respectively. In the 1766 Census there were no Terrys listed for the parishes of these two townlands.

Terrys, Barony of Imokilly

Terrys of Cloyne and Aghada

A James Terry, in 1727, delivered slate to Cloyne Cathedral.[55] Other records from Cloyne Cathedral for the period include,

> A Mrs Joan Terry was a witness and god-mother to the baptism of Robert Frankland in 1727.
> A Jane Terry was a witness to the baptism of Rachel Dover in 1730.
> A Joan Terry was a witness to the baptism of Sarah Jordan in 1734.
> A John Terry was a witness to the baptism of John Gallway.
> Married, 1736; Isaac Talon and Jone Terry.
> A Joan Terry named in 1743 as godmother to Sarah Harrington.
> Baptised, 1743; Richard, son of John Terry.
> Baptised, 1746; Charles, son of John Terry.
> Burial, 1747; Jane Terry.
> Baptised, 1749; James Terry, son of John Terry.
> Burial, 1753; Joan Terry, next of kin father, John.
> Baptised, 1756; William Terry, son of John Terry.
> A Richard Terry was a witness to the baptism of Richard Askew.[56]

In the records of the Cathedral Chapter of Cloyne, there are several references to Terrys in this period.

The 1766 Census gives lists of heads of named households for several parishes in County Cork.

These show that in Aghada parish, there was a John Terry, catholic, head of a household, and, in Cloyne parish, in the town, there were John, protestant, and David, catholic, named as heads of households.

Terrys in the barony of Fermoy

John Terry of Castleterry died in 1745 and is buried in Kilgallon Cemetery, Ballindangan. Also buried here is Fr Justin Therry in 1753. He studied in Salamanca and was ordained in 1751.

The will of James Therry, of Ballydangan, Killycroyne, and Ballybrittas, near Fermoy, is dated 3 June 1770.[57] James died on 21 June 1770.[58] His wife was Elizabeth Nagle. From the will it is clear that he had a brother John Terry (both forms of spelling in the same document), who was a captain and who died in 1795. There is no indication that Captain Therry was married in 1771.[59] James Therry had daughters, Elizabeth, Catherine and Mary. He also had a son John Joseph, who became a barrister, and was born in 1766 and died in 1853, as well as a number of sisters. Edmund Burke became the guardian of John Joseph, after his father's death.

In the deeds office, Dublin (289/191/190316), there is preserved a memorial dated 17 March 1772 registering 'Indentured Deeds of Lease and release' between Jon Therry late of Germany and now of the City of Dublin and Edmund Burke whereby Therry released to Burke half of the lands of Ballydangin, Killycroyne and Ballybrittas, in the barony of Fermoy.

A Nicholas Terry was a head of a household in Castletownroche in 1766.[60]

Terrys in the barony of Orrery and Kilmore

A James Terry was a head of a household in the town of Charleville in 1766.[61] Mary Terry, of Charleville, married George Gubbins, also of Charleville, in 1775. A John Terry was a witness to the wedding.[62]

Terrys elsewhere in Ireland

A number of Terrys are recorded in Dublin church records for this period.[63]

Concluding remarks on numbers and settlement of Terrys *c.*1700 and *c.*1750

The information on Terrys is sparse in and around 1700 in comparison to the earlier periods. Information that is available from army lists etc. is of limited use as, very often, a relationship between a named person and a place is not provided. However, based on the information that is available, it can be stated that the Old English families such as Terrys lost further ground in terms of their influence in the affairs of Cork. Many of those that supported King James II left Ireland for Europe after his defeat. An example of this is a military campaign in Savoy in 1690, where units of the Irish Brigade fought for King Louis XIV and distinguished themselves. These included the Regiments of Mountcashel and O' Brien. Battles were fought around the current day province of Isère in France.[64] A Dominick Terry was adjutant in Mountcashel's Regiment, while it was stationed in Cork and Waterford.[65] In King James's Irish army list, a Dominick Terry is Lieutenant in Lord Mountcashel's Infantry. A Major William Terry was in Sr. John Fitzgerald's Regiment in France in 1700.[66] The Venetian Republic, threatened by Turkey, recruited an Irish Unit in 1702 under Francis Terry who later became Brigadier General, see Ch. 12.[67]

In this period, *c.*1750, Terrys were still involved in the political affairs of Cork City. They are recorded as merchants and traders, one was a maltster, another a silversmith, and some were barristers. Others were recorded as farmers. The merchants and traders were predominantly Protestant. There is mention of a Captain John Terry. In terms of their religion at this time, there were both Catholic and Protestant Terry families. Some Terrys emigrated to America, and emigration to Spain is also observed. The close knit intermarriage with other Old English families of former times has loosened. Marriage into families that had then come to prominence, through either land ownership or position, such as Carden and Franklyn, is observed. Terry marriages to a Gallway and a Hoare are recorded.

The Religious Census of 1766 provides some information on Terrys in East Cork.

Named household heads are provided for about 70 per cent of the parishes in the Barony of Imokilly and two Terry families are recorded. On a pro rata basis, for the entire Barony, there were possibly three Terry families. As the barony of Barrymore contains several parishes in the Cork Diocese for which there is no information available, the percentage of parishes with household head lists is about 40 per cent. As there was only one Terry recorded this in the parish of Aghada, on a pro rata basis the total number of Terry families in the Barony of

Barrymore would be about two or three. Combining the information for the three baronies of Cork, Imokilly, and Barrymore, one arrives at a total of 71 parishes, with heads of households recorded in the case of 30 of these. On a pro rata basis, there were possibly seven Terry families in the three baronies in 1766.

The Catholic records of St Mary's and St Anne's go back to the middle of the 18th century, and list several Terry families in this parish of Cork City. None of these Terrys appears in bibliographical notices abstracted from newspapers for the period, nor in land deed records. If the Catholic records went back as far as 1700, there would presumably be a certain number of Terry families recorded.

They are given the freedom of the City on a number of occasions. They never again hold the position of Mayor. This is the first period, in which records are available, that shows a number of marriages into Irish families such as Sullivan and Murphy.

10

THE 19TH CENTURY

In this chapter the incidence and distribution of Terry families in Cork for the periods *c.*1800 and *c.*1850 are examined. This information is examined from the perspective of the occupation of Terrys at these two periods, genealogical links, where they resided and any discernible pattern of marriage with other families. For the period, 1850, the incidence of Terrys in other parts of Ireland, as gleaned from Griffith's Valuation, is provided.

1800

CORK CITY

Some parish records for this period include:

St Mary's & St Anne's Parish, Catholic, and St Anne's, Protestant

The following parents had children baptised in St Mary's and St Anne's Parish, during this period.[1]

Parents	Children, year of baptism in brackets
Hopkin Therry/Margaret Short	Catherine (1821)
John Terry/Ellen Burke	Mary (1778)
John Terry/Honora Tape	Ann (1784)
John Thiery/Elizabeth Whitford	William , Honora (1782)
Owen Terry/Elizabeth Cox	Elizabeth (1807)
William Terry/Johanna Driscol	Margaret (1791)

The following Terry burials took place at St Anne's, Shandon in this period.[2]

Elizabeth – 1783	Honor – 1785
Hanna (protestant), 1803	Mary (catholic), 1808
Mary (catholic), 1811	Nicholas Therry, 1815
Dominick Therry – 1824	Dominick Terry – 1825
Elizabeth Terry – 1825	William Terry – 1825

St Peter & Paul's, Catholic

The following parents had children baptised in St Peter's and St Paul's Church, in this period:[3]

Parents	Children, year of baptism in brackets
Nicholaus Therry/Johanna Sullivan (Angel Lane, this lane was known as David Thirry's Lane 150 years earlier)	James (1795)
James Terry/Catherine Fogarty	Charles (1781), Mary (1785), Honora (1776)
Hugh Terry/Bridget O'Brien	Margaret (1789)
Richard Terry/Mary Terry	Ellen (1800)

St Finbarr's South, Catholic Parish

The following parents had children baptised in St Finbarr's South, during this period:[4]

Parents	Children, year of baptism in brackets
James Terry/Mary Luony	Judith (1806)
John Therry/Elizabeth Conolly, of Clark's Bridge	James (1793), Stephen (1795), Jane Anne (1800), David Stephen (1802), and Mary (1797)
John Terry/Nany Ferris	Mary (1802)
John Terry/Jane Keating	Byasa (1797), James (1797)
John Terry/Betty Kenely	John (1789)
Samuel Terry/Ellen Hickey	Edward and Ann (1798), twins

John Therry and Elizabeth Conolly also had a son John Joseph, born 1790.[5] The John Terry, married to Jane Keating, was originally from Castleterry, and is referred to in the next section.

In 1785, a William Terry of Fishamble Lane, married Elizabeth Hayes. They had children, Margaret (1792), William (1798) and Elizabeth (1800). Eugene Therry and Elizabeth Coxe married in 1798. Timothy Therry was a sponsor to a Connell baptism in 1815.

Information from Cork Directories

Selected information from Cork Directories for the period is now provided.

One John Terry was an attorney in the Grand Parade.[6] He had a son Roger, who graduated from T.C.D.; Irish Bar, 1824, knighted 1869 and he became a judge in New South Wales.[7]

There were two people with the name John Terry, who were attorneys of the exchequer, admitted to King's Inns in 1787.[8] One of these, a councillor at law, was from Castleterry, in the barony of Fermoy. His wife was Jane Keating. He was a son of James Therry of Ballydangan, barony of Fermoy.[9]

The second John Terry is linked in land transactions, in the barony of Imokilly, with Carden Terry of the city of Dublin.[10] Also in the marriage agreement of John Williams of Cork, merchant, and Jane Terry, sister of Carden, Henry Terry acts as a trustee. Carden Terry and John Terry witnessed the marriage agreement.[11] This John Terry marries a Miss Sarah Saunders in 1794.[12]

From the information in the Cork Directories, there seems to be a third John Terry, who was a merchant and trader in the Grand Parade, from Morrison's Island.

Fig. 10.1 *Carden Terry and Jane Williams. (Courtesy: John Williams)*

The silversmith Carden Terry, Fig. 10.1, was resident in Cork at this time. His daughter, Jane Williams, also a silversmith, is shown as well.

King's Inns admission papers include Carden Terry, 2nd son of Carden, Cork, goldsmith, and Catherine Webb, over 16, attorney exchequer, 1805.[13]

One William Thyrry married Catherine Meade, in the Diocese of Cork and Ross, 1782.[14]

Benj. Terry was a maltster cooper in Queen Street in 1810.[15]

BARONIES OF BARRYMORE AND IMOKILLY

Aghada Parish

Charles Tyrry of Whitewell and his wife Ann had a number of children baptised in Aghada Church in this period. These include:

Margaret, b1776	Mary, b1777
Michael, b1779	Michael Goold Tyrry, b1781
John, b1783	Hariett, b1792

Charles, whose signature is on some vestry minutes, spelt his surname 'Tyrry'. Sometime after 1781 he moved from Whitewell to Jamesbrook, and he is stated as being from Saleen in 1792.

From other records, it is clear that Charles and Ann had other children: Francis, Charles, William and Elizabeth.[16] Elizabeth married Stephen Wigmore in 1814 at Jamesbrook Church.

One striking feature of the children of Charles and Ann, is that while Charles was a protestant, and the children were baptised protestant, most, if not all, became catholics in the early 1800s. In the case of his son, John, who married Isabelle Buckmaster in 1815, in the church in Aghada (protestant), he had a child, Charles, baptised in the Catholic Church, Cloyne, in 1817. Another child, William, was baptised in Aghada in 1820, with an address at Scartlay.

There are a number of deeds registered in the Registry of Deeds, where a Michael Goold of Jamesbrook gave considerable land to Charles Tyrry of Rostellan. Family tradition has it that the illegitimate daughter of Michael Goold was Charles' wife, Ann. On 19 December 1780, Michael Goold of Jamesbrook, gentleman, granted leases for the term of 999 and 900 years respectively on two tracts of land at Kilva to Charles Tyrry, farmer, of Rostellan. The length of the lease was relatively unusual; more common between gentry of equal status than between gentry and peasantry. This of course is coloured by the Penal Laws which forbade long leases to catholics, but some catholics found ways around the laws. Other evidence indicates that Tyrry was a protestant.[17]

However, Goold went on to bequeath to Tyrry an annuity of £110 in perpetuity, drawn on the rents of extensive lands, both his own property in fee simple and lands held by him in fee farm. In 19th-century deeds the sum is described variously as 'Irish' or 'late currency'. The will is dated 26 January 1782. This, to me, is convincing evidence that Goold was under obligation to Tyrry, and the family connection is very likely.[18]

In 1806, Michael Goold Tyrry, lieutenant of the City of Cork Militia, married Miss Ann Lea of Leaborough, Co. Monaghan.[19]

Some Terry marriages were:

Laurence Buckley and Margaret Tyrry, 1800	Michael Cleary and Margaret Terry, 1809
William Cavanagh and Ann Tyrry, 1811	James Cahill and Mary Tyrry, 1812
William Mackey and Harriet Tyrry, 1819	John Clancy and Mary Terry, 1819

Cloyne and Kilmahon Parishes

Between 1780 and 1782, a William Thyrry was employed regularly in carpentry, roofing, and painting work for the cathedral church of Cloyne.

Terry information from Catholic Church records includes:

Charles Terry married Ann McKenna in Cloyne, 1814.

Michael Terry, Carrigtohill, married Catherine Cotter, Cloyne, 1792,

Five of the children of Charles Tyrry and Ann McKenna are listed in the Catholic Records for Cloyne. These were Charles, baptised, 1815, James baptised, 1821, Michael baptised, 1823, George baptised, 1827, and John baptised 1829.[20] George went to Australia where he died in 1902.[21] A Michael Terry from Cork enlisted in the Royal Irish Constabulary in 1845, aged 19 and a George Terry from Cork enlisted in 1851, aged 22.[22] In September 1893, a Michael Terry, aged 70, a police pensioner, died in Ballycotton. Mary Anne Terry, a spinster and farmer's daughter, from Kiva, died in 1894.[23]

Fig. 10.2 *Charles Terry 1815-99. (Courtesy: Mary Terry, Rhode Island.)*

Cobh

Elanor Terry, Cobh, married Robert Perman in Clonmel Church, 1782.
Abbigan Terry of Cobh married John Clifford in 1784, Clonmel Church.
Mary Terry of Cobh married Charles New in 1798, Clonmel Church.

Abigal Terry of Cobh married Charles Jones at St Mary's, Cobh in 1816.
John Terry, son of Mathew Terry and Johanna McGrath, baptised, 1817.[24]

Mathew Therry, son of Richard Therry and Honora Hannon, was baptised in 1814, and another son John was baptised in 1818.[25] In 1876, a Mathew Terry, aged 27, died.

In 1821 a Catherine Therry married a Timothy Keeffe, and in 1823 an Ann Therry married a William Hayes.

A Patrick Therry married Bridget Walsh in Cobh in 1823.[26]

Baronies of Fermoy and Orrery & Kilmore

John Therry of Castleterry was admitted to King's Inns in 1792, aged 26.[27] Roger, his fourth son was admitted in 1825. John Therry was appointed commissioner of revenue in 1806 and was the first catholic to hold high office in the central administration in Dublin after the relief acts of the 1790s.[28] John died at Cobh in 1853, aged 86 and is buried in Templerobin churchyard. He was married to Jane Keating, daughter of Lieutenant-General Sir Henry Keating. John and Jane had four sons and two daughters. His sons were James, John, Bryan Keating and Roger. His daughters were Anne and Jane. James died in 1841.[29] Roger became a judge in Australia, and he retired to England. Anne, as Sr Baptist, was a founder of the Loreto nuns in Ireland. Jane died at the age of 15, in 1820.[30] Bryan Keating married Dora Maria Shea in 1857 and Dora died in the 1870s, a resident of Ballintubber, Carrigtohill parish.[31]

In 1799, Mary Tearry, daughter of William Tearry, from Ballyhea parish was born. This family were Church of Ireland.[32]

SELECTED TERRY INFORMATION FROM THE TITHE APPLOTMENT BOOKS

The following is information on Terry families in some parishes from the Tithe Applotment Books and from the Mallow Heritage Centre.

Lisgoold Parish

A James Terry had three acres in Glengariff and Carrigane. There were no Terrys resident in this parish in 1766. James's wife was called Mary. A Michael Terry and Joan, his wife, had children baptised in Lisgoold parish in this period. Also, a John Terry and his wife, Mary, had children baptised here.[33]

Britway Parish

A Patrick Terry had 11 acres in Banafohane. There were no Terrys in this parish in 1766.

Imogeely Parish

A John Terry, and brother, had 37 acres in Ballnameeta. This family was closely connected to the Terrys in Ballingarrane, Kimahon parish.

Rathcormac Parish

A David Terry had 14 acres in Kilbrien. His wife was Abigail Cronin. David was possibly the son of James Terry and Ellen Moylan, and baptised in 1792. A James Terry and Mary Ryan had a daughter baptised here in 1799. A John Therry married Ellen Barry in Rathcormac in 1800.[34]

Castlelyons Parish

An Edmond Terry had one acre in Killsaiah Ann. There were no Terry families here in 1766. A Patrick Terry and Mary Kenna had a number of children baptised in Castlelyons in the early 1800s. Maurice Theary and Catherine Barry also had children baptised here in this period.[35]

Carrigtohill Parish

A Patrick Terry married a Bridget Geary in Carrigtohill, in 1823.[36]

Youghal Parish

Some Youghal baptisms in this period were:
John Therry and Mary Therry had a child baptised.
Charles Terry and Mary Kenna had a child baptised.
John Terry and Mary Flavan had a daughter, Mary, baptised in 1819.[37]

Ballintemple, Cork City

This parish was at that time part of the county, in the barony of Cork. Hence the information is provided on Carden Terry. The Tithe Applotment Books did not cover the City.

In the case of Lisgoold, Britway, and Castlelyons parishes in the barony of Barrymore, Terrys were not present 70 years earlier. In other cases where Terrys appear in the Tithe Applotment Books, there were Terrys in Cloyne and Cobh in 1750. Records do not exist to indicate whether or not Terrys resided in Rathcormac parish in 1750, although the parish was a former stronghold for Terrys. Likewise, there is no evidence to indicate whether or not Terrys resided in Mogeela parish in 1750.

Kilmoconoge Parish, Bantry barony

A Cross Terry resided here.[38]

Brigown Parish, Condons and Clongibbons barony

A Mo Terry resided here.

Bandon

James Terry and Joannan Sullivan were married in Bandon in 1805. An Owen Terry was a sponsor to a Mahony baptism in 1821.[39]

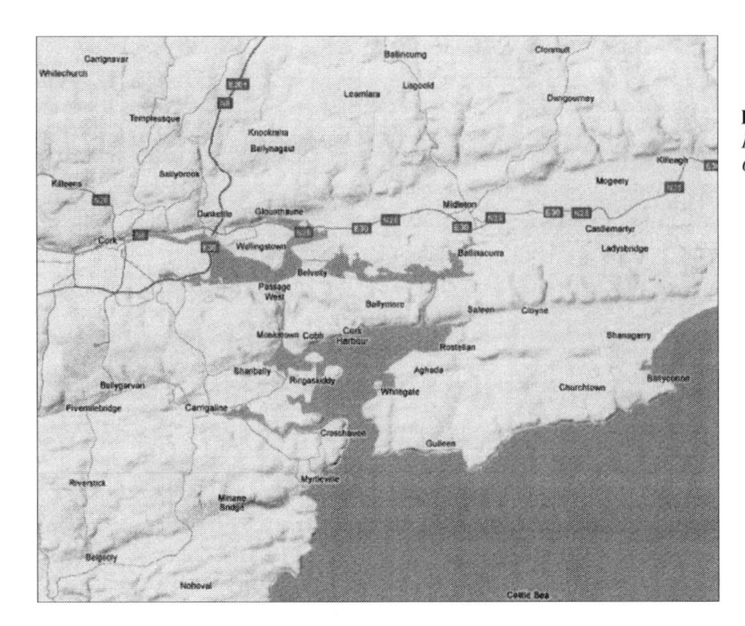

Fig. 10.3 *Cork Harbour area. (Source: Google Maps.)*

Griffith's Valuation

The period *c.*1850 is now considered. In total at this time there were *c.*29 Terry families in Cork predominantly in Cork City and the baronies of Barrymore and Imokilly. The settlement locations of some of these is identified in Fig. 10.3, which is a modern-day terrain map of the Cork Harbour area. Some of the families were:

Aghada Parish

Alexander Terry. An Alexander Terry, son of John Terry and Mary Ross, was born in 1818. Alexander, who was a carpenter by trade, died in 1878, aged 60, in Farsid. In 1861, James Therry, a son of Alexander Therry and Ann Connolly, was baptised in Aghada.[40] This James went to England and joined the Royal Navy.[41]

Cloyne Parish

Charles Terry, son of Charles Terry and Ann McKenna, in about 1844 married Nora O' Neil of the East Ferry and they had 13 or 14 children.[42] Charles was one of the delegates representing Cloyne at the county convention to select candidates for the Home Rule Party, chaired by Charles Steward Parnell in 1885.

Kilmahon Parish

John Terry and Thomas Terry.
John Terry and Abina Flynn married in 1868.

Mogeely Parish

Margaret Terry. In 1824, a John Terry and his brother had 37 acres in this parish. In 1834, one Mary Terry married a William Arnold of Glenbeg. In 1835, John Terry married Catherine Carey in Imogeely. Patrick Terry and Bridget Walsh resided in Ballinascarta. They married in Cobh a number of years earlier. In 1837, a Bridget Terry married a Patrick Barry of Garrykeale. In 1841 a Michael Terry and Judith Coughlan were married here.[43] In 1846, a Mary Terry married John Browne of Ballynemetach.

William Terry, labourer, of Kilbeg, and son of John Terry, labourer, Kilbeg, married Kate Walsh in 1870. Michael Terry, labourer, of Garranejames, son of John Terry, labourer, married Bridget Scully in 1872.

Killeagh Parish

Richard Terry. Richard Terry, widower, aged 90, from Castlemartyr, died in 1889. A Richard Terry, widower, from Killeagh, married Catherine Cunningham, widow, from Killeagh, in 1873.

A Bridget Terry married a William White in 1854.

In 1869 in Killeagh parish, Michael Molony married Mary Terry.[44]

Clonmel Parish

A Margaret Therry married a James Geary in 1826. A Mary Terry married John Gallagher in Cobh in 1838.

William Terry married Catherine Regan in 1832. A Charles Terry and Ellen Morrison were married in Cobh in 1838.[45] Mary Terry, of Clonmel married William Brooks in 1851, and a Margaret Therry married a William Lewis in 1867.[46] In 1854, Hannah Therry married Robert Daniels.

Richard Terry, village of Newtown, Ringmeen. John Terry, from Cobh, aged 25 and Mary Barry aged 27, were married in Cobh in 1864. John's father was Richard, a master mariner.

Templerobin Parish

John Therry. A John Terry and Mary Meehan were married in Cobh in 1845.[47]
Catherine Therry.
Margaret Terry.
A Patrick Terry was married to a Mary Gowra in the 1770s.

Rathcormac Parish

David Terry. A David Terry lived in Killbrien, Rathcormac, in 1824. Ellen Terry married James Collins in 1840. Frances Terry married Roger Keeffe in 1842.

Carrigtohill Parish

Patrick Terry. Patrick was a merchant in Carrigtohill and would appear to have had business interests in Cobh also. He was married to Ellen Hegarty. Dora Maria Therry, a widow from Ballintubber, died in the early 1870s aged 73. Dora's husband was Bryan Keating Therry.

Lisgoold Parish

John Terry. A James Terry resided in Lisgoold in 1824. In 1826, A Bridget Terry of Lisgoold married a William Hennessy of Lisgoold. A James Terry married Margaret Geary in 1830. A Patrick Terry married Catherine McCarthy in Lisgoold in 1832. A John Terry married a Johanna McCarthy in Lisgoold in 1833 and a Richard Terry married May Cashman in 1844.[48]

Templebodan Parish

Richard Terry. A Patrick Terry, weaver, from Ballincurrig, married Catherine O' Leary in 1874. Patrick's father was Richard.

Templenacarriga Parish

John Terry, of the townland Walshtown More (West). John was married to Ellen Barry.

Youghal Parish

A Nicholas Terry and Ellen Lynch were married in 1846.[49]

Castlemagner

In north Cork in the townland, Bettyville, a John Therry is recorded.

Rosscarbery

In 1875 Daniel Terry was a carpenter in Rosscarbery.[50]

A Donovan Terry was a sponsor to a Tobin baptism in Kilmacabea in 1851. Robert Terry and Abby Donovan had a son, Robert, born in 1867. Lionel Therry was a sponsor to a Carthy baptism in Scull West in 1850.

Clontead

William Therry was a sponsor to the baptism of a Kennifick in Clontead in 1848.

Cork City

Some Terry families in the City of Cork at this time were:

Charles Terry – Drawbridge St Charles was a publican. A Charles Terry and Mary Ann Gould had a son Dominic baptised in St Mary's and St Anne's Parish in 1859. A son James Alipius, born in 1844, went to America and died in 1878. A. Charles Terry and Ellen Hurley had a son Charles baptised in the same parish 28 years earlier, in 1831.[51] A James Terry and Maria Barry had a daughter Maria Elizabeth baptised in 1844.

John Terry – Drawbridge St John was an engine driver.[52]

John Terry – Carey's Lane.

John Terry – Paul St. In 1870, John Terry and Mary McCarthy married in South Main St. They had a number of children.[53]

A John Terry and Hannah Geary had a son Denis baptised in 1864.[54]

A John Terry and Ellen Coleman had a number of children baptised in St Mary's and St Anne's between 1873 and 1882.[55] John was a widower when he married Ellen in 1872. He was an engine driver and father of Jeremiah and Richard, detailed in Ch. 11. A John Therry and Ann Bernard had a daughter Mary Ann baptised in St Finbarr's South in 1855.[56] A Thomas Therry and Mary Cronin had a child Mary Ann baptised in St Mary's and St Anne's in the 1840s.[57]

Richard Therry, Devonshire St.

Richard Terry and Mary Murray had a daughter baptised in 1847, and a William Terry and Catherine Regan had a son Patrick baptised in 1837.[58] William and Catherine were married in Cobh in 1832.[59]

By 1875 all the Terrys who were significant merchants and traders over a number of centuries were gone. There were still several Terry families; these were all catholic, and had less wealth and income.

From Griffith's Valuations, Terrys also had land in Ballybeg, West, parish of Buttevant, barony of Orrery and Kilmore. A John Therry was the owner of land in Bettyville, parish of Castlemagner, barony of Duhallow. A John James Therry became tenant of *Springvale House*, Kildorrery, barony of Fermoy, in 1856. He was a Collector for the barony of Condons and Clongibbons.[60] John was grandson of John Joseph Therry of Castleterry, commissioner of revenue.[61]

Terrys elsewhere in Ireland from Griffith's Valuation

Griffith's Valuation gives the following incidence and distribution of Terry families.

Antrim	2	Armagh	1	Cavan	1
Clare	3	Cork	24	Down	1
Dublin	1	Kilkenny	1	Limerick	1
Laois	2	Monaghan	3	Tipperary	3
Waterford	25	Wicklow	1	Wexford	1

This gives a total of 70 families. Of the 24 families in Cork, 22 are within the area of east Cork including the city. The number of families given for Waterford is an approximation. As the same Christian name appears more than once in the same area, it was not possible without more detailed research to determine the exact number of families in the county. Most of these families are in the western portion of county Waterford.

From the mid-19th century the famine and emigration had a big impact on the population in Ireland. Close to 20 per cent of the Terrys in Ireland emigrated to New York in the five-year period 1846-51.

Some Conclusions

Around 1800 a number of Terrys were made freemen of Cork City. Some Terrys were involved in the legal profession, as a judge (New South Wales), and as merchants and traders, in banking, and as landowners. For another grouping of Terrys, from Catholic Church records, very little is known, other than who they married and the baptisms of their children. Many Terrys in the rural part of east Cork were tenant farmers; some owned their land outright.

A Fr John Joseph Therry was chaplain in Australia. A pattern of Terrys changing from the protestant religion to the catholic religion in the early 19th century is observed. There is no discernible marriage pattern for Terrys married in this and subsequent periods.

From the Tithe Applotment books there were a total of 62 Terry families in Ireland. This excluded cities. Of these 17 were from Waterford, 11 from Cork, nine from Tipperary, eight from Clare, seven from Donegal with a scattering from other counties.

By 1850, the Terrys who were merchants and traders in former times in the City had almost disappeared. The same situation was apparent with families that were in various professions. From Griffith's Valuation, the predominant occupation of the Terry families in rural areas was farming. Another occupation for several families was weaving.

11

Terrys in 1900

This chapter will examine settlement patterns in 1900. Consideration is given to the occupation of the families. Genealogical links and where they resided are also considered. Some reference will also be made to Terrys elsewhere in Ireland.

1901 Census Returns, and related information

When one browses the 1901 census returns for Ireland there are 246 entries for Terrys, 19 for the surname Tyrie, 13 for Torrie, three for Torry and three for Therry. In all there are about 70 Terry families in Ireland. The majority of these families are in Waterford and Cork with a scattering in some other counties. Some 18 counties return no Terrys. From Census Returns, the number of Terry families in Cork is about 22.

The 1911 Census shows about 310 Terrys in Ireland, or about 67 families. The highest number of families was in County Waterford with about 30 families, while Cork was next with about 13 families. Armagh had four Terry families and Dublin had five.

The 1901 Census Returns gives the following Terry families from Cork City

Jeremiah Terry, 34, Railway Engine Driver, St Ann's, Shandon.
Bridget Terry, 39, Music Teacher, St Mary's, Shandon.
John Terry, 50, Carpenter, St Ann's, Shandon. John was previously a shipwright and lived in Paul St.[1]
James Terry, 48, Clerk, Albert Place.
Edward Terry, 51, Commissioner Agent, St Peter's. Edward had nine children in all.[2] Ten years later Edward was living with his daughter in Suttons Buildings. Edward, the son, was married and living in Carragh Rd in 1911.
In 1884, Robert Ireland Torrie, son of Adam Frisken Torrie, grocer, 94, Patrick St., and Jemima (Ireland) Torrie was born.[3]

In the barony of Barrymore, there were the following Terrys:

Mary E. Terry, 62, Merchant, Carrigtohill. A niece, Josephine Terry, aged 19, lived with her. Another niece, Mary, married a William O' Grady. This family, according to local historian John Harte, had no family, and the O'Grady farm

Fig. 11.1 *Jeremiah Terry and Mary Ellen Terry. (Courtesy: Pat Chambers, Cobh.)*

was sold sometime around 1960. What follows is a verse of a song, 'The Bobbies of Carrig', connected to the attack on Carrigtohill Police Barracks, in 1920.

> Johnny at Terrys' he got a great fright;
> He was woke out of his sleep in the middle of the night;
> Jos opened the door, and it was his delight,
> And he slept on the sofa for the rest of the night.

John Harte, the local historian, informed me that Johnny was a young person, from an industrial school, who stayed at Terry's house, and 'Jos' refers to Josephine Terry.

Richard Terry, 80, Labourer, Templebodan.

Patrick Terry, 50, Wool Weaver, Gortroe. It would seem that this was the Patrick that lived in Glanworth ten years later.

Jeremiah Terry, 52, Market Gardener, Carrignafoy, Templerobin. This Jeremiah was a navigation pilot.[4] Sometime around 1905 Maryellen married a Patrick Cummins. Fig. 11.1 shows Jeremiah Terry (bowler hat) and his daughter (Mary) Ellen.[5]
A John and Margaret Terry lived in Templerobin in 1853.

In the barony of Cork there was the following Terry family:

John Terry, 58, Weaver, Rathcooney.

In the barony of Imokilly there were the following Terry families:

Edward Terry, 48, Labourer, Midleton.

William Terry, 60, Farm Labourer, Sheanliss, Cloyne.

Charles Terry, 52, Farmer, Cloyne.

John Terry, 33, Farmer, Ballintemple.

A John Terry, aged four, lived with his grandfather John Cusack, in Ballycotton in 1901.

Joseph Terry, 36, Farmer, Ballintemple. Joseph married Lizzie McCarthy, from Ballymacandrick, in Aghada in 1901.[6]

Of his children, Michael never married. Elizabeth (Lil) Terry married Tom Hennessy. Nora Terry did not marry. Kate Terry married Paddy Corbert from Dungourney.[7]

Bridget Terry, 60, Youghal. Bridget was born in Co Waterford.

Michael Terry, 59, agricultural labourer, St Mary's, Youghal. His wife was Bridget, aged 52, and they had the following children: John (23), William (19), Ellie (20), and Annie (16). They also had daughters: Bridget born 1878, Catherine born 1873, and May born 1874.[8] Michael was formerly from Garranejames, near Castlemartyr. Michael and Bridget married in 1872.

Mary Terry, 29, Ballycotton.

John Terry, 65, farmer, Kilmahon. John was married to Abina Flynn. John's father was also called John.

William Terry, 60, agricultural labourer, Castlemartyr. He and his wife Bridget (formerly Cronin) (50), were living with their son, Michael (28) and his wife Ellen (Sullivan) (26), and grandson Patrick (3). Ten years later, in the 1911 Census, William and Bridget are no longer shown as resident there. Michael, now indicated as being 45 years of age, and Ellen have the following children: Patrick, 10, William, 9, Bridget, 7, Charles, 6, and Mary, 5. They also had a number of children who died young. Michael had married Ellen in 1900, and was living in Ballynascarthy in 1911. Patrick and Charles emigrated to Boston, Massachusetts.[9]

The Census Returns include a John Terry, aged 30, as a servant in the household of Aherns in Kilbree, Castlemartyr.

In 1893, one James Terry, bachelor, aged 55, died. He was a shoemaker from Midleton.

In 1876, Redmond Terry, labourer, from Ballynascarta, son of Charles Terry, labourer, married May Barry, daughter of James Barry, farmer, in Ballintotis Chapel.[10] In 1896, William Cotter married Ellen Therry, daughter of Alexander Therry, of Aghada Hall.[11]

For Cork City, it would appear that there were six Terry families, one Terry family in the barony of Cork, four in the barony of Barrymore, and 10 in the barony of Imokilly. In Imokilly, the heads of these families were generally either farmers or farm labourers. All the Terry families in 1901 give their religion as catholic.

In terms of occupation, the Terrys, from the 1901 Census, in Imokilly and Barrymore were generally either farmers or labourers. There was one merchant family in Carrigtohill, and two families where the head of the household was a weaver. In the City the Terrys were involved in various trades. One Terry was a music teacher. The protestant Terry families had disappeared. There is evidence of Terrys emigrating to Australia and the United States.

Barony of Fermoy

Guy's Postal Directory of Munster, 1886, records the following Terry living near Fermoy:

John James Therry, J.P., Kilmagner.

The 1911 Census indicates a Patrick Terry and his wife Kathern with two children living in Glanworth. This family were living in Gortroe ten years earlier.

Barony of Kerrycurrihy

One Robert Edward Terry from Carrigaline married Ida Frances Roberts also from Carrigaline in St Mary's, Carrigaline, barony of Kerrycurrihy, in 1899.[12] Robert was English, born in Kent, and a lithographer by profession. He was in the U.K. in 1901 and emigrated to Canada in 1903. He died in the U.S. in 1936.[13]

Waterford

From the 1911 Census Returns there were about 30 Terry families in Waterford. All these Terrys were born in Waterford, with farming being the most popular occupation. All were catholic. The high proportion of heads of households who were farmers, relative to other occupations, would indicate a high level of emigration in the preceding decades. Of the Terrys in Dublin at this time, one, Kathleen Terry, was born in Waterford. There were three Waterford Terry families in Cork, one in Youghal and two in the city. In addition, a Kate Terry, a 22-year-old servant in Cork was born in Waterford. A Patrick Terry, agricultural labourer, from Tipperary, was born in Waterford. Another Patrick born in Waterford, an Irish teacher, was living in Carlow. The United States, England and elsewhere in the world must have attracted a large number of Terrys from this county.

Armagh

There were four Terry families in Armagh from the 1911 Census Returns. One of these, Edmund, a national school teacher, was born in Waterford.

Dublin

There were five Terry families in Dublin. The head of the household for four of these families was born in England and the fifth was born in Scotland.

12

Terrys in France of Cork Origin

This chapter will examine some Terrys in France whose ancestors came from Cork. Firstly, a brief background and context is provided. Secondly, the Terrys found in King James's Irish army lists are accounted for. Finally, some detail is provided on a number of Terrys in France of Cork extraction.

Background and context

From approximately 1600 the Irish began to emigrate to continental Europe in more significant numbers than previously. After many years of struggle and effort, England was solidifying its hold on the government of Ireland. The power of the remaining great Gaelic chieftains was broken, and the reluctance of a number of Old Anglo-Irish lords and gentry to welcome the new order, not least in matters of religion, was condemned and penalised.[1]

In the years towards the end of the 17th century, some 25,000 Irish left for mainland Europe. The soldiers in France were organised into a Jacobite army in French pay, nominally amounting to 20,000 men. In addition, some were part of the Irish Brigade in France under Mountcashel.

In 1697, an embattled France made peace at Ryswick, with England, Spain and other countries it was in conflict with, and, soon afterwards, drastically reduced the number of its Irish troops. Some of these redundant soldiers went to Spain to enlist in the Spanish army.

King James's Irish Army List

King James's Irish Army List includes the following Terrys:[2]

Colonel Justin MacCarthy's, now Lord Mountcashel, regiment of infantry: Lieutenant Dominick Terry.

Lord Kilmallock's regiment of infantry:

Lieutenant Terry, either Patrick or Stephen.

Colonel Owen Mac Cartie's regiment of infantry:

Lieutenant Terry, either Patrick or Stephen; Ensign Terry.

Mountcashel's regiment was sent to France in 1690 and were shortly afterwards involved in battles in Savoy. They were positioned on the river Isère. A later campaign for Mountcashel's regiment was one in Germany in 1694.

After the Jacobite defeat in Ireland, some 19,000 soldiers went to France, in addition to Mountcashel's regiment. Lord Kilmallock's regiment went to France.

In France, by 1692, there were two Irish forces: The Irish Brigade of the French Army under Justin MacCarthy, Viscount Mountcashel, and the Jacobite Army of James II under Patrick Sarsfield, Lord Lucan. After the peace of Ryswick in 1697, the Irish Brigade was retained, but the larger Jacobite Army was disbanded leaving the Irish to become beggars or highwaymen. Lord Kilmallock's regiment was broken up at this time, and the regiment of Limerick was absorbed into the regiment of Dillon. Some of the men of these regiments moved to Spain to enlist in the Spanish Army, including Patrick and Stephen Terry. Of the brigades of the second formation, in France, one was the Limerick regiment of infantry.[3] Sir John Fitzgerald was colonel of this regiment and William Therry was major. This Terry was the son of one Terry, who was deputy clerk of the Crown for the county of Cork. A Robert Thyrry Fitz-Robert, Sheriff in 1644.[4] Records show that from 1609-12, his father, Robert Tyrry, was deputy clerk of the Crown in Munster.[5] William had at least two brothers, Edmond and Captain Francis, and one of his sisters was married to Patrick Hurley.[6] Therry was still major in 1695.On 2 October 1694, in the parish of St Hugues, Grenoble, his son William, and that of his wife, Christine de Commine, was baptised. The godfather was Cornelius Murphy, Major in Clancarthy's regiment.[7] An account of Major Therry's fleeing France is contained in the Inchiquin Manuscripts.

The Venetian Republic, threatened by Turkey, recruited an Irish unit in 1702, under Francis Terry, who later became Brigadier General. The unit served Croatia and Bohemia. In 1717 the regiment became the Regiment of Terry and served Venice until the fall or the Republic in 1797.[8] A Laurence Terry, son of Robert Terry of Cork and Catherine McCarthy, was to join the Irish cadets in France.[9]

A William Terry, Clantark (presumably Kanturk), Cork, aged 40, enlisted in 1726 in the Irish cavalry regiment in France.[10] He had grey curly hair, full face, grey eyes, long pointed nose, large shoulders, and sturdy build. He left in 1729. D'Alton mentions that the Attainders of 1642 had the name Edmund Tyrry from Clonturk and those of 1691 had George and John Terry from Rathnagarde, near Kanturk.

A number of Terrys studied for the priesthood in France in penal times. Bishop William Tirry of Cork studied in the Louvain, and is first mentioned in 1606. Dominicus Therry of Cork and Ross is mentioned in 1690 and Edmondus Therry is mentioned in 1691. A Terry student in France in this period from the diocese of Cloyne was Justinus Terry, mentioned between 1726 and 1756.[11]

James Terry

James Terry, genealogist, was the son of John Terry and Mary Ronan, and was born in Limerick on 26 May 1660. James was grandson of Richard Terry, of Ballinterry, in the parish of Gortroe, Barony of Barrymore, and of Helen Fitzgerald. As a boy he entered the Irish army in Fleming's company of the Earl of Antrim's regiment. Abandoning a military career after a short period, he was by letters-patent appointed Athlone Herald by James II. After the Jacobite defeat in Ireland he emigrated to France and settled, with the Jacobite Court in exile, at Saint Germain-en Laye, at the cost of the King of France.

In that town, he was occupied for more than a quarter of a century in compiling a large number of pedigrees for expatriated Irish families, and particularly for those Irishmen upon whom James II and Louis XIV conferred peerages and titles. He died at Paris in 1725. In 1687, he married Mary Stritch of Limerick, by whom he had two sons William and John, and a daughter Margaret. The sons worked for James's brother, William, in Cadiz.[12]

William Terry

This is the William, who became a merchant and trader in Cadiz, born in Limerick. He was named Marquis of Cañada in 1730, and died in 1745. From Culligan and Cherici in their book, *The wandering Irish in Europe*,[13] William arrived in France in 1693. He joined the French army where he rose to the rank of general and served in the French forces sent to Spain in support of its new King, Philip V, in the war of the Spanish Succession in the early 1700s. He left the army when Philip V renounced his claim to the French throne. In his brother James's letters, referred to earlier, there is no reference to his military career.

Fig. 12.1 *Portrait of Emilio Terry (Artist: Salvador Dali)*

Several Terrys from Cork settled in Spain around 1700. Subsequently some of their descendants moved to Central America. A descendant of one of these returned to Paris in the 1880s, one Tomas Terry from Cuba.[14] Several of his daughters and grand-daughters married into prominent French families, the de Castellans, de la Tour d'Auvergne and Faucigny Lucinge. The famous French decorator Emilio Terry was also a member of this family; see Fig. 12.1.

Geneviève Terry

For several years, I corresponded with the late Geneviève Terry, from Lyon, France.

Geneviève had being researching the Terry family since 1962. The Irish connection in her grandfather's time was very strong. Her grandfather was a farmer, and had a number of siblings, one of whom, a brother, was called Etienne. Etienne had strong Irish features. From oral tradition given by her grandfather, Johany Terry, the family was descended from a very rich Irishman who settled in the village of Saint-Georges d'Esperanche, in the Department of Isère. This is said to have occurred in around the year 1800. The man who is believed to have emigrated from Ireland was her father's great-great-grandfather. This was close to the time that Castleterry passed from the Terrys to new owners. On a visit to Cork in 1962, Genevieve went to Christ Church where she came across the vaults of John Terry and his wife, Josepha.

However, it would appear that this family are in this part of France, in the Department of Isère, from at least the mid-17th century.

13
Spanish Terrys of Cork Origin

This chapter will examine descendants of Terrys, from the study area of Cork, that left and settled in Spain.

In 2011 there were 360 people in Spain whose first surname was Terry and 204 whose second surname was Terry. About 70 per cent of them were Spanish nationals. The highest occurrence was in the province of Cadiz. Many of these Terrys are descended from Terrys in Cork in former times.

From the 16th century there is evidence of Terry merchants trading with Spain, and, from the 17th century, settling there. Following the defeat of King James II, Terrys left Ireland and served in the armies of Spain. With a common religious background, and strong trading links, these families prospered in Spain, while those who remained in Ireland found a difficult political environment in which to prosper, unless they were Protestants. After the 1560s, as Spain found itself pitted against England for control of commerce in both Europe and the New World, the Spanish kings regarded the rebellious Irish as potential military allies.[1]

The Irish Regiments and the Spanish Army

Culligan and Cherici state that,

> All-Irish units were reintroduced into the Spanish military at the beginning of the eighteenth century when France lent the cavalry regiments of Daniel O'Mahony – famous for his defence of Cremona in 1701 – and Henry Crofton to Spain to bolster Spanish forces during the War of Spanish Succession.

King Charles II of Spain, who had no children of his own, left all the Spanish dominions to the Duke of Anjou, grandson of King Louis XIV of France, on the condition that the Crowns of Spain and France should never be united in one person.[2] The Duke of Anjou became King Philip V of Spain on Charles's death in 1700. In 1709, Spain formed the Ultonia, Hibernia, Limerick, Waterford and Irlanda Regiments. In 1733, the Waterford Regiment was incorporated into the Irlanda Regiment, and in 1735, the Limerick Regiment was transferred to the King of Naples. Throughout the 18th century, the officers from these Irish regiments distinguished themselves in battle, were frequently promoted to general, and were placed in command of Spanish troops, thereby exerting a widespread influence on the Spanish army.[3] O' Hart, in *Irish Pedigrees* gives slightly different dates for the formation of these regiments.

For the soldiers of the Irish regiments of the 17th and 18th centuries, life was hard. Although the regiments were headquartered in Spain, they were usually on operations in Flanders and Italy, and some contingents were even dispatched to Cuba and Mexico.[4] For many of the émigrés, the penalties of military life were heavier than the rewards. It could be so, even for the most successful. In 1712 Patrick Tyrry in Madrid wrote to his brother:

> I am the first brigadier of the king's army, commandant of his guards, and in six years that I am brigadier and most part of that time employed upon the frontiers in the army, may I never see the Lord in the face, if in this six years, I received more than three months and six days' pay ... I can assure you that this day to send my son Peter to his regiment, I was obliged to send my coffee pot to be pawned ... to supply him for his journey ... I assure you I love my child as well as a father can, yet notwithstanding at twelve years and nine months old, I sent him to the wars to scratch a livelihood as his father before him had done.

Shortly afterwards, Brigadier Tyrry was killed at the siege of Barcelona.[5] In 1912, the historical researcher C.E. Lart published some careful studies on records of the Jacobites in France and included invaluable information on Irish exiles. He later published a book on the genealogist James Terry which included the letter about young Peter Tyrry going to the wars. He ended his introduction with a pointed lament,[6] 'And little 'Peeter' where is his grave? And so many like him, child soldiers of fortune? They lie wherever the exiles fought for alien countries and a lost cause.'

Little Peter, however, may have proved sturdier than that. Some of the records of the Irish College at Salamanca have survived. They tell how, in the 1740s, two young lay students were admitted to what was normally an ecclesiastical college because they came from an Irish family of distinction. They were nephews of the Tyrry who was Marquis de la Cañada in Cadiz and they were sons of Don Pedro Tyrry of the Council of His Majesty in the tribunal of the high audit. Now, it is not certain but it looks possible that this distinguished Don Pedro was little Peter of 1712. His father and the merchant William, who became the first Tyrry Marquis of Cañada, were brothers.[7]

Merchant Adventurers

During the 15th century, a large number of merchant families in the port cities of Galway, Cork and Waterford had become wealthy by trading with European countries. They mostly shipped Irish butter and beef to the continent on English merchant vessels, which then returned to Ireland with casks of wine.[8]

Culligan and Cherici go on to state:

During the reigns of Henry VIII and his daughter Elizabeth, the lord deputies of Ireland placed many restrictions on Irish merchants. Merchants who did not convert to the new Anglican religion found themselves harassed by customs agents, and sometimes they had their premises sacked by soldiers. As O'Neill's rebellion spread across Ireland in the late 16th century, Irish merchants were heavily taxed by the English to pay for the defence of Irish cities against a rebel army that many of them sympathised with. In addition, the continual strife between the warring sides and the scorched-earth policy of the English army frequently cut the merchants off from their interior markets for their imported goods and also from the domestic goods they exported. Seeing their revenues plummet with little likelihood of recovery, many Irish merchants moved their headquarters to European port cities such as Cadiz and Bilbao in Spain with which they had been trading for many years while continuing to operate in Ireland as best they could.

> The majority of merchants in Ireland and Spain were small businessmen, usually employing only family members. With the base of operations shifted to Spain and business prospects in Ireland uncertain, they changed their business activity to importing goods and materials from the new world and the Far East and distributing these goods to other European countries. In the ports of Cadiz, Bilbao, and Barcelona, the Irish merchants imported coffee, cocoa, rum and other products and made arrangements to send them to other European countries. To ensure that their affairs abroad would be handled effectively and reliably, the Irish merchants often sent their sons or nephews to cities in Europe, the new world, and the far east to be their agents. In many parts of Europe, though, the Irish merchants did not need to dispatch an agent to handle their affairs because they could call upon members of their clans who had emigrated to do this. This was often the case in France and Austria and even faraway Russia. Having clan members they could rely on in foreign countries usually gave the Irish an advantage over their business rivals.

One of the most successful Irish families who went into business in Spain were the Terrys. They were supporters of James II, and established themselves as an influential and wealthy family in Cadiz and El Puerto de Santa Maria. There were a number of families. One family were from Limerick, where they had settled for a number of decades in the mid-17th century, having moved from Cork. Another branch, based in Malaga, was natives of Cork. The founder of the Cadiz branch was William, son of James. William Terry, one of the Wild Geese arriving in France in 1693, played a major role in the growth of the export of sherry from Spain to all parts of Europe. He was also responsible for the famous Lippizaner horses of Austria. Of this family, there are details of accounts between William Tyrry and Company in Cadiz, and Edward Gibbon, in 1719-20.[9] These accounts show transactions in 'rialls'.

Over three generations, the family built up a vast commercial enterprise, based principally on trade with the Americas and, by 1760, they owned three ships dedicated to this business.[10]

William Terry obtained an estate with vineyards near the southern city of Jerez, in the region of Andalusia. Terry improved the method of production of grapes on his farm and this became a profitable business for him. He began to produce fortified sherry. William Terry led the way in stimulating not only greater production, but also greater exports, laying the foundation for Andalusia to become the most important viable wine-growing area of Spain. Terry descendants still live in this region of Spain. Terry was also involved in breeding Carthusian horses.

The grandson of William, also called William (1726-79) inherited the titles of 'Marques' and 'caballero de Santiago' (Knight of Santiago), and led an intensive public life in his capacity as 'Alferez Mayor' or royal representative in council affairs.

The Terry family's trading activity continued to prosper and in 1762 William became the owner of several farms mainly dedicated to the production of wine and olives. He became known for his magnificent collection of antiques and medallions. His collection was displayed at his home in Calle Aurora in El Puerto de Santa Maria. William's wife was Maria Francisca Lacy, who was of Irish descent and had been lady-in-waiting to Queen Maria Louisa de Palma. Apparently, William was vain and died from a fit induced by an insult.[11]

The Terrys of El Puerto de Santa Maria were involved in supplying goods and provisions to the galleons crossing the Atlantic to the Americas. As indicated earlier, some members of the family quickly became leaders in different areas of public life, both in their adoptive city and in the capital, and came to occupy important civic positions.[12]

Genealogical links of the Terrys in Spain

As mentioned in the previous section there were a number of branches of Terrys living in Spain from the 17th century. The first branch examined is centred on James Terry, of Limerick and France, whose descendants live in some number in Andalusia. James was born in 1660 in Limerick. He died in Paris in 1725, and was Athlone Herald to King James II. James had three brothers: William, born 1663, Stephen, born 1669, and Patrick, born 1667. These brothers were born in Limerick, although the father was originally from Cork. In 1702, Patrick entered the military order of Santiago, followed by Stephen and William in 1712.

In all probability these three were three of the four brothers mentioned earlier. In the course of my research, a Pat Terry in the army near the Rhine in 1697 was discovered. This may well be the same person as Patrick, Knight of Santiago. The name William is missing from those attained; he was involved in business and trade with Spain, and is recorded as living in El Puerto de Santa Maria.[13] He may not have been involved in the Williamite wars in Ireland. He was a merchant of Cadiz and London. In 1702, after the Anglo-Dutch looting of El Puerto de Santa Maria, he went to live in Cadiz. He married Senorita Elizabeth Sanchez Silveira, in 1707, daughter of Don Diego Sanchez Silveira of Cadiz. They in turn had a daughter, Francisca Maria Terry, who married a son of James's (the Athlone Herald), John – her first cousin. James, the Athlone Herald, and his wife: Mary Stritch, had two other children in addition to John; William, and Margaret.

Guillermo was granted the title Marquis of Cañada de Tirry by Royal Dispatch on 28 September 1729;[14] he established himself definitively in El Puerto in 1737, and he died in 1745. Francisca, his daughter, and John, his nephew, had a son Guillermo, and this Guillermo in turn married Doña Francisca de Lacy y White.

The second Terry family is centred on Don Ramon Terry, of Malaga, Spain. Don Ramon was an officer in the service of the King of Spain. Don Ramon's parents were William Terry, born 1715, and Margaret MacNamara, born 1716, who married in Malaga Cathedral in 1734.[15]

His grandparents on his father's side were Ignatius Terry, born 1686 and Catherine Stackpoole, born 1691. William had a brother Dominick (Domingo), born in Limerick.[16] Domingo married Elena Macnamara and was a resident and merchant of the city of Malaga.[17] Another brother was a Philip who married Mary Hayes. William had a sister Jane, who married one Christopher Weldon, and another brother James.[18] Ignatius Terry's parents were William Terry of Cork and Mary Wolfe of Limerick. They married in 1684. A great grandson of

Fig. 13.1 *Antonio Terry y Rivas. (Courtesy: Luisa Garcia, the Netherlands.)*

Domingo was Antonio Terry y Rivas, 1838-1900, Admiral of the Spanish Navy and Senator from the province of the Canary Islands, see Fig 13.1.[19]

The third branch of the Terrys, with present-day links to Cadiz, can trace the genealogy back to one Don Antonio Maria de Terry and Dona Maria Angela Andreano, originating in Genoa, Italy. They were married in Finale Marino (Italy) and had six children.[20] Of the son, Andreas, born in 1728 and married twice, was born, Santiago, in 1750. From him (Santiago) was born Don Santiago Jose de Terry in 1783, who in Cadiz, during the Spanish Parliament of 1812, organised the committee of government and defence. It is also said that a Don Fernando de Terry y Brucet, born in Cadiz in 1783, was one of those who organised the defence of the city during the Peninsular War. Documents about this branch suggest that the Terrys settled in Spain during the 16th century.[21]

Don Santiago Jose de Terry, born 1783, had four children: Emilia, Eduardo, Fernando M., and Santiago. In 1865, Fernando Matias de Terry decided to devote his time completely to viti-viniculture, not only as a trader but also as a producer, and it was he who was to be the true founder of Bodegas Terry. Fernando Matias married Dona Maria Teresa Carrera, by whom he had three children, Carolina, M. Tresa and Fernando Angel. Taking charge of this last born was Dona Margarita Carrera, sister of the mother, who occupied herself with his upbringing and education, living with him until after his marriage to Dona Josefa de Cuvillo y Sancho.[22] Fernando A. de Terry was then to give an extra push to the family business and take the famous yellow net brand to all corners of Spain.[23] Don Fernando Matias married a second time to Dona Maria Teresa Urizar, by whom he had four children: Elena, Emilia, Maria Luisa and Santiago. Maria Luisa married Don Pedro de Leon, and stayed in El Puerto. The other three left for Central America. There, one of the female relations of Santiago, mentioned earlier, married with a Belaúnde of Peru, who later became President of that country.[24]

Tomas Terry y Adáns, who was born in the early 1800s in Caracas, Venezuela, was a son or grandson of one of the Terrys of Cadiz, Spain.[25] Tomas came to Cuba in the 1830s, as a poor immigrant from Venezuela, and was probably the richest man on the island in the late 19th century.[26] He moved to New York in the 1860s and from there to Paris.[27]

14

Terrys in Latin America of Cork Origin

This chapter will examine descendants of Terrys, from Cork, who settled in Latin America. Their arrival in Latin America from Cork was through a circuitous route. Some Terrys of Cork origin, who settled in continental Europe, moved to Latin America from the 18th century. From this time there is evidence of Terry merchants from Spain trading with the Americas.

As outlined in previous chapters, since approximately 1600, the Irish began to emigrate to continental Europe in more significant numbers than previously. After many years of struggle and effort, England was solidifying its hold on the government of Ireland. The power of the remaining great Gaelic chieftains was broken, and the reluctance of a number of Old Anglo-Irish lords and gentry to welcome the new order, not least in matters of religion, was condemned and penalised.[1] From the mid-17th century, apart from a brief interlude during the reign of King James II of England, it became increasingly difficult for Catholics to own land and to hold civic and political positions. Increasingly, some of them began to leave Ireland for continental Europe.

In the years towards the end of the 17th century, some 25,000 Irish left for mainland Europe.

Irish joined the armies of France and Spain. For the soldiers of the Irish regiments of the 17th and 18th centuries, life was hard. In the case of regiments in the Spanish army, they were usually on operations in Flanders and Italy, and some contingents were even dispatched to Cuba and Mexico.[2]

It was from Spanish links with the New World that the Terrys became involved in trading across the Atlantic. Some of this family settled and prospered in Latin America.

In 1733, one of Guillermo Terry's ships, the *San Felipe* – also known as *El Lerri*, *El Terri*, or *Tyrri* – was shipwrecked off the coast of Florida on a return journey from the West Indies to Spain.

A first cousin of William, Pedro Tyrry, was born in Spain in 1700. He was the son of Patrick Tyrry, brigadier and Knight of Santiago, from Limerick and Isauel Lambert.[3] His father was brother of James Tyrry. This family originated in Cork City and Ballinterry, near Rathcormac.

Pedro was appointed Director of the South Sea Company in 1737, for Spain. Tyrry was ordered to return to Spain, prior to the declaration of war by England in 1739.[4] In the Irish College in Salamanca, there were 169 letters written by Pedro, from Madrid, to the rector, John O'Brien. These were written in 1748-56. These are now in the National University of Ireland, Maynooth. Some of these letters refer to the slave trade. In one letter, in 1749, he offers his opinion that an expedition bound for Caracas, Venezuela, was in actual fact going to Havana, Cuba.

The genealogical links are now more closely examined in the case of four Terry members, Juan Tirry y Lacy, Tomas Terry y Adáns, Jose Antonio Terry Campos and Fernando Belaúnde Terry.

Juan Tirry y Lacy, Marquis de Cañada

Juan Tirry y Lacy, born in Spain, was descended from the Terrys of Cork City and Ballinterry, near Rathcormac. His parents were Guillermo and María. His grandparents, on his father's side, were Juan and Francisco María, both Terrys and first cousins. His paternal great-grandparents were James Terry of Limerick and Mary Stritch. Juan, residing in Cuba, inherited the title Marquis de Cañada, in 1824.[5]

In 1759-60, Juan's father, Guillermo, now the Marquis of Cañada, visited the Americas and West Indies.[6]

There is evidence of one John Tirry, in 1658, who was working for the King of Spain in paying his army in Flanders, and also having the protection of the English lord protector to traffic in the Barbados and other islands.[7]

In 1787, the commander Juan Terry y Lacy, who was a navy officer, presented a report to the Count of Santa Clara, on how to organise the colony on the isla de Pinos, modern day Isla de la Juventud.[8]

Juan Tirry y Lacy was responsible for mapping the Isla de la Juventud, where he went with the mission of analysing the pine trees to see if they could be used for the ships in the Spanish navy. In honour of his contributions to geography, the northernmost point of the island was called Punta de Tirry. Juan was made a Knight of Santiago in 1793 and in the following year he married María Jesus Loinaz y Lizundía. In Havana Juan Tirry was the engineer general, was twice mayor of the city and Governor of Matanzas in 1816, a city where one of the streets bears his name. The title Marquis Cañada de Tirry, which he inherited in 1824, he retained until he died 15 years later.[9] His son, Don Guillermo Tirry y Loynaz, born in Havana in 1799, was subsequently Marquis of Cañada.

Tomás Terry y Adáns

In the case of Tomás, first the Spanish link is detailed.

Don José Terry and his wife Doña María Mendoza had a son:

Don José Antonio Terry y Mendoza, born in Cadiz, went to Peru and to the city of Caracas, Venezuela.[10] He married twice. His first wife was Doña Tomasa Adáns y Espána, a native of Caracas and daughter of José and Manuela. They had two sons:

- Don Tomás Terry y Adáns, born in the city of Caracas, Venezuela, 1808. He went to Cuba and established himself in Cienfuegos in 1830.[11]
- Antonio, born in Venezuela.

His second wife was Doná Maria Ortega, a native of Extremadura. They had the following children:

- Josefa: She was a native of Curaçao. She married Don Tomás Arcay y Arritegui, a native of Granada, and son of José Manuel and Inés.
- Antonio.
- Eduardo: A native of the city of Puerto Cabello, on the Casta Firme, married in Cienfuegos in 1850 to Doña Ana Franciscade Borja y Ballagos, a native of Holguín and daughter of Don Francisco Del Mármol y Valdés-Llarcés and Doña Ana María Ballagas y Guerra.
- Guillermo: A native of the island of Curaçao. He met his demise in Havana, in the parish of Manserrate, 1879. He married Doná Curidad Latté in Cienfuegos.
- Teresa
- Emilia
- José Domingo: He was baptised on the island of Curaçao, in the Catholic Church on 17 December 1826. He married on the island of Cuba to Doña María Felipa Figueroa y Véliz, a native of Nueva Bermeja and daughter of the graduate Juan José Luis de Figuero y Hernández, Registrar and Provincial Lord Mayor of Jaruco, and Doña Ana Jarefa Véliz y Ganzález. They had the following children:
  - José Domingo, who was a pharmacist.
  - Alfredo who was baptised in Cienfuegos in 1860 was also a pharmacist.
  - Eduardo, was baptised in Cienfuegos in 1867, married Doña Inés María Arcay y Terry, daughter of Don Tomás Arcay y Arritegui and Doña Josefa Terry y Ortega.[11]

Tomás Terry y Adáns was the most successful of the planters in Cuba in the mid-19th century. He became the great boss of Cienfuegos, the 'Cuban Croesus'. He enjoyed a very good name with his slaves and employees: he was friendly with Congolese Negroes and gave them money to found clubs in the towns

Fig. 14.1 *Tomás Terry Theatre, Cienfuegos. (Source: Linda Blicher Brestgaard, Denmark.)*

of Cruces and Lajas.[12] He moved to New York in the 1860s and from there to Paris.[13] Tomas married Dona Teresa Dorticos y Gómez de Leys, a native of Oberon, France, in 1837. Teresa's family were French settlers from the Bordeaux area of France, who founded Cienfuegos in 1819. They had 12 children:

- Teresa who married Don Nicolás Acea.
- María Del Carmen. She obtained the title of Marquesa of Perinat by royal despatch in 1893. She married Don Guillermo Perinat y Ochoa in 1863.
- Natividad who married Baron Alberto de Blanc, Italian diplomat and Minister of Promotion.
- Emilio, who was a lawyer and married Doña Silvia Alfonso y Aldama,
- Eduardo, who married Doña María Isolina Sedano y Agramonte, in 1877.
- Antonio, who married Grace Dalton. A daughter of this marriage, Doña Natividad Terry y Dalton married in Paris in 1902, Prince Guy-Charles de Fancigny-Lueinge e Coligny.
- Francisco, who married Doña Antonia María Sánchez y Sarría. They had the following children:
  - Odette, who married the Prince of La Tour St. Auverge;
  - Natividad, who married Count Estanislao de Castellane;
  - Francisco, who belonged to the French Air Forse in the First World War in 1914. He married Nelly Ormond and had a daughter Elena Terry y Ormond.
- Andrés, who married Doña Carmen Gutiérrez y García. They had the following children:
  - María Isabel, who married Don Fernando Varona y Gonzalez Del Valle,

Andrés, who married Doña Blanca García-Montes y Hernández. They had a son Don Tomás, who married Doña Herminia Saladrigas y Fas.[14]

- Tomas,
- Josh Eduardo,
- Juan Pedro and
- Isabel.[15]

The famous French decorator Emilio Terry was also a descendant of Tomás.

When elections were held in Cuba, in 1866, Tomas Terry y Adán was returned for Cienfuegos.[16]

After making a fortune as a sugar merchant and planter, Tomas Terry became a powerful financier on the government bond and currency markets of continental Europe. He later moved much of his capital from Europe to the United States, putting millions into shares of mining and railroad companies on the New York stock market.[17]

He moved to New York in the 1860s before finally settling in Paris. He was probably the richest man on the island in the late 19th century, leaving $25m at his death in 1886.[18]

Of his children, Emilio Terry was the owner of two sugar estates, at the beginning of the 20th century. On Cuba's independence he served as Minister of Agriculture. Antonio was the owner of another sugar estate.[19]

José Antonio Terry Campos

Before considering José Antonio Terry Campos, some information is given on his ancestors. One Antonio Terry y Adriano came to Peru in 1765. He was the son of Antonio Terry and Angela Adriano. He came from Finale, which used to belong to Spain, and later to Genova, before the reign of Italy was established. The family moved to Finale for two generations from Cadiz, Spain, where they remain (in Cadiz) also up to today.[20]

Antonio Terry y Adriano married in Cadiz, Spain, Antonia Álvarez Campana. They had the following children: Bernarda, José, María, Pedro,[21] Pablo, José (2), José Antonio, 1763. [22]

Fig. 14.2 *José Antonio Terry Costa.*

One Andres Terry Alvarez married, in 1798, Rita Francisca Campos Rodriguez. Presumably this was another son of Antonio and Antonia. One of the sons from this marriage was José Antonio Campos, 1803-1866, in Argentina. In turn José Antonio had a son, José Antonio, 1846-1910. This José was a minister in the government of Argentina, and he in turn had a son the Argentine painter, José Antonio Terry, 1878-1954. Reference is made to José Antonio's descent from the Marques de la Cañada.[23] José Antonio Costa, Argentine government minister, and his son, the painter, are shown in Figs. 14.2 and 14.3. José married Rosa de Salazar y Pardo de Figueroa. A son married Jacoba Del Real y Solar, and they had a son Teodorico Terry del Real.

Antonio and Angela moved at a later stage to Peru, and in 1780 Antonio made a will.

Fig. 14.3 *José Antonio Terry, Argentine painter.*

Fernando Belaúnde Terry

I now turn to Fernando Belaúnde Terry. The José, son of Antonio and Antonia, referred to above, married Rosa de Sulazar y Padro de Figueroa. A son, Pedro, married Jacoba del Real y Solar, and they had a son, Teodorico Terry del Real.

Teodorico married in Arequipa, Peru, 1883, Jesús Garcia Pacheco y Vásquez de Oricaín and had the following children:

- Teodorico was a military engineer, married Rosa Elejalde Chopitea.[24] A son of this marriage was Teodorico Terry Elejalde.
- Pedro, 1889-1964, an engineer,
- Ernesto,

- Hortensia,
- Lucila, who married in Lima, Peru, 1907, Rafael Belaúnde Diez-Canseco. One of the children of this marriage was Fernando Belaúnde Terry, architect and future President of Peru.
- Jesús,
- Blanca Rosa,
- Flor de María,
- Graciela, who married Guillermo Rey y Lama.[25]

Fernando Belaúnde Terry was born in 1912. His mother was Lucila Terry y García.[26] He was President of Peru for two periods, 1963-8 and 1980-5. A successful architect, he served in the chamber of deputies (1945-8), formed the Popular Action party in 1956, and ran unsuccessfully for president in the same year. He succeeded in 1963. He effected social, educational, and land reforms; opened up the rich interior to settlement by constructing a vast highway system across the Andes; established a self-help programme for the country's indigenous inhabitants; and encouraged industrial development. However, an inflationary spiral set in, and Belaúnde antagonised nationalistic army leaders by failing to expropriate U.S. controlled oil fields and operations. Deposed by an army coup in 1968, he fled to the United States, where he subsequently taught architecture at Harvard and Columbia. Restored to the presidency in 1980, he attempted to combat inflation by denationalising industries and encouraging foreign investment in the petroleum industry.[27]

Belaúnde died in 2002.

This is one example of members of a Cork family, who emigrated from the 16th century for financial, religious and political reasons. Coming to France, Spain and Italy, for a period, some descendants finally settled in the New World. They brought their expertise in trade and commerce and political acumen. They settled in Cuba, Peru and Argentina, as detailed in this chapter.

Fig. 14.4. *Fernando Belaúnde Terry.*

Fig. 14.5 *Signature of Fernando, on a wine barrel in the Terry bodega, El Puerto de Santa Maria, Spain. (Source: Kevin Terry.)*

15

Terrys in England of Cork Origin

Irish sojourners were finding their way to Britain as early as the Middle Ages and had begun to form permanent settlements in London by the Elizabethan period. The 18th century saw further developments of this type, with Irish migration mirroring the wider growth of urban and industrial centres. The flow of migrants from Ireland reached new heights after the French Wars (1793-1815), with thousands entering British ports each year.[1] Between 1815 and 1840 was by far the most important period for Irish migrants to Britain.[2] From this time onwards America took over as the dominant destination for Irish emigrants. Significant numbers still settled in Britain. In 1901 there were more than 600,000 Irish in Britain.[3]

I will now give some thought to Terrys from Ireland who settled in Britain. Particular consideration is given to Terrys from Cork who settled in England. From Scottish census records, a number of Irish Terrys also settled in that country. It should be remembered, as outlined in the earlier part of this book, that the Terrys of Cork, in all probability, came from England some eight hundred years ago.

A distribution of the Terry surname in England from data in the 1891 census indicates the highest occurrence, at 1475, in Kent.

The 1851 Census of England would indicate about twenty Terry families from Ireland residing in England. About seven of these families were from Cork. These included:

Ann Terry, born *c.*1785, and living in Middlesex
Elizabeth Terry, born *c.*1830, and living in Kent
Henry Terry, born *c.*1787, and living in Somerset
Stephen Terry, born *c.*1796, who was a visitor staying in Middlesex.

It is not always indicated on the Census Returns in what part of Ireland a person was born.

In addition, the 1861, 1871, 1881, and 1891 England Census provide information of a number of Terrys residing in England of Cork birth.[4] In the case of married females, I do not know if the Terry name provided is the married name.

1861
Riche Terry, Royal Navy, born in Cork *c.*1831.
Ellen Terry, Kent, a boarder, born in Cork *c.*1835.

1871
Margaret Terry, Hampshire, born in Cork *c.*1808.
Catherine Terry, Kent, born in Cobh *c.*1842.
Ann Terry, London, born in Cork *c.*1803.
Ann Terry, London, born in Cork *c.*1833.
1881
Sarah Terry, Kent, born in Cork *c.*1846.
Julia Terry, Lancashire, born *c.*1841 in Cork.
1891
Elizabeth Terry, London, born *c.*1858 in Cork.
James Terry, Durham, born *c.*1843 in Cork.
James Terry, Hampshire, born *c.*1862 in Cork.
Laura Terry, London, born *c.*1836 in Cork.
Mary L G Terry, Lancashire, born *c.*1853 in Cork.
Frank Terry, Somerset, born *c.*1860, in Cobh. Frank was a barrister, and married to Adelaide Gibbons.

The 1901 Census indicates about thirty Terry families, from Ireland, in England. About ten of these would be from Cork. Again the Census Return does not always show what part of Ireland the family came from. Among those from Cork were:

Jeremiah Terry, aged 24, born in Cobh, and
Paul Terry aged 36, born in Cloyne.

Reference to the wider family of Jeremiah is made in Ch. 11. James Terry, born in Aghada in 1861, served in the Royal Navy and was discharged from the RFR Devonport in 1911 on age grounds.[5]

From correspondence with Ernie Terry from Surrey, one of his ancestors came from Crookhaven, West Cork, in the 17th century.[6] He emigrated to England after the Cromwellian Wars in Ireland and settled in the Sunderland area. Some of Ernie's relations now live in America.

One English branch of Cork Terrys is only four generations old and stems from Paul McKenna Terry who was born at Kilva on 2 July 1864.[7]

Paul graduated from both and also from the Faculty of Physicians and Surgeons, Glasgow, all in 1891.[8]

Paul married Anne Elizabeth Murtough, in 1899.

Of his children:

– Nora Ellen was born in 1899.
– Charles born in 1901.
– Sheila Mary Terry was born in 1902.
– Paul McKenna (Mac) was born in 1904.
– Bernard Murtough Terry was born in 1905.
– Patricia Mary Terry was in 1907.
– Phillip O'Neil Terry was born in 1908.
– Terrence Peter Patrick Terry was born in 1909.
– John Desmond Terry was born in 1913.

16

Australian Terrys

In writing this chapter consideration is given to a number of Terrys in Australia, of Cork origin. The first are descendants of John Therry and Elizabeth Conolly from Cork City. The second is Sir Roger Therry from north Cork. Finally there are some descendants of Cloyne Terrys. One of these was Bernard Murtough Terry, born in England in 1905.

Descendants of John Therry and Elizabeth Conolly

Two sons, a daughter and grandson of John Therry and Elizabeth Conolly went to Australia. One of these sons was Fr. John Joseph Therry (1790-1864).[1] He had brothers, James, Stephen and David Stephen baptised in St Finbarr's South parish in Cork City in 1793, 1795 and 1802 respectively. He had sisters, Mary and Jane Anne, baptised in the same parish in 1797 and 1800.[2] He was educated privately and at St Patrick's College, Carlow. Ordained priest in 1815, he was assigned to parochial work in Dublin and then Cork, where he became secretary to the bishop, Dr Murphy. He is recorded as sponsor to a Barry baptism in January 1819, in St Peter's and Paul's, Cork. Therry was sent as one of two Roman Catholic chaplains to New South Wales in 1820. He sailed from Cork under a senior priest, Father Philip Conolly, in the *Janus*, which carried more than a hundred prisoners. They arrived in Sydney, authorised by both church and state, in May 1820.[3]

Fig. 16.1 *Fr John Joseph Therry. (Erected at Cobh Heritage Centre; photo, Kevin Terry.)*

Therry described his life in Australia for the next 44 years as 'one of incessant labour very often accompanied by painful anxiety'. For five years he was the only priest on the mainland in Australia.

Articulate and thorough, he set himself the task of attending to every aspect of the moral and religious life of the Catholics. He travelled unceasingly, living with his scattered people wherever they were to be found, sometimes using three or four horses in a day. His influence was impressive among the protestant settlers and outstanding among the convicts. His correspondence shows the trust they placed in him. He also formed a lasting interest in the aboriginals, who became very attached to him.[4]

He built the original church of St Mary's in Sydney.[5]

In 1835 he was appointed parish priest of Cambelltown, where he remained until 1838 when he was appointed Vicar-Gereral of Van Diemen's Land.[6]

He was removed from his official situation as chaplain and his salary was withdrawn sometime around 1826. Despite frequent and general protest he was not reinstated until 1837.[7]

In April 1838 he was sent by Bishop Polding to Van Diemen's Land as vicar-general. He visited the interior and attended to the convicts. His church building at Hobart and Launceston was assisted by Sir John Franklin's spasmodic patronage, but on St Joseph's Hobart, and on the schools demanded by the free settlers, he overreached himself. In 1846, he went to Melbourne as parish priest where he remained until April 1847.

Therry was at Windsor in New South Wales as parish priest until June 1848 when he returned to live in Van Diemen's Land for six years. His efforts to settle affairs there were unsuccessful and, after a period of adjustment in New South Wales, he went in May 1856 to Balmain where he spent the rest of his life. Mellowed and serene, he continued to be an energetic pastor, watching the growth of the church in whose establishment he had played such a definitive part, the coming of the religious Orders, and the completion of his own church at Balmain and the first St Mary's, generously contributing whenever he could to every new development. He became spiritual director to the Sisters of Charity at St Vincent's, and in 1858 was made archpriest, taking precedence after the vicar-general. In 1859 he was elected a founding fellow of the council of St John's College within the University of Sydney. He had been given or had bought a number of properties which he tried to develop for the provision of more schools and churches for the growing Catholic community. Notable among these were his farms at Bong Bong and Albury, a property which is now the suburb of Lidcombe, and 1,500 acres (607 ha) at Pittwater, where he tried unsuccessfully to mine coal.[8]

A legend in his own lifetime, he died in 1864, aged 73 years.[9] A plaque erected to this Fr. Therry, is in the Heritage Centre, Cobh, and is shown in Fig. 16.1.

His remains are now in the crypt of St Mary's Cathedral, where the Lady Chapel was erected as his memorial.

A sister and brother of Fr. J. J. Therry resided in Harrington St., Sydney, and they died within a few weeks of each other in December 1874 and January 1875.[10]

James Therry, grandson of John Therry and Elizabeth Conolly, arrived in Sydney in 1862 from Ireland.[11] Her was formerly a supervisor in the inland revenue in Ireland, and had retired. He brought with him his wife Maria and eight children. James had a farm in the Pittwater area for a period. Six of these children were Gerald, Edward, James J., John N., Eugine and Helena G.

SIR ROGER THERRY

Sir Roger Keating Patrick Therry (1800-74), judge, was born at Cork, Ireland, and educated at Clongowes College and Trinity College, Dublin.[12] He was

Fig. 16.2 *Sir Roger Therry (1800-1874). (by Richard Read, 1834, courtesy of Mitchell Library, State Library of New South Wales. Call no: ML180.)*

the son of John Therry, of Castleterry, and Jane Keating. A brother and sister, Byasa and James, were baptised in St Finbarr's South, in 1797.[13] Another brother and sisters were Bryan Keating, Jane, and Anne.[14] In 1822 at Dublin Roger became secretary of the national society for the education of the poor in Ireland; he was called to the Irish bar and actively associated with Daniel O'Connell in the campaign for catholic emancipation. In 1827 he was called to the English bar. In the next year he edited *The Speeches of George Canning*, and wrote a memoir on the life of that statesman. On 9 August 1827 at Dublin he married Mrs Ann Reilly, née Corley. They had the following children: John H., Anne Huskisson, George J.J. Canning, Jane F. and Sophia.[15] In April 1829 he was appointed commissioner, with the right of private practice, of the Courts of Requests (small debts) in New South Wales. He arrived in Sydney with his wife in November.[16]

From March 1841 to August 1843 he acted as attorney-general and, as such, sat in the Legislative Council. In June 1843 he stood for election to the new part-elective Legislative Council as the representative of Camden and was elected. He vacated his seat in January 1845 but returned to the legislature in May 1856 as a nominee member of the first Legislative Council under responsible government.[17]

In December 1844 he was appointed resident judge at Port Phillip. In 1846 he was transferred to the Supreme Court of New South Wales. In 1850 he presided at the first sitting of the Supreme Court, on circuit, at Brisbane. He was the primary judge in Equity.[18]

Roger Therry was a close friend of Fr. Therry, although no close relation. Both men had siblings baptised in the same parish in Cork City around the same time.[19]

When he resigned his judgeship in 1859, Therry retired to England. There in February 1863 he published his *Reminiscences of Thirty Years' Residence in New South Wales and Victoria*.

Therry was always politically minded, and, as a member of the several Legislative Councils, he was in close touch with leading men and measures in an exciting period of Australian history. His deep and active interest in the promotion of education at all levels was lifelong.

Therry was knighted in 1869 and died at Bath in May 1874.[20]

DESCENDANTS OF CLOYNE TERRYS

George Paul Terry, son of Charles Tyrry and Ann McKenna of Kilva, Cloyne, was born in 1827. He went to New South Wales, Australia. He worked in the Bathurst post office department, Sydney. George and his wife Ann had four daughters: Frances born in 1865 and died in 1950, Ann born in 1867 and died in 1940, Mary born in 1869 and died in 1949, and Eugenie born in 1872 and died in 1942. George's wife Ann died in 1874 and he himself died in 1902.[21] In 1894, Mary (Bridie), George's third daughter, married at St James' Forest Lodge, Sydney, Jeremiah Foley, whose family originated from Saleen, Co Cork.[22]

A grand-nephew of George, Joseph, who left Ireland sometime after 1901, died in Sydney in 1909, aged 25.[23] Bernard Murtough Terry (Barney), the fifth child of Dr Paul Terry and Ann Elizabeth Murtough, was born on 22 September 1905. He arrived in Perth, Australia sometime around 1927, having emigrated from England.[24]

17
Some Terrys in North America

This chapter outlines emigration to North America, in particular, with reference to Terrys up to *c.*1900. It is not possible to trace all those Terrys who emigrated to America from Cork. However, an indication of the number of Terrys who emigrated is provided, together with an indication of the various periods in which they emigrated. While the predominant destination for Terrys was the United States, some also immigrated to Canada. Information on some of these Terrys is provided.

There are also descendants of some Cork Terrys who settled in the United States, in an indirect way. After the defeat of King James II, some Terrys from Cork moved to France and subsequently Spain. Descendants of some of these Terrys moved to Central America. One Tomas Terry, a sugar magnate from Cuba, in the mid-19th century, was descended from these Terrys.[1] He moved to New York in the 1860s before finally settling in Paris. One of his great-grandchildren, Juan Terry Trippe, founded Pan American.

Kenny refers to four principal waves of Irish emigration to America: colonial, pre-famine, famine and post-famine.[2] Popular legend holds that mass emigration from Ireland commenced with the famine of the 1840s; yet, Irish migration to America actually began in the 17th century and assumed the characteristics of a mass movement as early as 1720.[3] According to Kenny, very little is known about the early catholic settlers in America, this in contrast to our knowledge about the presbyterians from Ulster who emigrated to America in this period.

Terry Emigration in the Colonial Period

Stephen and John Terry, brothers, are believed to have come to Dorchester, Massachusetts in 1630 and moved to Windsor, Connecticut, *c.*1637.[4] These brothers were not of Irish descent, but were said to be the first Terrys in America. They were from Barnet, near London. An early Terry from Cork that emigrated to Long Island, New York, was a Quaker.[5] Some of the descendants of this family now reside in Nova Scotia, Canada. A Rachel Torrey married a Dennis Carrie in Hanover, Massachusetts, in 1738.[6] Two brothers of the Cork silversmith, Carden Terry, went to America. One of these brothers Paul, born in 1748, was never heard of after he went to America. The other brother George was born in 1743, and he, likewise, was not heard of again.[7] A John Terrey arrived in America on the brig *Ann and Margaret* from Ireland in 1767.[8] The Muster Rolls of the Virginia Companies, organised for the defence of the Frontier during

'Lord Dunmore's War' in 1774, included Peter Torrey.[9] A curious incidence of some early settlers from Cork is now outlined.

THE LOST TOWN OF CORK, MAINE

During the 17th and 18th centuries that part of the colony of Massachusetts Bay now embraced in the state of Maine, was a great centre of colonial activity, chiefly because of its fine harbours, rivers, forests and protected valleys, which attracted European settlers to its shores. O'Brien states:

> In a chronological collection of events, under the title of '1,400 Dates of the Town and City of Bath, Maine,' published by Levi P. Lemont in 1874, we are informed that in the year 1640 one Christopher Lawson acquired from the Indians a large tract of land on the banks of the Kennebec and named it *Ireland*, and that, 'in 1720 Robert Temple purchased the Lawson plantation and settled it with families from Cork, in Ireland, and it still retains the name of Ireland'. In the collections of the Maine Historical Society (vol. 4, 2nd series, p.240) this place is named *Cork*.

The town of Cork in Maine was named after the city of Cork in Ireland. O'Brien states that Lemount was incorrect in assigning Cork to the Lawson plantation, instead of to a tract of land on the opposite side of the Kennebec River. Here, Temple settled the town of Cork. However, the settlement did not last long and was abandoned a couple of years later. To this day the bend of the Eastern River where the old town of Cork was located is known locally as *Cork Cove*.

EMIGRATION BEFORE THE FAMINE

While Irish immigrants to America in the 18th century had been mainly protestant, the immigrants of the 19th century were overwhelmingly catholic. By the 1830s, Catholics exceeded Protestants in the transatlantic migration from Ireland for the first time since 1700. Mass emigration from catholic Ireland occurred in the pre-famine era, 1800-44.[10] Some Irish Terrys who immigrated in America in this period include Michael who arrived in New York in 1827, James and Edward who arrived here in 1832 and 1837 respectively. One Thomas Terry arrived in 1840 and a Pat Terry in 1841. Other Terrys arrived in Boston: James in 1821, Mary and presumably her young child, Michael, in 1837. Arriving in Boston also were John Therry from Limerick in 1827 and Lawrence Therry in 1829. Thomas Terry, of Cork or Waterford birth, is recorded as residing in Richibucto, Canada in 1861.

On the internet for this period is some Terry information, from Breathitt County:[11]

> Ike C. Terry came to Breathitt in about 1839 at the age of19. He came from Pike County and settled on Long's Creek where he lived for three to four years. He fell among the Gabbards and married. His first child lived to be two years old, died, and was buried on Terry's Ranch. Afterwards they came to Turkey Creek. He settled there and raised a large family, of 12 or 13 children. Two of the boys were captured in the Civil War and died at Lake Eire. Ike C. Terry was raised in Pike County. His father, Thomas, came from Virginia, by foot.[12] They owned large boundaries of land. A number of the Terrys were teachers, some were merchants, and all were of Irish descent.

Emigration during the Famine

During the famine decade, 1846-55, from a population of 8.5 million at the beginning of the famine, 2.1 million fled the country, 1.8 million of these to North America (all but 300,000 of these to the United States).[13]

Between 1846-51, over 40 Irish Terrys left from Liverpool and Cobh (Queenstown) and arrived at the Port of New York.[14] About ten per cent of all Terrys in Ireland left for the United States during this period. Their names, ages and occupations were:

Name	Age	Occupation	Name	Age	Occupation
James Terry	16	Labourer	Jno Terry	37	Farmer
William Terry	30	Labourer	Jas Terry	30	Servant
Michael Terry	20	Labourer	J. Terry	29	Labourer
James Terrey	40	Unknown	Mary Terry	30	Servant
Mary Terry	13	None	Wm Terry	40	Labourer
Wm Terry	22	Labourer	George Terry	10	Servant
Stephen Terry	16	Servant	Judy Terry	16	Unknown
Julia Terry	21	Servant	Edmund Terry	15	Unknown
Margaret Terry	24	Servant	Richard Terry	40	Farmer
Betty Terry	17	Labourer	Pat Terry	25	Farmer
Mary Terry	16	Labourer	Eliza Terry	20	Spinster
Michael Terry	11	Labourer	John Terry	50	Farmer
Chas. Terry	16	Unknown	Caroline Terry	15	Unknown
Walter Terry	28	Farmer	Ann Terry	13	Unknown
Benjamin Terry	40	Farmer	Francis Terry	11	Unknown
Edward Terry	1	Child	William Terry	9	Child
Benjamin Terry	40	Unknown	Martha Terry	5	Child
Sarah Terry	38	Unknown	Sarah Terry	4	Child
Wm. Terry	16	Farmer	John Terry	7	Child
George-W. Terry	20	Jeweller	Julia Therry	20	Carpenter
Pat Terry	35		John Terry	21	
James Terry	14				

Table 17.1 *Terrys arriving at New York, 1846-51.*

Of these close to half were from counties Cork and Waterford. Based on a national population of 4.5 million in 1800, 8.3 million in 1841, and the number of Terry families in East Cork in 1800 and 1850, and other immigration data provided by Glazier and Tepper, about thirty per cent of these were from East Cork. The death notice of George W. Terry, of Antietam Creek MD, appears in the *Cork Examiner* on 7 October 1862.

Additional Terrys from Ireland that arrived in the United States, all to New York, up to the end of 1855, are tabulated in Table 17.2.[15]

Name	Arrival Year	Name	Arrival Year
Ellen	1852	Isabella	1855
James (12)	1852	Jane	1852
Johan	1853	Johanna	1853
Johannah	1852	John	1853
Margaret	1852	Martha	1852
Michael	1855	Pat	1853
Robert	1852	Robert	1852
William	1852	Ellen	1855
Jane	1853	James (4)	1852

Table 17.2 *Terrys arriving at New York, 1852-5.*

Terrys also immigrated to other U.S. ports such as Philadelphia and Boston. The 1850 United States Federal Census lists 137 Terrys living in that country of Irish birth. Counties and states with in excess of ten Irish Terrys were New York County in New York State with 38 Irish Terrys and Middlesex, Massachusetts, with 11 Irish Terrys.

The 1851 Census of Canada East, Canada West, New Brunswick and Nova Scotia indicates the following Terrys who were born in Ireland:[16]

Name	District and Province	Estimated year of birth
Mary	Prescott County, Ontario	1836
Elizabeth	Prescott County, Ontario	1838
Michael	Prescott County, Ontario	1840
Michael	Prescott County, Ontario	1799
Catherine	Prescott County, Ontario	1799
Thomas	Prescott County, Ontario	1830
John	Prescott County, Ontario	1834
Mary	Duex Montagnes, Quebec	1802
Michael	Quebec County, Quebec	1802
Margrett	Quebec County, Quebec	1807
Elizabeth	Kent County, Ontario	1831
Dr	Kent County, Ontario	1805
Mrs	Kent County, Ontario	1815

Table 17.3 *Some Irish Terrys in Canada from 1851 Census.*

One Albert Wesly Terry, born around 1856 in Co Cork, moved to Canada around 1888.[17]

Emigration after the Famine

Kenny defines this period as being between 1855 and 1921.[18] It was during this period that the greatest number of Irish emigrants went to the United States. The Irish-born population of the United States reached a historical peak of 1.9 million in 1890. In this year there were also 2.9 million second-generation Irish Americans. In the post-famine era, emigration was numerically and proportionately heaviest from the provinces of Munster and Connacht.[19] Boston elected its first Irish-born Mayor, Hugh O' Brien, in 1884.[20] The number of Terrys from Ireland, who emigrated to the United States for each five-year period between 1855 and 1924, as taken from the John F. Kennedy Trust and Ancestry.com databases, is illustrated in Table17.4.

Period	Number of people
1855-1859	15
1860-1864	21
1865-1869	42
1870-1874	27
1875-1879	19
1880-1884	23
1885-1889	13
1890-1894	4
1895-1899	7
1900-1904	10[21]
1905-1909	12
1910-1914	2
1915-1919	0
1920-1924	2
Total	195

Table 17.4 *Terrys arriving in United States, 1855-1924.*

The majority of these Terrys left from Liverpool, Cobh (Queenstown) and Derry (Londonderry) and arrived at New York port. As many as 90 of these Terrys were from Cork. The death notice of one of them, one James A. Terry, son of Charles, aged 33, appears in the *Cork Examiner* on 4 September 1878. James married Mary Keady and they had children Mary, Cecilia, Charles and Emma.[22] He lived in Brooklyn, New York, and was formerly from Cork City. Significant numbers of Terrys were also from Waterford and Donegal. It can be seen that, after 1910, the number decreased to single figures.

Thomas Terry, son of William and Kate Terry from near Castlemartyr, arrived in Boston in 1900. Sometime after 1911, Patrick and Charles Terry, from Ballinascarta, Midleton, emigrated to Boston.[23] Charles died shortly after emigrating. In 2009, I met Parnell Terry and his family from Maine. Parnell is the son of William and grandson of Patrick.

One Terry, from Co. Waterford, who emigrated to the United States in this period was the paternal great-grandparent of Patrick L. Terry of Baraboo Town, Patrick E. Terry.[24] Patrick L., from this information, is a lifelong farmer in the towns of Baraboo and Dellona.

One Thomas Terry, from Ireland, son of Michael, married Margaret McGrath in Ontario, Canada, in 1878.[25]

The 1870 United States Federal Census lists 243 Terrys living in that country of Irish birth. New York Passenger lists for the period 1820-70 indicate 137 Terrys of Irish ethnicity arriving at the port. Thirty years later, in 1900, the census lists 232 Terrys of Irish birth, with the New York Passenger lists indicating the arrival of 231 Terrys of Irish ethnicity. In 1870, the highest concentrations of Terrys were in New York county, 38, and Kings, 10, in the state of New York, and Middlesex, 12, in the state of Massachusetts. By 1900, the most popular locations for Terrys of Irish birth were New York (Manhattan), with 19 Terrys, Philadelphia, with 17, Suffolk, Massachusetts, with 13, and Kings (Brooklyn), with 11.

In 1900 then, for every two Terrys living in Ireland, there was one Terry of Irish birth living in the United States. In all probability there were more first and second generation Irish Terrys living in the United States at this time than there were in Ireland itself. The main states where Terrys of Irish birth resided, in 1900, are indicated in Table 17.5.

State	Number of Terrys of Irish birth
New York	50
Massachusetts	43
Pennsylvania	36
Illinois	11
Ohio	9
Wisconsin	9

Table 17.5 *Principal States in U.S. with Irish Terrys, 1900.*

Charles Terry born in 1898, from Ballylanders, Cloyne, the son of John Terry and May Fitzgerald, emigrated to the United States in 1923. His brothers John and Paul did likewise. Descendants of these brothers live in Rhode Island and elsewhere.[26]

In 1920, there were 105 Terrys in the U.S. of Irish birth.[27]

18
Conclusions

Chapter one of this book examined the background and context of the subject matter of the book. The origin of Terrys in Cork, as well as the early Norman period, the historical setting, and settlement of Terrys in the 14th century was examined. Terrys are generally accepted as being an Anglo-Norman family. They are recorded as having settled in Cork from the 13th century. Records show that they were a landed family and were royal servants. They acted as jury members and were witnesses to a number of acquisitions. However, in this early period, there is no evidence that they were urban-based in Cork. The information in the second chapter showed how, for the Terrys, the initial steps towards an urban élite in Cork City were undertaken from the mid-15th century. From this period they are recorded as buying and mortgaging property, on a regular basis, in both the city and the suburbs. They were favoured and trusted by the King. In 1499, two of their members, William and Edmund, were appointed to govern the city. There is general evidence of a change in the families that gave Cork City its civic leaders and merchants in the 15th century. The main focus of the book then follows in the succeeding four chapters covering the period 1420-1644. A new grouping of families came to prominence and retained this position until they were expelled from the city in 1644. As merchants and traders, Terrys were one of about a dozen such families that dominated the civic and economic life of the city for 200 years, from the mid-15th century. In looking at this period, Terrys had a limited role, based on available records examined, in the mid-15th century, but by the end of the century they played a significant role in Cork City. An example of this is where one Edmund Tyrry is referred to as a citizen of Cork in 1438, in a deed involving a land transaction, while some 14 years later he is referred to as a burgess and merchant of the city in land transaction deeds. From the records available it would seem that this Edmund was the first significant merchant of Cork City, and from him an increasing number of, and more influential, Terry merchants and traders prospered in the city over the following two centuries. He was the first of the Terry merchant gentry.

Some historians have taken the view that enterprise was quite dormant in this period; others that there was active and prosperous commercial and trading sectors. There appears to be general agreement that income from trading activity was much more lucrative than rental income from land holding. In the 16th century, Terrys firmly established their power base in the city, providing a mayor for the first time in 1505, and on several other occasions during the century. They continued to expand their land base and their trading activities with other parts of Europe. Also, the number of Terry families in the city increased. At times in this period Terrys were the leading merchant family, particularly in the reigns of Henry VIII and James I. As well as being merchants and traders in the city, they had extensive land holding in the surrounding countryside, particularly in east Cork and around the harbour. They owned extensive land in Carrigtohill.

The Desmond wars in the 16th century caused a lot of difficulty in Cork, and the decline of the Desmonds created an unstable situation around Cork. However, the city merchant families survived this, and they also steered a course of non-involvement in the lead up to and the actual Battle of Kinsale. Generally, they provided support for the Queen. Terrys worked closely with the monarchy and agents for the monarchy.

The Reformation had, in time, an unfortunate outcome for the old merchant families of Cork City, including the Terrys. These are now being referred to as the 'Old English'. At the time of the reign of Henry VIII, the changing religious thinking, in the form of the Reformation, did not present a major difficulty for the established families; Dominick Terry accepted the bishopric of Cork from the King. However, towards the end of the 16th century, division on religious affiliation became more acute, and the 'Old English' sought to adhere to the Catholic religion, and at the same time remain loyal to the Crown. As events unfolded in the 17th century, it was not possible to hold this position successfully.

By the year 1600, the Terry families were in a powerful economic position in the city. Some members began purchasing land in more remote parts of county Cork. Other family members moved to Limerick City and to Clare, while still others settled in Cadiz, Spain.

By the beginning of the 17th century, Terrys were more prevalent in Cork City and the Barony of Barrymore than in the remainder of Cork. At this time there were between 20 and 30 Terry families in Cork City, eight recorded Terry families in Barrymore, two in Cork and possibly one or two families in Imokilly. Terrys may have represented as much as eight per cent of the City population in 1600.

Some of the attributes of Terrys in Cork City, at this time, that gave them significant power and wealth, and assisted them in maintaining it included:

- They were merchants and had strong trading links with Europe
- They had extensive land holdings in rural areas, such as in the Barony of Barrymore
- They held significant sway in the political and civic affairs of the City
- They were in a position to support laws that extended privileges, in trade and civic positions, to their children. In this they were able to exclude outsiders.

In the Barony of Barrymore there were Terry strongholds in Rathcormac, Carrigtohill and Cobh. The Terrys sold their holdings, in Carrigtohill, to the Earl of Cork in the 1620s. The families from these strongholds had strong links with their city cousins and, in many cases, the Terrys from the city owned land, and lived, in these rural areas. The Terrys mixed socially and married into other merchant families of Cork. These families included Sarsfields, Gallways, Goulds, Ronans, Skiddys etc. No evidence of strong social interaction of this type with the Barrys of Barrymore is available. There is also no evidence of a strong Terry presence in the Barony of Imokilly in this period, although they did own some property in Youghal.

In Cork, for four decades from the year 1600, the merchants including the Terrys held onto their privileged positions, despite the problems that arose for them in adhering to the Catholic religion. Indeed, in 1627, a King's letter was issued ordering that David Terry be made a baronet of Ireland for his services performed for the King and for his other merit. In the 1640s affairs became untenable for catholic families and for royal families, in Cork. To hold one's position and property one had to be protestant and 'show constant good affection to Parliament'. Terrys were strongly adhering to the catholic religion, with evidence of some six Terry priests in the first half of the 17th century. In 1644, the Catholic families were thrown out of the city, and the functioning of the Corporation terminated. In the subsequent victory of the parliamentarians over the King, the Terrys were further offside. In the Cromwellian settlement, the ancient natives and inhabitants of the city were allowed to transfer to the baronies of Muskerry and Barrymore, as distinct from Connacht. Terrys lost considerable property and position in this period. Some converted to Protestantism and remained in the city. Others retained a certain position in the surrounding countryside. Still others emigrated. But the interconnecting links – such as – inter-marriage between Old English families, property holdings in the city and surrounding districts, civic role and merchant and trading activities – were now substantially broken. A new grouping, the 'New English', was now dominant.

The remainder of the book provides selected material on descendants of the merchant gentry family. From the begining of the 16th century, an approximation is made, based on fairly exhaustive research, on the number and location of Terry families at intervals of about fifty years for the city and the baronies of Barrymore, Cork and Imokilly. This information is provided in Fig. 18.1.

Year	Cork City	Barony of Cork	Barony of Barrymore	Barony of Imokilly	Total
1600	20-30	2	8	1-2	31-42
1650	17	Included in City	5	1-2	23-24
1700	6	2	5	3-4	16-17
1750	18	1	2	5	26
1800	24	1	11	5	41
1850	8	0	15	8	31
1900	6	1	5	10	22

Table 18.1 *Number of Terry families, 1600-1900.*

In 1600, Terrys were more prevalent in Cork City and the Barony of Barrymore than in the remainder of east Cork. Available records do not indicate that the decrease in the number of Terry families in the city during the 17th century was matched by a corresponding increase in other areas of east Cork over this period. Possible reasons include, one, or a combination of the following factors:

Older generations expired and were not replaced.

Families settled elsewhere in Ireland other than east Cork.

They emigrated abroad in particular to the continent of Europe.

Their presence is not fully recorded in extant documents.

In Cobh and Rathcormac, in the barony of Barrymore, Terrys forfeited land in the 17th century. Terrys did hold onto some land in Cobh.

Many Terrys from Cork left Ireland from the 17th century, and even earlier. Some settled and prospered in Spain while others went to France, South America, and the United States and beyond. Some chapters of this book trace Terry families in some these countries. In addition, Terrys from Cork who emigrated to England and Australia are considered.

At a general level, it can be deduced that Terrys in Cork, from 1644 onwards, lost significantly in terms of a viable and identifiable foothold in the affairs of the area. For those in the City, where records are available, it is clear that some traded in intellectual services, such as law, and in crafts, such as that of the silversmith. In the rural areas, the emergence of Terry families in the Barony of Barrymore was recorded, and Terry families still held land in Cobh.

A number of interconnecting factors that had made the Terrys a powerful family grouping in former times were now broken. These links included:

Intermarriage with other Old English families who were merchants and traders

Strong involvement in the civil affairs of the city

Strong trading links with other countries, particularly Spain

Ownership of land in rural areas coupled with merchant activities in the city. The merchant and trade grouping of Terrys in the city had disappeared by 1850.

Endnotes

Chapter 1

1. O'Hart, John, *Irish Pedigrees or The Origin and Stem of the Irish Nation* (1876).
2. Hanks, Patrick and Hodges, Flavin, *A Dictionary of Surnames*, Oxford University Press (1988).
3. Hodgkin, Thomas, *The Barbarian Invasion of the Roman Empire*, Volume III, The Ostrogoths, The Folio Society (2001), pp.476-535.
4. Reaney, P.H., *The Origin of English Surnames*, Routledge & Kegan Paul (1967).
5. MacLysaght, Edward, *More Irish Families*, Irish Academic Press (1982).
6. *Ibid.*
7. Private correspondence with Professor Signe Horn Fuglesong, University of Oslo, and Dr Gillian Fellows-Jensen, Institut for Navnefarskning, Copenhagen; genealogy prepared by James Terry in 1690 at St Germain on the 'ancient and noble family of Tyrry', copy in MacSwiney Papers, Royal Irish Academy.
8. O' Connell, Morgan John, *The Last Colonel of the Irish Brigade*, Tower Books (1977).
9. O'Connor, Bryan, *The Genealogy and ensigns armorials of Messrs William Terry, Dominick Terry, James Terry and Philip Terry, negotiants in Malaga and Cadiz ... sons of Ignatius Terry of the City of Dublin*. This was given to me by Julian Walton of U.C.C.
10. Wagner, Anthony, *Pedigree and Progress*, Phillimore (1975).
11. *Calendar of the Charter Rolls, 1257-1300*, pp.71-2. Nightingale, Pamela, 'Some London Moneyers and Reflections on the Organisation of English Mints in the Eleventh and Twelfth Centuries', *Numismatic Chronicle*, 142 (1982), pp.34-50.
12. Nightingale, Pamela, op.cit., pp.34-50.
13. Private correspondence with David Terry, England.
14. Bolster, Evelyn, *History of the Diocese of Cork*, Irish University Press, Shannon (1972).
15. O'Buachalla, Liam, *History of Carrigtwohill*, Clann na Greine Teo.
16. MacCotter, Paul, *A brief history of Medieval Ballincollig*, http://ballincollig.wordpress.com/medieval-ballincollig/.

17. Collins, J., 'The Old Castles around Cork Harbour', *Journal of the Cork Historical and Archaeological Society*, Vol XXI (1915).
18. Fairbairn, *Book of crests of the families of Great Britain & Ireland* (1905); Terry or Tyrry of Baghyoghis, Co. Cork. *See also* Cork Deeds in marsh's Library, C78 reference to Bellaghoghellie alias Tinestown in Barriemore countrie. While I have not been able to ascertain exactly where Baghyoghis is, I think it is in Carrigtohill.
19. Fairbairn, *op.cit.*
20. Carpenter, David, *The Struggle for Mastery*, Penguin Books (2003).
21. Otway-Ruthven, A.J., *A history of medieval Ireland*, Ernest Benn Ltd, London (1980) p.109.
22. *Ibid*, p.115.
23. Nolan, William, *The shaping of Ireland, the geographical perspective*, The Mercier Press (1986), pp.54-62.
24. Mills, James (ed.), *Calendar of the Judiciary Rolls of Proceedings in the Court of the Justiciar of Ireland, 1295-1303*, HMSO (1914); information supplied by Dr Kenneth Nicholls (Records Commissioners Calendars of Plea Rolls, R.C.7/6, p.112).
25. *Calendar of Documents Relating to Ireland, 1285-1292*, Longman & Co. 1875, Thomas de Clare was the brother of the earl of Gloucester, and was married to the daughter and presumptive heiress of the great Geraldine baron Maurice fitz Maurice. King Edward granted the whole of Thomond to Thomas in 1276; *see* Nicholls, K.W., *Gaelic and Gaelicized Ireland in the Middle Ages*, Lilliput Press (2003), pp.182-3.
26. O Buachalla, Liam, *An early fourteenth-century place name list for Anglo-Norman Cork, Dinnseanchas* (1966), p.50.
27. Clonteyd is possibly Clontead parish, near Kinsale. An old placename in this parish is 'Tyrrestowne', *see Court of Claims Submissions and Evidence 1663* (ed.) Tallon, Geraldine, Irish Manuscripts Commission, p.344.
28. The Terry deeds in the Sarsfield Papers are dealt with and referenced in a subsequent chapter.
29. Carpenter, David, *op.cit.*, p.392.
30. O'Sullivan, William, *The economic history of Cork City from the earliest times to the Act of Union,* Cork University Press (1937), pp.22-6.
31. *Ibid*, p.25.
32. Carpenter, David, *op.cit.*, p.393.
33. *Ibid*, pp.394-5.
34. From Kent Archives Service.
35. Gilbert, J.T., *Historic and Municipal Documents of Ireland, A.D. 1172-1320*, Longman, Green & Co. (1870).
36. *Ibid*, pp.136-40; *Nouum Forum* is a Latin name for Newmarket, Cambridgeshire. *Forum* is the Latin name for Cheap, London. From, Martin, C.T., *The Record Interpreter*, Phillimore (1999). Terrys owned land in Cheap some 900 years ago; *see* Nightingale, Pamela, 'Some

London Moneyers and Reflections on the Organisation of English Mints in the Eleventh and Twelfth Centuries', *Numismatic Chronicle*, 142 (1982), pp.34-50.

37. Otway-Ruthven, A.J., *A history of medieval Ireland*, Ernest Benn Ltd, London (1980), p.124.
38. Carpenter, David, *op.cit.*, pp.395-7.
39. The fitz Ellis family were a prominent merchant family from Oxfordshire in the 13th century.
40. Carpenter, David, *op. cit.*, p.399.
41. *Ibid, op.cit.*, p.399.
42. *Ibid, op.cit.*, p.402.
43. *Calendar of Documents Relating to Ireland, 1171-1251*, Longman & Co. (1875); a son of John, who came to Ireland in 1170, was named Stephen (from James Terry's 1690 genealogy).
44. *Calendar of Documents Relating to Ireland, 1293-1301*, Longman & Co. (1875), Collectors were appointed by the king for that purpose, and were later known as bailiffs; see O'Sullivan, William, *The economic history of Cork City from the earliest times to the Act of Union,* Cork University Press (1937), p.33.
45. *Calendar of Documents Relating to Ireland, 1285-1292*, Longman & Co. (1875).
46. *Calendar of the Judiciary Rolls of Proceedings in the Court of the Justiciar of Ireland, 1295-1303*, HMSO (1914).
47. Carpenter, David, *op. cit.*, p.403.
48. *Ibid, op.cit.*, p.409.
49. Gilbert, John T., *Register of the Abbey of St Thomas, Dublin*, HMSO (1889), pp.202-16.
50. Carpenter, David, *op.cit.*, p.436.
51. Nicholls, K.W., *Gaelic and Gaelicized Ireland in the Middle Ages*, Lilliput Press (2003), pp.106-7.
52. *Profession of obedience*, CCA-DCc-ChAnt/C/115/70, Canterbury Cathedral Archives.
53. Bliss, W.H., *Petitions to the Pope 1342-1419*, vol. IV: 2 Clement VI (1896), pp.39-53; *Calendar of Papal Registers, Papal Letters III, 1342-1362.*
54. Nicholls, Kenneth, 'The Development of Lordship in County Cork', 1300-1600, in *Cork History & Society*, eds, O'Flanagan, Patrick and Buttimer, Cornelius G., Geography Publications (1993), pp.158-9.
55. *Ibid*, p.159.
56. Taken from Nicholls, Kenneth, *op.cit.*, p.161.
57. Berry, Henry F., 'Sheriffs of the County Cork – Henry III to 1660', *Society of Antiquaries Journal* (1905), XXXI, pp.39-52.
58. Jefferies, Henry Alan, *Cork Historical Perspectives*, Four Courts Press (2004), p.69.

59. http://www.corkcorp.ie/aboutcork/history.
60. Green, Alice Stopford, *The Making of Ireland and its undoing 1200-1600*, Macmillan and Co. (1908), p.24.
61. Kelly, Maria, *A History of the Black Death in Ireland*, Tempus (2001), p.97.
62. O'Brien, A.F., 'Politics, Economy and Society; the development of Cork and the Irish South-Coast Region *c.*1170 to *c.*1583' in *Cork History & Society*, eds, O' Flanagan, Patrick and Buttimer, Cornelius G., Geography Publications (1993),p.114.
63. *Ibid*, p.115.
64. *Ibid*, p.117.
65. Nicholls, Kenneth, 'Two Islands, One Street', *Cork Examiner*, 13 March 1985. The evidence for Terry movement into the city would suggest that it was from the mid-15th century.
66. O'Brien, A.F., *op.cit.*, p.118.
67. Jefferies, Henry Alan, *op.cit.*, pp.71-2.
68. *The Receipt Roll of the Irish Exchequer, 1301-2* (E101/233/16); Paul Dryburgh and Brendan Smith, *Handbook and Select Calendar of sources for Medieval Ireland in the National Archives of the United Kingdom*, Four Courts Press (2005), p.112.
69. *Calendar of the Justiciary Rolls, Ireland*, HMSO, 1914, pp.296-439.
70. *Calendar of the Justiciary Rolls, Ireland I to VII years of Edward II*, Stationary Office, Dublin, pp.72-4.
71. *Calendar of the Justiciary Rolls, op.cit.*, pp.201-2.
72. *Calendar of the Justiciary Rolls, op.cit.*, pp.287-97.
73. *Calendar of the Justiciary Rolls, op.cit.*, p.292.
74 O'Connell, Morgan John, *The Last Colonel of the Irish Brigade*, Tower Books (1977), p.320. From Tuckey's *Cork Remembrancer*, the first named Terry mayor was in 1505. There are many gaps in the list of mayors prior to 1310.
75. Windele, John, *Sarsfield and other Papers relating to Cork*, Blair's Castle (1847), p.1.
76. O'Brien, A.F., 'Irish Exchequer Records of Payments of the Fee farm of the City of Cork in the Later Middle Ages', *Analecta Hibernica*, No.37 (1998).
77. Translated into English for the author by Richard Samways, Dorset.
78. Irish Manuscripts Commission, 'Coram Rege Roll, No 364 (Trinity, 1351)', *Analecta Hibernica*, No. 23; translated into English for the author by Richard Samways, Dorset.
79. Nicholls, Kenneth, *op.cit.*, p.176.
80. Irish Manuscripts Commission, *op.cit.*, p.23.
81. Windele, John, *op.cit.*, p.3.
82. Translated into English for the author by Richard Samways, Dorset.

Chapter 2

1. Brooks, Eric St John, 'Unpublished charters relating to Ireland, 1177-82', *Proceedings of the Royal Irish Academy* (1936).
2. *See* Charter details below.
3. Dennehy, Rev. Henry Edward, *History of Great Island The Cove of Cork, and Queenstown*, Tower Books (1990).
4. Gilbert, John T., *Register of the Abbey of St Thomas, Dublin*, HMSO (1889). Richard Samways, Dorset, translated these charters for the writer.
5. In Bolster, Evelyn (1), *A History of the Diocese of Cork from the earliest times to the Reformation*, Irish University Press (1972), p.129; Ynespic is identified as Spike Island and Kairultan as Caherultan, Castlemartyr.
6. John T. Gilbert, *op.cit.*
7. *See* Caulfield's 'Records of the Sarsfield Family', in the *Journal of the Cork Historical and Archaeological Society*, vol. XXI, 1915, p.85. Keppagh is identified as Kippane, now included in Kilrush, Mogeely parish, and Ballymolyn, with Ballinwillin, Gortroe parish, by O'Buachalla, L., *Dinnseanchas* (1966-7). Speristown and Tybtotistown adjoin Carrigtohill. Caulfield, R., 'Chartae Tyrryanae', *Topographer and Genealogist*, iii Chapt (1958), pp.119-22. Windele gives a different place name for the third place name on this list; he gives the place name as Ballymortiri [Castlemartyr] as distinct from Ballymoilyn. *Report on private collections, No 309, Sarsfield Papers*, National Manuscripts Office, Dublin.
8. A messuage is a house with outbuildings and a parcel of land or yard. Downgarwan is the present North Main St. area of Cork City. Caulfield, R., *op.cit.*, pp.110-22.
9. Bolster, Evelyn (2), 'A Landgable Roll of Cork City', *Collectanae Hibernica*. Bolster states that the document belongs to the period 1377-1413. Windele's Cork, dates the document to the period 1377-98. Jefferies' *Cork Historical Perspectives* dates it in the 15th century. On reading it in conjunction with Terry Deeds, it appears to me that it probably dates from *c.*1442.
10. Windele, John, *Sarsfield and other Papers relating to Cork*, Blair's Castle, Cork (1847).
11. Caulfield, R., *op.cit.*, p.113, Caulfield states that the island of Inys ewenaghe may have been called Spike Island. This island is Haulbowline.
12. *Report on private collections, No 309, Sarsfield Papers*, National Manuscripts Office, Dublin.
13. *Ibid.*
14. *Cork Constitution*, 8 February 1867. 'A report on a meeting of the Cork Cuvcerian and Archaeological Society where Dr Caulfield exhibited two original Tyrry wills of 1454 and 1479'.
15. According to Windele, it is Walshe in another deed of the same date.
16. This and subsequent details are from, Caulfield, R., *op.cit.* These cover Terry deeds in the period 1438 to 1529.

17. Tuckey indicates that David was mayor in 1521. Tuckey, Francis H., *Cork Remembrancer* (1st published 1837), Tower Books, Cork (1980).
18. Johnson, Gina, *The Laneways of Medieval Cork*, Cork City Council (2002).
19. *Ibid.*
20. O. Murchada, Diarmuid, in 'The Ui Meic Thire of Imokilly', *Journal of the Cork Historical and Archaeological Society*, July-December 1977, states that this townland appears in a patent of James I as 'Knockanmacterrie' and associates it with the Un Meic Thire sept.
21. Dennehy, Rev. Henry Edward, *op.cit.*
22. Power, Rev. Professor Patrick, 'Place-Names and Antiquities of S.E. County Cork', *Proceedings of the Royal Irish Academy*, vol. 36 (1921-4).
23. Bliss, W.H., *Petitions to the Pope 1342-1419*, vol.IV: 2 Clement VI, 1896, pp.39-53; *Calendar of Papal Registers, Papal Letters III, 1342-62.*
24. Caulfield, R., *op. cit.*, pp.119-22. *Report on private collections, No 309, Sarsfield Papers*, National Manuscripts Office, Dublin.
25. *Calendar of Papal Registers, 1441*, vol. IX.
26. *Ibid, 1444-5*, vol. IX.
27. *'Lateran Regesta 547:1459' Calendar of Papal Registers Relating to Great Britain and Ireland, vol. 12: 1458-71* (1933), pp.42-8.
28. Wilson, Fr James, *Cloyne Parish Priests.*
29. Bolster, Evelyn (1), *op. cit.*, pp.497-8.
30. *Calendar of Papal Registers*, vol. XII, 1461.
31. *Calendar of Papal Registers, op. cit.*, 1464-5.
32. Nicholls, K.W., *Gaelic and Gaelicized Ireland in the Middle Ages*, Lilliput Press, Dublin (2003), p.106.
33. Caulfield, R., *op. cit.*
34. Carpenter, David, *The Struggle for Mastery*, Penguin Books (2003), p.436.

CHAPTER 3

1. D'Alton, E.A., *History of Ireland*, The Gresham Publishing Co., London, p.412.
2. Ellis, Stephen G., *Ireland in the Age of the Tudors 1447-1603*, Longman (1995), p.32.
3. *Ibid*, p.32.
4. Nolan, William, *The Shaping of Ireland*, The Mercier Press, Cork and Dublin, p.64.
5. O'Brien, A.F., 'Politics, Economy and Society: The Development of Cork and the Irish South-Coast Region, *c.*1170 to *c.*1583', p.133 in *Cork History & Society* (eds), O'Flanagan, Patrick, and Buttimer, Cornelius G., Dublin.
6. *Ibid*, p.40.
7. Curtis, Edmund, *A History of Medieval Ireland from 1086 to 1513*, Methuen & Co. Ltd, London (1923), pp.413-5.

8. Bolster, Evelyn, *A History of the Diocese of Cork*, Irish University Press, Shannon (1972), p.427.
9. Colgan, E., *For Want of Good Money*, Wordwell Ltd. (2003), p.46.
10. *Ibid*, p.54.
11. Nicholls, K.W., *Gaelic and Gaelicized Ireland in the Middle Ages*, Lilliput Press, Dublin (2003), pp.144-5.
12. Green, Alice Stopford, *The Making of Ireland and its Undoing 1200-1600*, Macmillan and Co. (1908), pp.172-3.
13. Lydon, James, *The Lordship of Ireland in the Middle Ages*, Four Courts Press, Dublin (2003), p.178.
14. *Ibid*, p.179.
15. Nicholls, K.W., *Gaelic and Gaelicized Ireland in the Middle Ages*, Lilliput Press, Dublin (2003), p.54.
16. McCormack, Anthony M., *The Earldom of Desmond 1463-1583*, Four Courts Press (2005), p.41.
17. Lydon, James, *op. cit.*, p.197.
18. Nicholls, Kenneth, 'The development of lordship in County Cork, 1300-1600' in *Cork History & Society* (eds), O'Flanagan, Patrick & Buttimer, Cornelius G., Geography Publications (1993), pp.172-6.
19. D'Alton, E.A., *op.cit.*, pp.430-2.
20. Jefferies, H.A., *Cork Historical Perspectives*, Four Courts Press (2004), p.72.
21. Caulfield, Richard, *Council Book of the Corporation of Cork*, Appendix C.
22. Windele, John, *Roche, Fitzgerald and Sarsfield Papers*, Blair's Castle (1845), pp.318-48.
23. D'Alton, John, *King James's Irish Army List (1689)*, vol. 1, John D'Alton, p.109.
24. Bolster, Evelyn, *A landgable Roll of Cork City*, Collectanae Hibernica.
25. Caulfield, R., *op.cit.*, pp.114-5.
26. Windele, John, *Sarsfield and other Papers relating to Cork*, Blair's Castle, Cork (1847).
27. *Cork Constitution*, 8 February 1867, 'A report on a meeting of the Cork Cuvcerian and Archaeological Society', where Dr Caulfield exhibited two original Tyrry wills of 1454 and 1479.
28. Dryburgh, Paul and Smith, Brendan, *Handbook and Select Calendar of Sources for Medieval Ireland in the National Archives of the United Kingdom*, Four Courts Press (2005), p.281.
29. *Calendar of Patent Rolls, Henry VII, 1485-94*, HMSO (1914).
30. *Oath of the Citizens (of Cork), 1498,* transcript from PRO E/30/1564; McCarthy, C.F.J., 'An Antiquary's Note Book 19', *Cork Historical and Archaeological Society Journal.* Caulfield's *Council Book of the Corporation of the City of Cork*, gives two different Christian names for Terrys, than those indicated by McCarthy. In place of the Edwards, he has Edmund and Dominick Fz Piers. These, based on other information for this

period, I take to be the correct Christian names. The image of the oath, with seals attached, was provided by The National Archives, UK.

31. Fuller, J.F., 'Carden Terry', *Journal of the Cork Historical and Archaeological Society*, vol. IX, 1903, p.68;. J. Hughes, James L., *Patentee Officers in Ireland, 1173-1826*, Irish Manuscripts Commission (1960), p.129.

CHAPTER 4

1. Lennon, Colm, *Sixteenth Century Ireland*, Gill and Macmillan (1994), p.1.
2. *Ibid*, p.21.
3. *Ibid*, p.22.
4. Duplessis, Robert S., *Transitions to Capitalism in Early modern Europe*, Cambridge University Press (1997), p.38.
5. Putting-out is similar to modern day sub-contracting, with the sub-contractor responsible for his own plant and equipment.
6. Sheehan, Anthony, 'Irish Towns in a Period of Change, 1558-1625', in *Natives and Newcomers*, eds, Brady, Ciaran and Gillespie, Raymond, Irish Academic Press (1986), p.98.
7. Gillespie, Raymond, *The Transformation of the Irish Economy 1550-1700*, Dundalgan Press (W. Tempest) Ltd. (1991), p.8.
8. Sheehan, Anthony, *op.cit.*, pp.98-9.
9. Jefferies, H.A., *Cork Historical Perspectives*, Four Courts Press (2004), p.84.
10. Green, Alice Stopford, *The Making of Ireland and its Undoing 1200-1600*, Macmillan and Co., p.37.
11. Jones, Evan Thomas, 'The Bristol Shipping Industry in the Sixteenth Century', PhD Thesis, University of Edinburgh, unpublished (1998). These percentages are based on trade figures for three selected years, 1541-2, 1542-3 and 1545-6.
12. Jefferies, H.A., *op. cit.*, p.87.
13. O'Sullivan, William, *The Economic History of Cork City from the earliest times to the Act of Union,* Cork University Press (1937), p.70.
14. Lennon, Colm, *op. cit.*, p.25.
15. *See* Edwards, David, *The Ormond Lordship in County Kilkenny 1515-1642*, Four Courts Press (2003), p.31.
16. Sheehan, Anthony, *op. cit.*, pp.100-1.
17. *Ibid*, p.101.
18. Taken from Nicholls, Kenneth, 'The Development of Lordship in County Cork, 1300-1600', in *Cork History & Society* (ed.), O'Flanagan, Patrick & Buttimer, Cornelius G., Geography Publications (1993), p.195.
19. Source: Tuckey's *Cork Remembrancer.*
20. Sheehan, Anthony, *op. cit.*
21. Edwards, David, *op. cit.*, p.32.

22. Gillespie, Raymond, *op. cit.*, p.5.
23. Duplessis, Robert S., *op. cit.*, p.90.
24. Gillespie, Raymond, *op. cit.*, pp.15-9.
25. *Ibid*, p.26.
26. J.C., 'The old castles around Cork Harbour', *Journal of the Cork Historical and Archaeological Society*, Vol. XXI, pp.86-7.
27. O'Dowd, Mary (ed.), *Calendar of State Papers Tutor Period 1571-1575*, Public Records Office & Irish Manuscripts Office (2000), p.59.
28. Nicholls, Kenneth, *op. cit.*, p.178.
29. Fraser, Antonia (ed.), *The lives of the Kings & Queens of England*, Weidenfeld & Nicolson (1998).
30. Edwards, David, *op. cit.*, p.ix.
31. *Ibid*, p.1.
32. Lordship territories.
33. Edwards, David, *op. cit.*, p.1.
34. *Ibid*, p.12.
35. Jefferies, H.A., *op. cit.*
36. Lennon, Colm, *op. cit.*, p.13.
37. *Ibid*, p.113. The 'Old English' were catholic descendants of Anglo-Norman settlers who monopolised government positions until the Reformation.
38. Curtis, Edmund, *A History of Medieval Ireland from 1086 to 1513*, Methuen & Co. Ltd (1923), p.365.
39. O'Brien, A.F., 'Politics, Economy and Society: The Development of Cork and the Irish South-Coast Region *c.*1170 to *c.*1583', in *Cork History & Society* (ed.) O'Flanagan, Patrick and Buttimer, Cornelius G., Geography Publications (1993), p.142.
40. *Ibid.*
41. Lennon, Colm, *op. cit.*, p.135.
42. *Ibid*, p.142.
43. Elton, G.R., *England under the Tudors*, The Folio Society (1997), pp.178-9.
44. Jefferies, H.A., *op. cit.*, p.80.
45. *Ibid*, p.105.
46. *Ibid*, p.114.
47. Bagwell, Richard, *Ireland under the Tudors*, Longmans, Green and Co. (1885), vol. I, pp.332-3.
48. Ellis, Stephen G., *Ireland in the age of the Tudors 1447-1603*, Longman (1998), p.265.
49. *Ibid*, p.289.
50. O'Connor, Brian, 'Genealogia, Insignias y Blasones de la familia Terry', unpublished (1753).
51. O'Down, Mary, *op. cit.*, p.437.
52. *See* Chapter on, 'Terrys in Tutor Cork', in *Terrys of Cork 1600-2000*, and compare with Chart 1.1 Edwards, David, *The Ormond lordship in*

County Kilkenny 1515-1642.

53. Edwards, David, *op. cit.*, p.27.
54. Canny, Nicholas, *Making Ireland British 1580-1650*, Oxford University Press (2001), p.149.
55. Jefferies, H.A., *op. cit.*, p78.
56. *Ibid*, p.115.
57. Ford, Alan, *The Protestant Reformation in Ireland, 1590-1641*, Four Courts Press (1997), pp.38-9; Recusant: a person in the 16th and 17th centuries, usually a catholic, who refused to attend Anglican services and denied the ecclesiastical supremacy of the Crown.
58. Lennon, Colm, 'The Counter-Reformation in Ireland, 1542-1641', in *Natives and Newcomers, essays on the making of Irish Colonial Society, 1531-1641*, (eds) Brady, Ciaran and Gillespie, Raymond, Irish Academic Press (1986), p.84.
59. Ford, Alan, *op. cit.*, p.39.

CHAPTER 5

1. This and subsequent details are from Caulfield, R., 'Chartae Tyrryanae', *Topographer and Genealogist*, iii (1958). These cover Terry deeds in the period 1438 to 1529.
2. Tuckey indicates that David was mayor in 1521.
3. An abbey near Midleton.
4. I take *maðro* to mean a cleric with a Master's degree.
5. Ainsworth's report on private collections, no. 309, *Sarsfield papers*, Manuscripts Department, National Library of Ireland.
6. O'Brien, Alph, 'Commercial relations between Aquitaine and Ireland *c.*1000 to *c.*1550', in *Aquitaine and Ireland in the Middle Ages*, ed. Picard, Jean-Michel, Four Courts Press (1995), p.63.
7. Lodge, *Records of the Rolls*, National Archives Ireland, vol.1, pp.167-8.
8. *Ibid.*
9. Windele, John (1), *Sarsfield and other Papers relating to Cork*, Blair's Castle, Cork (1847), p.24.
10. *Calendar of State papers Ireland 1592-1596*, p.482. Lord Burghley, William Cecil, was the principal adviser to Queen Elizabeth I through most of her reign, from *Encyclopaedia Britannica*, 15th Edition, Micropaedia, vol.II, p.664.
11. Green, Alice Stopford, *The Making of Ireland and its undoing 1200-1600*, Macmillan and Co. (1908), p.175.
12. *Calendar of State Papers Ireland 1588-1592*, p.17; LDS film #823809, vol.14, p.2,576.
13. *Ibid*; also *Lodge Manuscripts*, National Archives Ireland, vol.1, p.213.
14. Windele, John (1), *op. cit.*, p.79.
15. Windele, John (2), *Roche, FitzGerald and Sarsfield Papers*, Blair's Castle, Cork (1845).

16. Nicholls, Kenneth, *Chancery Bills, survivals from pre-1922 Collection*, National Archives, Dublin, unpublished.
17. Ainsworth, *op.cit.*
18. Caulfield, Richard (1), 'Early Charters relating to the City and County of Cork', *Gentleman's Magazine*, April (1865).
19. Casey, James, 'Land Ownership in North Cork', PhD Thesis, U.C.C., unpublished (1988).
20. Nicholls, Kenneth, 'The Development of Lordship in County Cork, 1300-1600', in *Cork History & Society*, (eds) O'Flanagan, Patrick and Buttimer, Cornelius G., Geography Publications (1993), p.202.
21. Caulfield, Richard (2), 'Early Charters relating to Kinsale', *Gentleman's Magazine*, April (1865), p.454.
22. Lart, Charles, *The Pedigrees and Papers of James Terry, Athlone Herald, at the Court of James II in France, 1690-1725*, William Pollard & Co. Ltd (1938).
23. Genealogical Office, Dublin, *g.o.218*, p.266.
24. Hackett, Michael Benedict, *A Presence in an Age of Turmoil, English, Irish, and Scottish Augustinians in the Reformation and Counter-Reformation*, Augustinian Historical Institute (2001), p.116; www.ancestry.co.uk.
25. Caulfield, Richard (3), 'Wills and Inventories, Cork temp. Elizabeth and James I', *Gentleman's Magazine* (1861), p 502.
26. O' Connor, Brian, 'Genealogia, Insignias y Blasons de la familia Terry', unpublished (1753).
27. Caulfield, Richard (1), *op. cit.*
28. Caulfield, Richard (4), 'Cork Wills', Church of Ireland Records, unpublished, RCBL, Dublin.
29. *C46, Oct 4, 1560, Cork Deeds*, Marsh's Library, Dublin. Details provided by Fr Michael Hackett, O.S.A.
30. Caulfield, Richard (1), *op. cit.*; *D.25, 925-14*, National Library of Ireland.
31. Nicholls, Kenneth, *op. cit.*
32. Jones, Evan, *Bristol 'particular' accounts, 1503-4*, TNA E122 199/1, University of Bristol (2006). The column headed 'Port' refers to the port from which the ship came. The column headed 'Destination' refers indicates where a ship is sailing to or from.
33. www.bris.ac.uk/History/Ireland/, *Bristol 'Particular' Customs Account, 1516-7*, reference e122212; *see also* Jones, Evan, 'The British Shipping Industry in the Sixteenth Century', unpublished PhD Thesis, University of Edinburgh (1998).
34. Bernard, Jacques, *Navires et Gens de Mer a Bordeaux, 1400-1550*,SEVPEN (1968), vol.III, pp.388-9.
35. O'Brien, Alph, *op. cit.*, p.63.
36. www.bris.ac.uk/History/Ireland/, *op. cit.*, *1525-6*.
37. www.bris.ac.uk/History/Ireland/, *op. cit.*, *1542-3* and *1545-6*, reference e 1221994 and e 1222115.

38. My guess is that 'Kyrry' should be spelt 'Tyrry'.
39. *A Calendar of Material relating to Ireland from the High Court of Admiralty Examinations, 1536-1641*, Irish Manuscripts Commission (1992).
40. *Calendar of State Papers Ireland, 1574-1585*, Longmans, Green, Reader & Diver (1867), pp.473-6.
41. Jefferies, Henry Alan, *Cork Historical Perspectives*, Four Courts Press (2004).
42. Caulfield, Richard (5), 'Wills and Inventories, Cork', *Gentleman's Magazine*, April (1862).
43. Caulfield, Richard (4), *op. cit.*
44. Windele, John (1), *op.cit.*, pp.16-7.
45. *C 65 Aug 4 1584, Cork deeds*, Marsh's Library, Dublin. Details provided by Fr Michael Hackett, O.S.A.
46. Courtesy of the Cork Archives Institute.
47. Candon, Anthony, 'The Cork Suburb of Dungarvan', *Journal of the Cork Historical and Archaeological Society* (1985), p.98.
48. Windele, John (1), *op. cit.*; Windele, John (2), *op. cit.*; Caulfield, Richard (3), p.262.
49. Caulfield, Richard (6), *op. cit.*
50. An abbey near Midleton.
51. I take this to mean a cleric with a Master's degree.
52. Tuckey, *op. cit.*, p.47.
53. Tuckey, *op. cit.*
54. Caulfield, Richard (3), *op. cit.* pp.454-5; in a handwritten footnote to the copy of this deed that I received from Kenneth Nicholls is the following additional Information. Bally na Monwylyg is Mansfieldstown. In the Sarsfield Ms., Letter of attorney of Philip Gogan appoints Walthur Gallway and George Tyrry, merchants, his attorneys re. Richard Tyrry in possession of lands, 1539.
55. Coleman, J., 'The Old Castles around Cork Harbour', *Journal of the Cork Historical and Archaeological Society*, vol.XXI, pp.6-7.
56. Casey, James, 'The Barony of Kerrycurrihy, Co. Cork, an archaeological and historical study', M.A. Thesis, unpublished, U.C.C. (1982).
57. MacCarthy, C.J.F., *Thomas Ronan in sixteenth century Cork*, C.J.F. MacCarthy (1990)
58. Bolster, Evelyn, *A History of the Diocese of Cork*, p15.
59. *C 47 March 4 1559(60), Cork Deeds*, Marsh's Library, Dublin. Details provided by Fr Michael Hackett, O.S.A.
60. Caulfield, Richard (5), op.cit.
61. Windele, John (1), op. cit., p.15.
62. Genealogical Office, Dublin, *g.o. 218*, p.267.
63. Windele, John (2), op.cit, p. 40.
64. Caulfield, Richard (4), op.cit.
65. Caulfield, Richard (5), op.cit, pp.710-1.
66. Caulfield, Richard (2), p 21. Windele's date for this deed is 1584, but

in the original deed in Marsh's Library it is dated 1589.

67. *C 74 Oct 4 1589, Cork Deed*, Marsh's Library, Dublin. Original in Latin, a transcript by Fr Michael Hackett, O.S.A.
68. Caulfield, Richard (2), op.cit.
69. *Calendar of State Papers Ireland 1588-1592*, p.17.
70. Caulfield, Richard (7), *Council book of the Corporation of Cork*, Appendix C.
71. Caulfield, Richard (2), op.cit.; John Windele (2), op.cit., p232
72. MacCarthy, C.J.F., op.cit. The city did not have sheriffs until later. A John Terry was one of the bailiffs in 1537.
73. Windele, John (1), op.cit., p.55.
74. Caulfield, Richard (2), op.cit.
75. Caulfield, Richard (2), op.cit.
76. *C II 17 Nov 17 1538, Cork Deeds*, Marsh's Library, Dublin.
77. *C II 31 June 6 1540, Cork Deeds*, Marsh's Library, Dublin.
78. *C 71 June 5 1540, Cork Deeds*, Marsh's Library, Dublin. Details provided by Fr Michael Hackett, O.S.A.; Tuckey indicates that William was mayor in 1538 and Richard was mayor in 1540.
79. Caulfield, Richard (2), op.cit.
80. MacCarthy, C.J.F., op.cit., p.21.
81. O'Dowd, Mary, ed., *Calendar of State Papers Ireland Tudor Period 1571-5*, Public Records Office & Irish Manuscripts Office, 2000, p. 47.
82. President of Munster.
83. O'Dowd, Mary, op.cit. p241.
84. O'Dowd, Mary, op.cit., p.272.
85. Hughes, James L.J., *Patentee Officers in Ireland, 1173-1826*, Irish Manuscripts Commission (1960), p. 132.
86. O'Dowd, Mary, op.cit., p.286.
87. O'Dowd, Mary, op.cit., p.825.
88. O' Connor, Brian, op.cit.
89. Caulfield, Richard (4), op.cit.
90. Caulfield, Richard (2), op.cit.
91. *Calendar of State Papers Ireland, 1574-85*, Longmans, Green, Reader & Diver (1867), pp.473-6.
92. *Calendar of State Papers Ireland, 1574-85*, op.cit., pp.473-6.
93. Caulfield, Richard (2), op.cit.
94. Bolster, Evelyn, *A History of the Diocese of Cork, from the earliest times to the Reformation*, Irish University Press (1972), p.311.
95. It would seem that Edmund and David, and other Terrys were commissaries, who exercised spiritual jurisdiction by commission of the bishop.
96. Brady, W.M., *Clerical and Parochial Records of Cork, Cloyne, and Ross*, Longman, Green, Longman, Roberts, and Green (1864).
97. Bolster, Evelyn, op.cit., p.493.
98. Brady, W.M., op. cit.

99. Ibid.
100. Bolster, Evelyn, op.cit., p.44.
101. Ibid, p.47.
102. Jefferies, Henry Alan, op.cit.
103. Brady, W.M., op.cit.
104. Ibid.
105. Caulfield, Richard (3), op.cit., p.262.

CHAPTER 6

1. Terry, Kevin, et al., *Terrys of Cork 1600-2000 a local historical perspective* (Kevin Terry) 2005, pp.27-8.
2. Nicholls, Kenneth, 'The development of Lordship in County Cork 1300-1600', in *Cork History and Society*, ed. O'Flanagan, Patrick and Buttimer, Cornelius G., Geography Publications (1993).
3. O Buachalla, Liam, *History of Carrigtwohill*, Clann na Greine Teo.
4. Power, Rev. Professor Patrick, 'Place names and antiquities of SE Cork – Barony of Barrymore', *Proceedings of the RIA,* vol. 36 (1921-4), Part III; see chapter 1, note 24 on p.134.
5. Nicholls, Kenneth, op.cit.
6. Hajba, Anna-Maria, *Houses of Cork vol. 1: North Cork*, Ballinakella Press (2002).
7. O' Brien, Michael, *Drawings of Cork*, The O'Brien Press (1974).
8. Johnson, Gina, *The Laneways of Medieval Cork*, Cork City Council (2002).
9. Ibid.
10. McCarthy, Mark, 'Geographical change in an early modern town: Urban growth, economy and cultural politics in Cork, 1600-41', *Journal of the Cork Historical and Archaeological Society*, vol. 105 (2000).
11. Johnson, Gina, op.cit.
12. Healy, James N., *The Castles of County Cork*, The Mercier Press.
13. Clarke, Aidan, *The Old English in Ireland, 1625-1642*, Four Courts Press (2000), p.15.
14. Foster, R.F., *Modern Ireland 1600-1972*, The Penguin Press (1988), p.16.
15. Foster, R.F., Ibid, p.16.
16. Clarke, Aidan, op.cit., p.15.
17. Hackett, Michael Benedict, *A Presence in the Age of Turmoil, English, Irish and Scottish Augustinians in the Reformation and Counter-Reformation*, Augustinian Historical Institute (2001), Chapter 6.
18. Dennehy, Rev. Henry Edward, *History of Great Island*, Tower Books (1990).
19. Tuckey, Francis, *Cork Remembrancer*, Tower Books (1980), p.71.
20. Beckett, J., *The Making of Modern Ireland 1603-1923*, Faber and Faber

(1966), p.46.

21. Hackett, Michael Benedict, op.cit., p.116.
22. Dickson, David, *Old World Colony Cork and South Munster 1630-1830*, Cork University Press (2005), pp.3-28.
23. Connolly, S.J., *Religion, Law and Power – the making of Protestant Ireland, 1660-1760*, Clarendon Press, Oxford (1992), p.7.
24. Clarke, Aidan, op.cit., p.236.
25. Tuckey, Francis, op.cit., p.86.
26. Connolly, S.J., op.cit., p.13; *City of Cork – Survey of Valuation (circa AD 1663-1664).*

Chapter 7

1. Caulfield, Richard (1), *The Council Book of the Corporation of the City of Cork from 1609 to 1643, and from 1690 to 1800.* J. Billing & Sons: Guildford (1867). Once admitted to the freedom of a corporate town and entered on the register of freemen, a man was permitted to practise his trade and vote in parliamentary elections. Freedom was attained through the completion of an apprenticeship, through descent from one's father, by marriage into the family of a freeman or by grace of the mayor and corporation.
2. Caulfield, R. (1), Ibid.
3. *Sarsfield Papers*, National Library of Ireland, Manuscripts Department.
4. *Court of Claims submissions and evidence 1663*, ed., Tallon, Geraldine, Irish Manuscripts (2006), p241.
5. Fuller, James F. (1), 'Terry Pedigree', *Journal of the Cork Historical and Archaeological Society*, vol. IX (1903), p.276.
6. While Windele would indicate that this was before 1609, the reference to Edward, bishop of Cork and Ross, would date it much later in the 17th century.
7. Terry genealogy by O Connor, Bryan (1753); Tuckey's Cork Remembrancer.
8. *Lismore Papers*, vol. IV.
9. Windele, John, *Sarsfield and other papers relating to Cork*, Blairs Castle, Cork (1847).
10. Windele, John, Ibid.
11. *Court of Claims submissions and evidence 1663*, op.cit., p.241.
12. Caulfield, Richard (1), op.cit.
13. Fuller, J. F. (2), 'Notes and Queries', *Cork Historical and Archaeological Society Journal, Second Series*, vol. IX (1903), p.275.
14. Tuckey, Francis H., *The County and City of Cork Remembrancer*, Tower Books, Cork (1980).
15. This name appeared twice on the list.
16. This name appeared twice on the list.
17. This name appeared twice on the list.

18. This name appeared twice on the list.
19. *Ref. n548,* p.135 Paris: Bibliotheque National, microfilm copy in the National Library of Ireland.
20. Lart, Charles, *Pedigrees and Papers of James Terry, Athlone Herald at the Court of James II in France (1690-1725),* William Pollard & Co Ltd (1938).
21. *Ref. n548 p.135,* op.cit.
22. Lart, Charles, Ibid.
23. Caulfield, Richard (2), 'Wills and Inventories, Cork, temp. Mary, etc.', *The Gentleman's Magazine,* April (1862), pp.443-4. Caulfield, Richard (3), 'Early Charters relating to the city and county of Cork', *The Gentleman's Magazine,* August (1865), p.177.
24. Caulfield, Richard (2), op.cit.
25. Commentary by Fr Michael Hackett, OSA. unpublished. Caulfield, Richard (3), op.cit., p.177.
26. Windele, John, op.cit., pp.29-30.
27. This suggestion from Paul MacCotter, M.A. in conversation; Office of Public Works, *Archaeological Inventory of County Cork Volume 2: East and South Cork,* Stationery Office Dublin (1994), p.245.
28. Bangs, J., *Dirk Van der Ples – Cork Deeds,* deposited with the Cork Archives Institute.
29. Windele, John, op.cit. in Roche papers.
30. Windele, John, *MSS 12.I.4,* p.738.
31. Ohlmeyer, Jane and O'Ciardha, Eamonn, ed., *The Irish Statute Stable Books, 1596-1687,* Dublin Corporation (1998).
32. From the Welsh cantref. the cantred was the administrative subdivision of the Anglo-Norman county, corresponding to the later barony.
33. Fuller, J. F. (2), op.cit., p.275; *Lodge Records of the Rolls,* vols II & III.
34. O' Mahony, Colman, *The Maritime Gateway to Cork,* Tower Books (1986).
35. Genealogical Office, Ms 159, *Terry Family of,* p.264.
36. *Inquisitions Post Mortem,* 13 April (1624). Tuckey, Francis H., op.cit., pp.74-8.
37. Hayes, Richard, *Manuscript Sources from the History of Irish Civilisation,* 1st Supplement D26.003 'Sarsfield Papers (Associated Families)'.
38. *Lismore Papers,* vol. 1.
39. Caulfield, Richard (1), op.cit., p.111.
40. Irish Manuscripts Commission (IMC), *A Calendar of material relating to Ireland from the High Court of Admiralty Examinations, 1536-1641,* IMC (1992).
41. Ibid.
42. *Betham Abstracts from Prerogative Wills/ Administrations.*
43. Clayton, Margaret Curtis, ed., *The Council Book of the Province of Munster c.1599-1649,* I.M.C., p.17.
44. Caulfield, Richard (1), op.cit., p.141. As well as the chief clerk there

shall be six clerks known as Attorneys of the Court, from *The Council Book of the Province of Munster.*

45. Foster, Joseph, *The Register of Admissions to Gray's Inn 1521-1889,* The Hansard Publishing Union, London (1889), p.204.
46. Dickson, David, *Old World Colony Cork and South Munster 1630-1830,* Cork University Press (2005), p.16.
47. Windele, John, op.cit.
48. Dennehy, Rev. Henry Edward, *History of Great Island, the cove of Cork, and Queenstown,* Tower Books (1990).
49. Dennehy, Rev. Henry Edward, op.cit.
50. Coleman, J., 'The Old Castles around Cork Harbour', *Cork Historical and Archaeological Society Journal,* Vol XXI (1915).
51. Casey, James, 'Land ownership in North Cork, 1584-1641', Ph. D. Thesis, U.C.C., unpublished (1988); Roper was a captain, lieutenant, colonel and councillor of the Council of the Province of Munster, one of the New English. Dominick Sarsfield was Attorney General, Munster, 1600-4, Chief Justice 1604-8, and Chief Justice of the Common Pleas, in Ireland, 1616-34. He was married to the daughter of Edmund Tirry, Joan.
52. *1641 Depositions,* T.C.D. library, fol. 220r-221v.
53. *Court of Claims submissions and evidence 1663,* op.cit., p.268.
54. Treadwell, Victor, *The Commission of 1622,* I. M. C., 2006, p.497.
55. Henchion, Richard, *East to Mahon,* Dahadore Publications (2005), p.177.
56. Windele, John, *Windele's Cork – Historic and Descriptive notices of the City of Cork,* Guy & Co Ltd (1910), p.24.
57. O' Buachalla, Liam, *History of Carrigtwohill,* Clann na Greine Teo, Carrigtwohill.
58. *Lismore Papers,* vol. 2.
59. Townsend, Dorothy *The Life and letters of the great Earl of Cork,* Duckworth & Co., London (1904).
60. A messuage is a house with out buildings and a parcel of land or a yard.
61. *Pedigree, LDS films # 100135,* vol. 217, p.28.
62. *Lismore Papers,* vol. 1; *Court of Claims submissions and evidence 1663,* op.cit., p.241.
63. Ring, Denis Paul, *Macroom through the Mists of Time,* Castle House Publications (1995).
64. Power, Rev. Patrick, 'Historical and Topographical Notes', *Journal of the Cork Historical and Archaeological Society,* vol XIII (1907), p.152.
65. *1641 Depositions,* op.cit.
66. Simmington, R.C., The Civil Survey 1654-1656: *County Waterford, Vol. VI, with appendices. Also Valuations, 1663-1664, for Waterford and Cork Cities,* The Stationery Office, Dublin (1942).
67. Coppinger, W.A., ed., *History of the Copingers or Coppingers of the County of Cork, Ireland, and the counties of Suffolk and Kent, England,*

London (1884). From Caulfield's *Council book of the Corporation of Cork*, Appendix C, Edmond Terry was mayor in 1604, and William Terry fz Francis and David Terry were bailiffs in this year. David Terry fz David was bailiff three years earlier, and in 1605-6, John Terry was one of the bailiffs. David was one of the bailiffs again in 1607.

68. Windele, John, op.cit., pp.28-9; Gibson, C.B., *The History of the County and City of Cork*, vol. II, Ch. VIII, The Fercor Press (1974), pp.388-9.
69. Francis H. Tuckey, op.cit., pp.74-8.
70. *Lismore Papers*, 2nd Series.
71. Tuckey, Francis H., op.cit., pp.74-8.
72. Windele, John, op.cit. p29; Genealogical office, Dublin, 218, *Anglo-Irish Families*, iv, p254.
73. Caulfield, Richard (1), op.cit.
74. Clayton, Margaret Curtis, op.cit., pp.53 and 76.
75. Tuckey, Francis H., op.cit.
76. Treadwell, Victor, op.cit., p.410.
77. *Lismore Papers*, vol. 5.
78. Tuckey, Francis H., op.cit.
79. Clayton, Margaret Curtis, op. cit., pp.135-7; Hackett, Michael B., O.S.A., *A presence in the age of turmoil – English, Irish and Scottish Augustinians in the Reformation and Counter-Reformation*, Augustinian Historical Institute, Villanova University (2001), p.118.
80. Caulfield, Richard (1), op.cit.
81. Mulcahy, John, 'Patrick Lavallin and the Popish Plot', *Journal of the Cork Historical and Archaeological Society*, vol.99 (1994), p.83.
82. A member of a city corporation or town council next in rank in the order of citizens to the mayor. He was appointed for life. The alderman played an important role in the appointment of the mayor and bailiffs. In modern times the councillor elected first in each ward is called alderman. This title was abolished recently.
83. Caulfield, Richard (1), op.cit.
84. Ibid.
85. Ibid.
86. Tenison, C.M., 'Cork M.P.s 1559-1800', *Journal of the Cork Historical and Archaeological Society*, vol. II 2nd Series (1896), p.326; Caulfield, Richard (1), op.cit.
87. O' Connor, Bryan, 'The Genealogy and Ensigns Armorials of the Terry family', unpublished (1753).
88. O' Connor, Bryan, op.cit.; Caulfield, Richard (1), op.cit.
89. Tenison, C.M., op.cit. p326.
90. D'Alton, John, *King James's Irish Army List (1689)*, 2nd edition, vol. 1, John D'Alton, p.110.
91. *1641 Depositions*, T.C.D., various folios; fol.128r.
92. Tenison, C.M., op.cit., p.326; *Sarsfield Papers*, National Library of Ireland, Manuscripts Department.

93. Windele, John, op.cit.
94. Buckley, Rev. Cornelius, 'Story of the R.C. Bishops of Cork, Cloyne and Ross since the Reformation', *Journal of the Waterford & South-East of Ireland Archaeological Society*, vol. VI (1900), pp.205-14.
95. Dickson, David, op.cit., p.9.
96. Bolster, Evelyn, *A History of the Diocese of Cork from the Reformation to the Penal Era*, Tower Books (1982), p.173.
97. Hackett, Michael B., op.cit.
98. Bolster, Evelyn, op.cit.
99. O' Mahony, S. C., 'Discalced Carmelites in Ireland, 1641', *Collectanea Hibernice*, No 17, Leinster Leader Ltd (1974-5), pp.7-14.
100. *Sarsfield Papers*, National Library of Ireland; Foley, Henry, Records of the English province of the Society of Jesus, 1875; Finegan, Fr Francis, 'A Biographical Directory of Irish Jesuits in the time of the Society's third Irish mission 1598-1773', unpublished.
101. O Connor, Bryan, op.cit.
102. There was no Catholic bishop of Cork between 1603 and 1622, see Bolster, Evelyn, op.cit., p.137. However, as indicated earlier this event occurred probably when Edward Wettenhall was bishop of Cork and Ross, from 1678-99.
103. David Tyrry fz Edmond, of Cork, was granted the chief rent and messuages in Youghal, by the Chancellor of the Diocese of Lismore.
104. Dickson, David, op.cit., p.9.
105. Caulfield, Richard (1), p.273.
106. *1641 Depositions*, T.C.D., fol. 186r.
107. O'Hart, John, *Irish Pedigrees*, Murphy & McCarthy (1923).
108. Ohlmeyer, Jane and O'Ciardha, Eamonn, eds., op.cit.

Chapter 8

1. Ellis, Peter-Berresford, *Hell or Connaught – the Cromwellian Colonisation of Ireland 1652-1660*, The Blackstaff Press (1975).
2. Connolly, S. J., *Religion, Law and Power – the making of Protestant Ireland, 1660-1760*, Claredon Press, Oxford (1992), p.13.
3. Ibid., p.15.
4. *City of Cork – Survey of Valuation (c.AD 1663-4).*
5. *History of Confederation & War in Ireland, 1643-4*, vol. III pp.235-6.
6. Ibid.
7. O' Hart, John (1), *The Irish and Anglo-Irish Landed Gentry*, Irish University Press (1969), pp.278-85.
8. Also spelt Thyrry and Thirry, see Martin, Rev. F.X., 'The Tirry Documents in the Archives de France, Paris', *Archivium Hibernicum*, 20 (1957), pp.67-97.
9. Ring, Denis Paul, *Macroom through the Mists of Time*, Castle House Publications (1995).

10. Pender, S., ed., *A Census of Ireland circa 1659*, Irish Manuscripts Commission, Dublin (1939).
11. *Van der Plas Cork Deeds*, Cork Archives Institute, U675/58.
12. Simington, Robert C., *The Civil Survey 1654-6 County of Waterford*, Stationery Office (1942), p.xlv.
13. O' Hart, John (1), op.cit., pp.325-6.
14. Tuckey, Francis H., *The County and City of Cork Remembrancer*, Tower Books, Cork (1980), p.308.
15. *Van der Plas Cork Deeds*, op.cit., U675/50.
16. Hood, Susan, *Register of the parish of Holy Trinity (Christ Church), Cork 1643-1669*, Representative Church Body Library (1998).
17. Ohlmeyer, Jane and O'Ciardha, Eamonn, eds., *The Irish Statute Stable Books, 1596-1687*, Dublin Corporation (1998). Glancullanne is actually Glankittane, in the North Liberties of the City. This land was forfeited and restored to the Terry family. Richard was a Terry who converted to Protestantism while David remained catholic.
18. Dennehy, Rev. Henry Edward, *History of Great Island, the cove of Cork and Queenstown*, Tower Books (1990).
19. O Hart, John (2), *Irish Landed Gentry when Cromwell came to Ireland*, James Duffy & Sons (1887), p.278.
20. Caufield, R., *Council Book of the Corporation of Kinsale.*
21. A messuage is a house with out buildings and a parcel of land or a yard.
22. *Ref. n548* p.135, Paris: Bibliotheque National.
23. Lart, Charles, *Pedigrees and Papers of James Terry, Athlone Herald at the Court of James II in France 1690-1725*, William Pollard & Co Ltd (1938).
24. Waters, Ann, 'A distribution of forfeited land in the county of Cork, returned by the Downe Survey', *Journal of the Cork Historical and Archaeological Society*, vols 38 and 39.
25. Genealogical Office, Dublin, G.O.69, *Funeral entries*, vol. 6, p.158.
26. Waters, Eaton W., 'The Waters Family of Cork', *Journal of the Cork Historical and Archaeological Society*, 2nd Series, pp.33-4: Genealogical Office, G.O. 218 *Anglo-Irish Families*, p.265.
27. Tallon, Geraldine, ed., *Court of Claims Submissions and Evidence, 1663*, Irish Manuscripts Commission (2006), p.183.
28. Ibid., pp.220 and 391.
29. Private research carried out by Paul MacCotter, M.A., Historian and Genealogist, for the author.
30. Windle, John, *Sarsfield and other papers relating to Cork*, R.I.A. (1847).
31. 'Historical and Topographical notes', *Journal of the Cork Historical and Archaeological Society* (1911), p.68; It refers to Castle Terry being in Co Limerick. Castle Terry is in Co Cork.
32. Dublin (COI), *St Peter*, http://churchrecords.irishgenealogy.ie

Chapter 9

1. *Vestry minutes of Christ Church, Cork*, National Archives, Dublin.
2. Fuller, J.F., 'Notes and Queries', *Journal of the Cork Historical and Archaeological Society*, vol. IX, 2nd Series, 1903, p.68.
3. Welply, William Henry, 'Abstracts of Munster Wills, 1528-1859', O Kief, Coshe, Mang, *Slieve Lougher & Upper Blackwater in Ireland* (1965).
4. *Deed 14 100 5264*, Registry of Deeds.
5. *Betham Abstracts for Prerogative Wills, Administrations.*
6. *Notes from Wills of the Cork Diocese 1660-1700*, National Archives, M2760.
7. Keane, Edward, Phair, P. Beryl, and Sadlier, Thomas U., eds., *Kings Inn's Admission Papers, 1607-1867*, IMC (1982).
8. Sturgess, H.A.C., *Register of Admissions to the Honourable Society of the Middle Temple*, Butterworth & Co. (1948), p.254.
9. Brown, Josiah, *Report of cases upon appeals and writs of error, in the High Court of Parliament, from the years 1701-79*, vol. 1, London (1779-83).
10. Registry of Deeds, Dublin, vol. 2, p.471, no. 574.
11. Tuckey, Francis H., *The County and City of Cork Remembrancer*, Tower Books (1980).
12. Smith, Charles, *The ancient and present state of the city and county of Cork*, Dublin (1774).
13. Swanzy, Henry B., 'Militia Commissions, Co. Cork, 1727-56', *Journal of the Cork Historical and Archaeological Society*, vol. XXXII No. 135.
14. Blackhall, Sir Henry, 'The Galways of Munster', *Journal of the Cork Historical and Archaeological Society*, vol. 72 (1967), pp.20-49.
15. Registry of Deeds, Dublin, vol. 2, p.351, no. 12245.
16. Welply, William Henry, op.cit.
17. Genealogical information received from Fr M.B. Hackett, O.S.A.
18. Linhan, T.A., ed., *Bishop Dive Downe's Visitations of his Diocese, 1699.*
19. Refausse, Raymond and Smith, Heather, 'W.H. Welply's Absrtacts of Irish Chancery Bills, 1601-1801', *The Irish Genealogist.*
20. *Betham Abstracts for Prerogative Wills, Administrations.*
21. Lart, Charles, *The Pedigrees and Papers of James Terry, Athlone Herald, at the Court of James II in France, 1690-1725*, William Pollard & Co Ltd (1938).
22. *MCFI 30*, National Archives.
23. Information supplied by Cobh Genealogical Project.
24. Wikipedia information about Buttevant.
25. O'Hart, John, *Irish Pedigrees; or the origin and stem of the Irish Nation*, Murphy & McCarthy, New York (1923), vol. 1, p.126.
26. *Will of James Therry*, Public Records Office, The National Archives, U.K., Prob 11/641.
27. Ffolliott, Rosemary, *Biographical Notices (primarily relating to counties Cork and Kerry) collected from newspapers, 1756-1827.*

28. Welply, William Henry, op.cit.; see *O'Donnell Papers*, Blackwater, Co. Clare, www.limerickcity.ie/collection list/. This John, I think, is the father of James the Athlone Herald, and was originally from Cork.
29. Dublin (COI), *St Audoen*, http://churchrecords.irishgenealogy.ie.
30. *Terry MSS, Puerto de Santa Maria*, kindly given to me by Julian Walton.
31. Some of this information is provided by Wynn Parker, New Zealand, descendant of Carden Terry.
32. Ffolliott, Rosemary, op.cit.
33. O'Shea, John, vol. II, *Indexes to Cork City Council Book*.
34. The Church of Jesus Christ of Latter-Day Saints, Salt Lake City.
35. *Deed 193 481 128523*, Registry of Deeds; Rosemary Ffolliott, op.cit.
36. John O'Shea, op.cit.
37. *Deed 167 395 112952*, Registry of Deeds.
38. Genealogical Office, 404, pp67-68, *Pedigree of John Terry of Cork and Castleterry, Co. Limerick*.
39. Information supplied from the Cork City Ancestral Project, c/o Cork County Library.
40. O'Shea, John, op.cit.
41. Keane, Ed, Phail, P. Beryl and Sadlier, Thomas W., op.cit.
42. Welply, William Henry, op.cit.
43. Welply, William Henry, op.cit.
44. Keane, Ed, Phail, P. Beryl & Sadlier, Thomas W., op.cit.
45. Ffolliott, Rosemary, op.cit.
46. O'Shea, John, op.cit.
47. Welply, William Henry, op.cit.
48. O'Shea, John, op.cit.
49. Ffolliott, Rosemary, op.cit.
50. St Ledger, Alice, ed., *Register of the Cathedral of St Finbarrs, Cork, 1753-1804*, Representative Church Body Library, Dublin (2008).
51. Casey, Albert Eugene, 'Index to Administration Bonds, Diocese of Cloyne, 1630-1857', *O'Kief, Coshe, Mang, Slieve Lougher & Upper Blackwater in Ireland* (1965). MF, National Archives.
52. MF, National Archives.
53. *Deed Number 223522*, Registry of Deeds.
54. Henchion, R., 'The Gravestone Inscriptions of Co. Cork', *Journal of the Cork Historical and Archaeological Society*, vol. XCV No. 254, pp.124-41.
55. C12 Records of the Cathedral Church of St Colmans, Cloyne, RCBL.
56. Ibid.
57. Fuller, J. F., 'Carden Terry', *Journal of the Cork Historical and Archaeological Society*, vol. IX (1903), p.68.
58. Sutherland, Lucy S., ed., *The correspondence of Edmund Burke*, University Press, Cambridge (1960).
59. Sutherland, Lucy S., ed., op.cit.
60. From the *Religious Census of the Diocese of Cloyne in 1766*.

61. Ibid.
62. From the Mallow Heritage Centre.
63. http://churchrecords.irishgenealogy.ie.
64. Bredin, Brigadier A.E.C., *A history of the Irish Soldier*, Century Books (1987), p.121.
65. Historical Manuscripts Commission, *The Marquis of Ormonde – the castle of Kilkenny*, vol. I.
66. Ainsworth, John, ed., *The Inchiquin Manuscripts*, IMC (1961), p.270.
67. The Society of the Irish Brigade, web page.

Chapter 10

1. Information provided by the Cork City Ancestral Project, Cork County Library.
2. Information supplied by the Cobh Genealogical Project.
3. Information from the Church Records of St Peter's and St Paul's Church, Cork City.
4. Information supplied by Mr Joe O' Reilly, St Finbarr's South parish.
5. O' Brien, Eris M., *The Life of Archpriest J. J. Therry*, Angus & Robertson (1922).
6. Haly, *Cork Directory* (1795).
7. Kennedy, Maire, 'The Cork Library Society of 1801', *Cork Historical and Archaeological Society*, vol. XCIV, No.53, p.71.
8. Keane, Ed., Phail, P. Beryl and Sadlier, Thomas W., *Kings Inn's Admission Papers, 1607-1867*, IMP (1982).
9. Private correspondence from PRO (NI) to Rev. Hackett, OSA, *Burke collection of pedigrees,* T559, V.37, p.246.
10. Registry of Deeds, *Book 572*, p.416.
11. Ibid, *439-415-285146*.
12. Ffolliott, Rosemary, *Biographical Notices (primarily relating to Cork and Kerry) collected from newspapers, 1756-1827*.
13. Keane, Ed., Phail, P. Beryl and Sadlier, Thomas W., op.cit.
14. From *O'Kief, Coshe, Mang, Slieve Lougher & Upper Blackwater in Ireland* (1965).
15. West, Will, *Directory and picture of Cork and its environs, Cork* (1810).
16. The source of this information is Church of Ireland Records in the National Archives, Bishop Street, Dublin, and deeds from the Registry of Deeds, Dublin.
17. UaConaill, Diarmuid (1), 'Tyrry and Goold', in *Terrys of Cork 1600-2000 a local historical perspective*, Kevin Terry (2005).
18. Ibid.
19. Ffolliott, Rosemary, op.cit.
20. UaConaill, Diarmuid (2), 'A family history specially selected for John Terry', *1994*, unpublished.
21. *The Sydney Morning Herald*, 2 August (1902).

22. Ancestry.co.uk
23. From the records of the Superintendent Registrar of Births, Deaths and Marriages, Southern Health Board.
24. The source of this information is Church of Ireland Records in the National Archives, Bishop Street, Dublin, and deeds from the Registry of Deeds, Dublin.
25. Information supplied by the Mallow Heritage Centre.
26. Ibid.
27. Keane, Ed., Phail, P. Beryl and Sadlier, Thomas W., op.cit.
28. Information supplied by C. J. Woods, Kildare.
29. *The Sydney Morning Herald*, 6 September (1841).
30. Ffolliott, Rosemary, op.cit.
31. See *The Irish-American newspaper (New York),* 1857, for a notice of the marriage.
32. Information supplied by the Mallow Heritage Centre.
33. Ibid.
34. The source of this information is Church of Ireland Records in the National Archives, Bishop Street, Dublin, and deeds from the Registry of Deeds, Dublin.
35. Information supplied by the Mallow Heritage Centre.
36. Ibid.
37. Ibid.
38. Ancestry.co.uk
39. Ibid; www.irishgenealogy.ie
40. Information supplied by the Mallow Heritage Centre.
41. The National Archives, KEW, Catalogue ref: *ADM/188/119.*
42. UaConaill, Diarmuid (2), op.cit.
43. Information supplied by the Mallow Heritage Centre.
44. Ibid.
45. Ibid.
46. Information supplied by the Cobh Genealogical Project.
47. Information supplied by the Mallow Heritage Centre.
48. Ibid.
49. Ibid.
50. Guy's *Directory of Cork, 1875-6.*
51. Information provided by the Cork City Ancestral Project, Cork County Library.
52. Registrar of Births and Marriages, Gratten Street, Cork.
53. http://churchrecords.irishgenealogy.ie.
54. Information provided by the Cork City Ancestral Project, Cork County Library.
55. Ibid.
56. Information supplied by Mr Joe O' Reilly, St Finbarr's South Parish.
57. Information provided by the Cork City Ancestral Project, Cork County Library.

58. Ibid.
59. Information supplied by the Mallow Heritage Centre.
60. Henry and Coughlan's General Directory of Cork, 1867.
61. Hajba, Anna-Maria, *Houses of North Cork*, vol. I, Ballinakella Press (2002).

CHAPTER 11

1. Registrar of Births, Marriages, Gratten St.
2. Terry, Brian, 'Some Terrys in Cork City', in *Terrys of Cork 1600-2000 a local historical perspective*, Kevin Terry (2005).
3. Registrar of Births, Marriages, Gratten St.
4. Information supplied by Pat Chambers, Cobh.
5. Ibid.
6. Registrar of Births, Marriages, Gratten St.
7. Information supplied by Joseph Terry, Ballymacotter.
8. Registrar of Births, Marriages, Gratten St.
9. Private correspondence with Parnell Terry of Maine.
10. Registrar of Births, Marriages, Gratten St.
11. Ibid.
12. Cobh Genealogical Project.
13. Ancestry.com.

CHAPTER 12

1. D'Arcy, Frank, *Wild Geese and Travelling Scholars*, Mercier Press (2001).
2. D'Alton, John, *King James's Irish Army List 1689*, D'Alton.
3. Lenihan, Maurice, *Limerick: its history and antiquities, ecclesiastical, civil and military*, Mercier Press (1967).
4. Tuckey, Francis H., *The County and City of Cork Remembrancer*, Tower Books (1980).
5. Clayton, Margaret Curtis, ed., *The Council Book of the Province of Munster c.1599-1649*, Irish Manuscripts Commission, pp.79-80, 135, 137; Hackett, Michael B., O.S.A., *A presence in the age of turmoil – English, Irish and Scottish Augustinians in the Reformation and Counter-Reformation*, Augustinian Historical Institute, Villanova University (2001), p.118.
6. *An appendix being an answer to a libel, intituled Patrick Hurly's vindication*, Dublin (1701); Ainsworth, John, ed., *The Inchiquin Manuscripts*, IMC (1961).
7. Barnwell, Stephen B., 'Some Irish in Grenoble, France, 1694 to 1771', *The Irish Genealogist* (1994).
8. The Honourable Society of the Irish Brigade, web page.
9. Molloy, Sheila, *French-Irish correspondence, vol. II, Dec. 1688-Feb. 1692*, IMC (1984).
10. Ó hAnnracháin, Eoghan, 'Corkmen in Eighteenth-Century France: Some additional evidence', *Journal of the Cork Historical and Archaeological*

Society, vol. 108 (2003), pp.147-54.
11. From the National Library of Ireland.
12. Lart, Charles, *The Pedigrees and Papers of James Terry, Athlone Herald, at the Court of James II in France (1690-1725).*
13. Culligan, Matthew J. and Cherici, Peter, *The Wandering Irish in Europe*, Constable, London (2000).
14. Private correspondence with Lodovico Blanc.

CHAPTER 13

1. Information on the statistics of Terrys in Spain was kindly provided by Beatriz Garcia, Granada. Culligan, Matthew J. and Cherici, Peter, *The Wandering Irish in Europe*, Constable, London (2000).
2. Darby, Graham, *Spain in the seventeenth century*, Longman (1994).
3. Culligan, Matthew J. and Cherici, Peter, op.cit.
4. Ibid.
5. D'Arcy, Frank, *Wild Geese and Travelling Scholars*, Mercier Press (2001).
6. Ibid.
7. Ibid.
8. Culligan, Matthew J. and Cherici, Peter, op.cit.
9. *The particulars and inventories of the estates of the late Sub-Governor, Deputy-Governor, and Directors of the South-Sea Company: and of Robert Surman late Deputy-Cashier, and of John Grigsby late Accountant.. Together with the abstracts of the same,*vol. 1, London (1721).
10. Fannin, Samuel, 'The Irish community in eighteenth-century Cadiz', in *Irish Migrants in Europe after Kinsale, 1602-1820*, eds., O'Connor, Thomas and Lyons, Mary Ann, Four Courts Press (2003).
11. Ibid.
12. *Terry brochure*; I left out some details. For example the brochure refers to Fernando's brothers. From other information, Fernando had one step-brother.
13. Beltran, Jose, Gasco, Fernando, eds., *La Antiguedad como argumento historiografia de arqueologia e historia Antigua en Andalucia, Sevilla* (1993).
14. Moya, Rafael Fernández (translated by Anette Leahy), 'The Irish Presence in the History and Place Names of Cuba', *Irish Migration Studies in Latin America*, vol. 5 No 3 (2007), p.192.
15. Private correspondence with Samuel Fannin.
16. Archivo Historico Provincial de Cadiz, Document Ref. 4.483, *Folios 854-8.*
17. Archivo Historico Provincial de Cadiz, Document Ref 4.516, *Folios 1085-8.*
18. O' Connor, Bryan, *Terry Genealogy* (1753), kindly given to me by Julian Walton, U.C.C.
19. National Library of Ireland, G.O. *Ms 164*, pp.125-8; information supplied by Beatriz Garcia, Granada.

20. Private correspondence with F. Javier de Terry y Del Cuvillo, Cadiz.
21. Literature supplied by Milagros Terry Martinez.
22. Private correspondence with F. Javier de Terry y del Cuvillo, and translated by Aoife Terry.
23. *Terry brochure;* op.cit.
24. http://gw.geneanet.org/fracarbo
25. Private correspondence with Lodovico Blanc, United States.
26. Speck, Mary, 'Prosperity, Progress, and Wealth: Cuban Enterprise during the Early Republic, 1902-27', *Cuban Studies* vol. 36 (2005), pp.50-86.
27. Private correspondence with Lodovico Blanc, United States.

CHAPTER 14

1. D'Arcy, Frank, *Wild Geese and Travelling Scholars*, Mercier Press (2001).
2. Culligan, Matthew J., & Cherici, Peter, *The Wandering Irish in Europe*, Constable, London (2000).
3. *Catalogo de las Disposiciones Testamentarias de Cadiz*, Folio 159-60, Archivo Historico Provincial de Cadiz; other accounts have Pedro's mother as Isabel Rocha from Limerick, see José Manuel de Molina, Terry (Tirri), www.andalucia.cc/habis/terry.htm.
4. Anes, Rafael Donoso, *Un análisis sucinto del Asiento de esclavos con Inglaterra (1713-50) y el papel desempeñado por la contabilidad en su desarrollo, Anuarío de Estudios Americanos, Julio-diciembre, 2007*; (translated for the writer by Aoife Terry); Hildner, Ernest G. Jr., 'The Role of the South Sea Company in the Diplomacy Leading to the War of Jenkins' Ear, 1729-39', *The Hispanic American Historical Review*, Vol.18, No.3 (1938).
5. Moya, Rafael Fernández (translated by Anette Leahy), 'The Irish Presence in the History and Place Names of Cuba', *Irish Migration Studies in Latin America*, vol.5 No.3 (2007), p.192; Tirry genealogy information supplied by F. Javier de Terry y del Cuvillo.
6. Beltrán, José, *La Antigüeudad Como Argumento. Historiografía de Arrqueología e Historia Antigua en Andalusia.*
7. Thurloe, John, *A collection of the state papers of John Thurloe, Esq; secretary, first, to the Council of State, and afterwards to the two Protectors, Oliver and Richard Cromwell*, London (1742).
8. *El Municipio de Isla de Pinos*, Guije.com; Moya, Rafael Fernández, op.cit., p.192.
9. Moya, Rafael Fernández, op.cit., p.192.
10. Slightly different accounts come from different sources; from the web one Pedro Terry indicates that Jose Terry Alvarez Bell was born in Cadiz in 1755, moved to Peru and then later to Guayra. He is the father of Tomás Terry y Adáns. Pedro Terry provides information on the ancestors of Tomás.
11. Santa Cruz y Mallen, Francisco I., *Historia de familias cubanas*, 6 vols.

Havana (1940-50); Lourdes Diaz Canto, Miguel Albuerno Mesa, *Cienfuegos y los Terry*, Edition Mecenas, Cienfuegos, Cuba, 2005.

12. Thomas, Hugh, *Cuba*, Picador (2001), p.86.
13. Private correspondence with Lodovico Blanc, United States.
14. Santa Cruz y Mallen, Francisco I., op.cit.
15. Private correspondence with Ludovico Blanc, United States; Will of Don Thomas Terry (from the web). Santa Cruz y Mallen, Francisco I., op.cit.
16. Thomas, Hugh, op.cit., pp.142-3.
17. Speck, Mary, 'Prosperity, Progress, and Wealth: Cuban Enterprise during the Early Republic, 1902-1927', *Cuban Studies*, vol.36 (2005), pp.50-86.
18. Speck, Mary, op.cit. Thomas, Hugh, *Cuba*, Picador (2001). The New York Times, 21 November 1886, valued his estate at $50,000,000.
19. Speck, Mary, op.cit., pp.50-86.
20. Message posted by Teodorico Terry Elejalde on the web in 1999.
21. Notes on one hundred families established in Peru – Luis Lasarte Ferreyros archive of Juan Miranda Costa.
22. http://gw.geneanet.org/fracarbo; de Rubinat, Pau Font, Revista Iberica de Exlibris, 1904, No.4, p.37.
23. Private correspondence with F. Javier de Terry y del Cuvillo, and translated by Aoife Terry.
24. Message posted by Teodorico Terry Elejalde on the web in 1999.
25. In Peru, Terry is one of the most renowned families. Its members have been very important for the development and progress of Peru. Magistrado of the Constitutional Tribunal is Guillermo Rey Terry; Message posted by Teodorico Terry Elejalde on the web in 1999.
26. Geneall.es. parents of Lucila were Teodorico Terry y del Real and María Jesús García Vásquez Pacheco y Oricaín.
27. *The Columbia Encyclopedia*, Sixth Edition.

CHAPTER 15

1. MacRaild, Donald M., *Irish Migration in modern Britain, 1750-1922*, Macmillan Press Ltd (1999), p.1.
2. Ibid., p.10.
3. Ibid., p.3.
4. Ancestry.co.uk
5. The National Archives, KEW, Catalogue Ref: *ADM/188/119*.
6. Private correspondence with Ernie Terry of Surrey. Ancestors of Ernie emigrated from West Cork during the famine to the North-East of England. Some members of the clan settled in the U.S. The Terry family appear in the Bantry area in the 1820s from the Tithe Applotment Books.
7. Terry, Christopher, 'Some Terrys in England', in *Terrys of Cork 1600-*

2000 a local historical perspective, Kevin Terry (2005).

8. Dr Paul McKenna Terry LRCP, LRCS.Ed, LRFPS, JP see BMA register 1949. He was Medical Officer at two Alverstoke hospitals and an Admiralty Surgeon at the Royal Naval Hospital, Haslar.

CHAPTER 16

1. Eddy, J., 'Therry, John Joseph (1790-1864)', *Australian Dictionary of Biography*, Online Edition, Australian National University (2006).
2. Information supplied by Mr Joe O' Reilly, St Finbarr's South Parish.
3. Eddy, J., op.cit.
4. McSweeney, John, *A Meddling Priest*, St Pauls Publications (2000).
5. Ibid.
6. Ibid.
7. Eddy, J., op.cit.
8. Eddy, J., op.cit.
9. *Cork Examiner*, 17 August 1864.
10. *The Sydney Morning Herald*, 23December 1874 and 18 January 1875.
11. *The Brisbane Courier*, 10 January 1865, p.3; *Pittwater Offshore*, December 2005.
12. Roger's other Christian names were provided by Tony Branigan; Currey, C. H., 'Therry, Sir Roger (1800 -1874)', *Australian Dictionary of Biography*, Online Edition, Australian National University (2006).
13. Information supplied by Mr Joe O' Reilly, St Finbarr's South Parish.
14. Information provided by Tony Branigan.
15. Ibid.
16. Currey, C. H., op.cit.
17. Ibid.
18. Ibid.
19. From information supplied by Mr Joe O' Reilly, St Finbarr's South Parish.
20. Currey, C. H.,op.cit.
21. *The Sydney Morning Herald*, 3 July 1874 and 2 August 1902.
22. *The Sydney Morning Herald*, 10 August 1894.
23. *The Sydney Morning Herald*, 19 June 1909.
24. The information on Barney is taken from Terry, Bernard, 'Australian Terrys', in *Terrys of Cork 1600-2000 a local historical perspective*, Kevin Terry (2005).

CHAPTER 17

1. Private correspondence with Ludvocio Blanc.
2. Kenny, Kevin, *The American Irish*, Pearson Education Limited (2000), p.131.
3. Ibid., p.7.

4. *Terry Family Historian*, vol. 1 June (1982), No.1, p.37.
5. Private correspondence with David Terry, Nova Scotia, Canada.
6. O 'Brien, Michael J., *Irish Settlers in America*, Genealogical Publishing (1979).
7. Information from the Genealogical Office, Dublin.
8. O 'Brien, Michael J., op.cit.
9. Ibid.
10. Kenny, Kevin, op.cit., p.45.
11. www.breathittcounty.com/BreathittWeb2/BCFamilies.html
12. From information provided by Kim Falzgraf, Thomas, according to family lore was a ship hand who emigrated from Ireland in 1832.
13. Kenny, Kevin, op.cit., pp.89-90.
14. Ira Glazier's and Michael Tepper's Volumns on the *Famine Immigrants*; Ancestry.com, New York *Passenger Lists, 1820-1957*.
15. From the John F. Kennedy Trust Database of Irish Emigrants.
16. From ancestry.com census databases.
17. Information supplied by David Terry, Nova Scotia.
18. Kenny, Kevin, op.cit., p.131.
19. Ibid., p.132.
20. Kennedy, Lawrence W., *Planning the City upon a Hill*, University of Massachusetts Press (1992).
21. Includes data from the Ellis Island Foundation, Inc.
22. Ancestry.com.uk
23. Private correspondence with Parnell Terry of Maine.
24. *Emerald Reflections Online*, April (1999).
25. Ontario, Canada, marriages 1801-1928.
26. Terry, Kevin, et al., *Terrys of Cork 1600-2000*.
27. Ancestry.com, *The Terry name in history*, The Generations Network (2007).

Bibliography

Primary Sources

A Calendar of Material relating to Ireland from the High Court of Admiralty Examinations, 1536-1641, Irish Manuscripts Commission (1992)

Bangs J., / Van der Ples, Dirk – *Cork Deeds*, deposited with the Cork Archives Institute

Betham Abstracts from Prerogative Wills/ Administrations, National Archives, Dublin

Bolster, Evelyn, ' A Landgable Roll of Cork City', *Collectanae Hibernica*

C46 Oct 4 1560 Cork Deeds, Marsh's Library, Dublin

C65 Aug 4 1584 Cork Deeds, Marsh's Library, Dublin

C47 March 4 1559(60), Cork Deeds, Marsh's Library, Dublin

C71 June 5 1540, Cork Deeds, Marsh's Library, Dublin

C74 Oct 4 1589, Cork Deeds, Marsh's Library, Dublin

C II 17 Nov 17 1538, Cork Deeds, Marsh's Library, Dublin

C II 31 June 6 1540, Cork Deeds, Marsh's Library, Dublin

Calendar of Documents Relating to Ireland, 1171-1251, Longman & Co (1875)

Calendar of Documents Relating to Ireland, 1285-1292, Longman & Co (1875)

Calendar of Documents Relating to Ireland, 1293-1301, Longman & Co (1875)

Calendar of Papal Registrars, Volumn IX

Calendar of Papal Registrars, Volumn XII

Calendar of State Papers Ireland Tudor Period 1571-75, Public Records Office & Irish Manuscripts Office (2000)

Calendar of Patent Rolls, Henry VII, 1487-1494, HMSO (1914)

Calendar of State Papers Ireland, 1574-1585

Calendar of State Papers Ireland 1588-1592

Calendar of State Papers Ireland 1592-1596

Calendar of the Charter Rolls, 1257-1300

Calendar of the Judiciary Rolls of Proceedings in the Court of the Justiciar of Ireland, 1295-1303, HMSO (1914)

Calendar of the Justiciary Rolls, Ireland, I to VII years of Edward II, Stationery Office, Dublin

Calendar of the Patent and Close Rolls of Chancery in Ireland of the Reigns of Henry VIII, Edward VI, Mary & Elizabeth, vol. I

Caulfield, Richard, 'Cork Wills', Church of Ireland Records (unpublished),

RCBL, Dublin
Caulfield, Richard, 'Early Charters relating to Kinsale', *Gentleman's Magazine*, April (1865)
Caulfield, Richard, 'Early Charters relating to the City and County of Cork', *Gentleman's Magazine*, April (1865)
Caulfield, Richard, 'Early Charters relating to the city and county of Cork', *Gentleman's Magazine*, August (1865)
Caulfield, Richard, 'Wills and Inventories, Cork', *Gentleman's Magazine*, April (1862)
Caulfield, Richard, 'Wills and Inventories, Cork temp. Elizabeth', *Gentleman's Magazine*, September (1861)
Caulfield, Richard, 'Wills and Inventories, Cork temp. Elizabeth and James I', *Gentleman's Magazine* (1861)
City of Cork-Survey of Valuation (*c*.AD 1663-4)
Cork Constitution, 8 February 1867, 'A report of a meeting of the Cork Cuvcerian and Archaeological Society'
Genealogical Office, Dublin, *g.o.218*, p.266
Genealogical Office, Dublin, *g.o.218*, p.267
Genealogical Office, Dublin, *218, Anglo-Irish Families, iv*, p.254.
Genealogical Office, *Terry Family of*, Ms. 159 p.264
Gilbert, John T., *Register of the Abbey of St Thomas*, Dublin, HMSO (1889)
Grosart, Alexander B., ed., *Lismore Papers*, 1st and 2nd Series, Chiswick Press, London (1886-8)
Inquisitions Post Mortem, 13 April (1624)
Irish Manuscripts Commission, 'Coram Rege Roll, No 364 (Trinity, 1351)', *Analecta Hibernica*
Lodge, *Records of the Rolls*, National Archives Ireland
Nicholls, Kenneth, 'Chancery Bills, survivals from pre-1922 Collection', National Archives, Dublin, Abstracts made by Kenneth Nicholls, unpublished
Oath of the Citizens of Cork, 1498, transcript from PRO E/30/1564
O' Connor, Bryan, *Terry Genealogy*, Terry MSS, 1753 (Courtesy of Julian Walton, UCC)
Profession of obedience, CCA-DCc-ChAnt/C/115/70, Canterbury Cathedral Archives
Ref. n548 p.135 Paris: Bibliotheque National (microfilm copy in the National Library of Ireland)
Report on Private Collections, No. 309, *Sarsfield Papers*, National Manuscripts Office, Dublin
Sarsfield Papers, Manuscripts Department, National Library of Ireland
Tallon, Geraldine (ed.), *Court of Claims Submissions and Evidence 1663*, Irish Manuscripts Commission (2006)
Treadwell, Victor, *The Irish Commission of 1622*, Irish Manuscripts Commission, 2006
Windele, John, *Fitzgerald and Sarsfield Papers*, Blair's Castle (1845)
Windele, John, *Sarsfield and other Papers relating to Cork*, Blair's Castle (1847)

Secondary sources

Ainsworth, John, ed., *The Inchiquin Manuscripts*, IMC, 1961

Anes, Rafael Donoso, 'Un análisis sucinto del Asiento de esclavos con Inglaterra (1713-1750) y el papel desempeñado por la contabilidad en su desarrollo', *Anuarío de Estudios Americanos*, Julio-diciembre (2007)

Bagwell, Richard, *Ireland under the Tudors*, Longmans, Green and Co. (1985)

Bellings, Richard, *History of Confederation & War in Ireland, 1643-1644,* M.H.Gill & Son

Bernard, Jacques, *Navires et Gens de Mer a Bordeaux*, 1400-1550,SEVPEN, vol. III (1968)

Berry, Henry F., 'Sheriffs of the County Cork – Henry III to 1660', *Royal Society of Antiquaries Journal* (1905)

Bolster, Evelyn, *A History of the Diocese of Cork from the earliest times to the Reformation*, Irish University Press (1972)

Bolster, Evelyn, *A History of the Diocese of Cork from the Reformation to the Penal Era*, Tower Books of Cork (1982)

Brady, Ciaran and Gillespie,Raymond, eds, *Natives and Newcomers, essays on the making of Irish Colonial Society, 1531-1641*, Irish Academic Press (1986)

Brady, W.M., *Clerical and Parochial Records of Cork, Cloyne, and Ross*, Longman, Green, Longman, Roberts, and Green (1864)

Brooks, Eric St John, 'Unpublished charters relating to Ireland, 1177-1182', *Proceedings of the Royal Irish Academy* (1936)

Buckley, Rev. Cornelius, 'Story of the R.C. Bishops of Cork, Cloyne and Ross since the Reformation', *Journal of the Waterford & South-East of Ireland Archaeological Society*, vol. VI (1900)

Butler, Professor W.F.T., 'Town Life in Medieval Ireland', *Journal of the Cork Historical and Archaeological Society*, vol. 7 (1901)

Candon, Anthony, 'The Cork Suburb of Dungarvan', *Journal of the Cork Historical and Archaeological Society* (1985)

Canny, Nicholas, *Making Ireland British 1580-1650*, Oxford University Press (2001)

Carpenter, David, *The Struggle for Mastery*, Penguin Books (2003)

Casey, James, 'Land Ownership in North Cork', PhD Thesis, U.C.C., unpublished (1988)

Casey, James, 'The Barony of Kerrycurrihy, Co. Cork, an archaeological and historical study', M.A. Thesis, UCC, unpublished (1982)

Caulfield, R., 'Chartae Tyrryanae', *Topographer and Genealogist*, iii (1958)

Caulfield, R., *Council Book of the Corporation of Kinsale*

Caulfield, R. 'Records of the Sarsfield Family', *Journal of the Cork Historical and Archaeological Society* (1915)

Caulfield, R., *The Council Book of the Corporation of the City of Cork from 1609 to 1643, and from 1690 to 1800.* J. Billing & Sons: Guildford (1876)

Clarke, Aidan, *The Old English in Ireland, 1625-1642*, Four Courts Press (2000)

Coleman, J., *The Old Castles around Cork Harbour*, Cork Historical and

Archaeological Society Journal, vol. XXI (1915)
Coppinger, W.A., ed., *History of the Copingers or Coppingers of the County of Cork, Ireland, and the counties of Suffolk and Kent, England*, London (1884)
Crowley, J.S., Devoy, R.J.N., Linehan, D., O'Flanagan, P., eds, *Atlas of Cork City*, Cork University Press (2005)
Culligan, Matthew J. and Cherici, Peter, *The Wandering Irish in Europe*, Constable, London (2000)
Curtis, Edmund, *A History of Medieval Ireland from 1086 to 1513*, Methuen & Co Ltd, London (1923)
Diaz Canto, Lourdes and Albuerne Mesa, Miguel, *Cienfuegos y les Terry*, Ediciones Mecenas, Cienfuegos, Cuba (2005).
D'Alton, E.A., *History of Ireland*, The Gresham Publishing Co., London
D'Alton, John, *King James' Irish Army List (1689)*, published by the author
D'Arcy, Frank, *Wild Geese and Travelling Scholars*, Mercier Press (2001)
Dennehy, Rev., *History of the Great Island*, Tower Books (1990)
Dryburgh, Paul and Smith, Brendan, *Handbook and Select Calendar of sources for Medieval Ireland in the National Archives of the United Kingdom*, Four Courts Press (2005)
Ellis, Peter-Berresford, *Hell or Connaught – the Cromwellian Colonisation of Ireland 1652-1660*, The Blackstaff Press (1975)
Ellis, Stephen G., *Ireland in the Age of the Tudors, 1447-1603*, Longman (1995)
Ellis, Stephen G., *Reform and Revival English Government in Ireland, 1470-1534*, The Boydell Press (1986)
Elton, G.R., *England under the Tudors*, The Folio Society (1997)
Fannin, Samuel, 'The Irish Community in eighteenth-century Cadiz', in *Irish Migrants in Europe after Kinsale, 1602-1820*. Eds O'Connor, Thomas and Lyons, Mary Ann, Four Courts Press (2003)
Fannin, Samuel, 'The Ryan and Terry families in Spain', *The Irish Genealogist*, vol. 10 No.2
Ford, Alan, *The Protestant Reformation in Ireland, 1594-1641*, Four Courts Press (1997)
Foster, Joseph, *Register of admissions to Grey's Inn 1521-1889*, The Hansard Publishing Union, London (1889)
Fuller, J. F., 'Notes and Queries', *Cork Historical and Archaeological Society Journal*, 2nd Series, vol. IX (1903)
Gibson, C.B., *The History of the County and City of Cork*, The Fercor Press (1974)
Gilbert, J.T., *Historic and Municipal Documents of Ireland, A.D. 1172-1320*, Longman, Green & Co. (1870)
Gillespie, Raymond, *Seventeenth Century Ireland*, Gill & Macmillan (2006)
Gillespie, Raymond, *The Transformation of the Irish Economy 1550-1700*, Dundalgan Press (W.Tempest) Ltd. (1991)
Glazier, Ira A, Editor, *The Famine Immigrants, Lists of Irish Immigrants arriving at the Port of New York, 1846-1851*, Genealogical Publishing Co Inc. (1983)
Green, Alice Stopford, *The making of Ireland and its undoing*, Macmillan and Co, London (1908)

Hackett, Michael Benedict, *A Presence in an Age of Turmoil, English, Irish, and Scottish Augustinians in the Reformation and Counter-Reformation*, Augustinian Historical Institute (2001)
Hajba, Anna-Maria, *Houses of Cork, North Cork*, vol. I, Ballinakella Press (2002)
Hanks, Patrick and Hodges, Flavin, *A Dictionary of Surnames*, Oxford University Press (1988)
Hayes, Richard J., *Manuscript Sources from the History of Irish Civilisation,* G.K. Hall (1965)
Healy, James N., *The Castles of County Cork*, The Mercier Press
Henchion, Richard, *East to Mahon*, Dahadore Publications (2005)
Henchion, Richard, *The Gravestone Inscriptions of the Cathedral Cemetery of Cloyne, Co. Cork*, Cloyne Literary and Historical Society (1999)
Hood, Susan, *Register of the parish of Holy Trinity (Christ Church), Cork 1643-1669*, Representative Church Body Library (1998)
Hughes, James L.J., *Patentee Officers in Ireland*, Irish Manuscripts Commission (1960)
Jefferies, Henry Alan, *Cork Historical Perspectives*, Four Courts Press (2004)
Johnson, Gina, *The Laneways of Medieval Cork*, Cork City Council (2002)
Jones, Evan Thomas, 'The Bristol Shipping Industry in the Sixteenth Century', PhD Thesis, University of Edinburgh, unpublished (1998)
Keane, Edward, Phair, P. Beryl, and Sadlier, Thomas U., eds, *Kings Inn's Admission Papers, 1607-1867*, IMC (1982)
Kenny, Kevin, *The American Irish*, Pearson Education Limited (2000)
Kelly, Maria, A *History of the Black Death in Ireland*, Tempus (2001)
Lart, Charles, *The Pedigrees and Papers of James Terry, Athlone Herald, at the Court of James II in France, 1690-1725*, William Pollard & Co Ltd (1938)
Lennon, Colm, *Sixteenth Century Ireland*, Gill and Macmillan (1994)
Lydon, James, *The Lordship of Ireland in the Middle Ages*, Four Courts Press, Dublin (2003)
Lough, Susan M., 'Trade and Industry in Ireland in the Sixteenth-Century', *Journal of Political Economy*, vol. 24, No 7, July (1916) pp.713-30.
MacCarthy, C.J.F., *Thomas Ronan in sixteenth century Cork*, C.J.F. MacCarthy (1990)
MacLysaght, Edward, *More Irish Families*, Irish Academic Press (1982)
MacLysagh, E., *A Guide to Irish Surnames,* Helicon, Dublin (1964)
McCarthy, Mark, 'Geographical change in an early modern town: Urban growth, economy and cultural politics in Cork, 1600-41', *Journal of the Cork Historical and Archaeological Society*, vol. 105 (2000)
McCarthy, Mark, 'The Historical Geography of Cork's Transformation from a late Medieval Town into an Atlantic Port City, 1600-1700', PhD Thesis, University College Cork, unpublished (1997)
McCarthy, Mark, 'Turning a world upside down: The metamorphosis of property, settlement and society in the city of Cork during the 1640s and 1650s', *Irish Geography*, vol. 33, 1 (2000)
McCormack, Anthony M., *The Earldom of Desmond 1463-1583*, Four Courts Press (2005)

McSweeny, John, *A Meddling Priest John Joseph Therry*, St Paul's Publications (2000)
Mulcahy, John, 'Patrick Lavallin and the Popish Plot', *Journal of the Cork Historical and Archaeological Society*, vol.99 (1994)
Mulcahy, Michael, 'A Cork City Grant of 1666', *Journal of the Cork Historical and Archaeological Society*, vol. 69 (1964)
Nicholls, K.W., *Gaelic and Gaelicized Ireland in the Middle Ages*, Lilliput Press (2003)
Nicholls, Kenneth, 'The Development of Lordship in County Cork, 1300-1600', in *Cork History & Society*, eds, O' Flanagan, Patrick and Buttimer, Cornelius G., Geography Publications (1993)
Nicholls, Kenneth, 'Two Islands, One Street', *Cork Examiner*, 13 March (1985)
Nolan, William, *The shaping of Ireland, the geographical perspective*, The Mercier Press (1986)
O'Brien, A. F., 'Irish Exchequer Records of Payments of the Fee farm of the City of Cork in the Later Middle Ages', *Analecta Hibernica*, No 37
O'Brien, A. F., Politics, 'Economy and Society; the development of Cork and the Irish South-Coast Region *c.*1170 to *c.*1583, in *Cork History & Society*, eds, O' Flanagan, Patrick and Buttimer, Cornelius G., Geography Publications (1993)
O'Brien, Alph, 'Commercial relations between Aquitaine and Ireland *c.*1000 to *c.*1550', in *Aquitaine and Ireland in the Middle Ages*, ed. by Picard, Jean-Michel, Four Courts Press (1995)
O Buachalla, Liam, 'An early fourteenth-century place name list for Anglo-Norman Cork', *Dinnseanchas* (1966)
O Buachalla, Liam, *History of Carrigtwohill*, Clann na Greine Teo
O' Connell, Morgan John, *The Last Colonel of the Irish Brigade*, Tower Books (1977)
O' Hart, John, *Irish Landed Gentry when Cromwell came to Ireland*, James Duffy & Sons (1887)
O'Hart, John, *Irish Pedigrees or The Origin and Stem of the Irish Nation* (1876)
O' Hart, John, *The Irish and Anglo-Irish Landed Gentry*, Irish University Press (1969)
O' Mahony, S. C., 'Discalced Carmelites in Ireland, 1641', *Collectanea Hibernica*, No 17, Leinster Leader Ltd (1974-5)
O'Sullivan, William, *The economic history of Cork city from the earliest times to the Act of Union*, Cork University Press (1937)
Otway-Ruthven, A.J., *A history of medieval Ireland*, Ernest Benn Ltd, London (1980)
Pender, S., ed., *A Census of Ireland c.1659*, Irish Manuscripts Commission, Dublin (1939)
Power, Rev. Professor Patrick, 'Place names and antiquities of SE Cork – Barony of Barrymore', *Proceedings of the RIA*, vol.36, Part III (1921-4)
Reaney, P.H., *The Origin of English Surnames*, Routledge & Kegan Paul (1967)
Ring, Denis Paul, *Macroom through the Mists of Time*, Castle House Publications (1995)

Santa Cruz y Mallen, Francisco I., *Historia de familias cubanas*, 6 vols. Havana (1940-50)
Sheehan, Anthony, 'Irish Towns in a Period of Change, 1558-1625', in *Natives and Newcomers,* eds, Brady, Ciaran and Gillespie, Raymond, Irish Academic Press (1986)
Simmington, R.C., *The Civil Survey 1654-6: County Waterford, with appendices, also Valuations, 1663-4, for Waterford and Cork Cities*, vol. VI The Stationery Office, Dublin (1942)
Smith, Charles, *The ancient state of the city and county of Cork*, Dublin (1774)
Sturgress, H.A.C., *Register of Admissions to the honourable society of the Middle Temple from the fifteenth century*
Tenison, C.M., 'Cork M.P.s 1559-1800', *Journal of the Cork Historical and Archaeological Society*, vol II 2nd Series (1896)
Terry, Kevin, 'Some Spanish Terrys of Irish Origin', *The Irish Genealogist*, vol. 10, No. 3 (2000)
Terry, Kevin et al., *Terrys of Cork 1600-2000, a local historical perspective*, Kevin Terry (2005)
Townsend, Dorothy, *The Life and Letters of the great Earl of Cork*, Duckworth and Co., London (1904)
Tuckey, Francis H., *Cork Remembrancer*, Tower Books, Cork (1980)
Wagner, Anthony, *Pedigree and Progress*, Phillimore (1975)
Waters, Ann, 'A distribution of forfeited land in the County of Cork', *Journal of the Cork Historical and Archaeological Society*, vols. 38 and 39
Welply, William, 'Abstract of Munster Wills, 1528-1859', in *O'Kief, Coshe Mang, Slieve Lougher, and Upper Blackwater in Ireland*, Casey, Albert Eugene, Amite and Knocknagree Historicall Found (1961)
Wilson, Fr James, *Cloyne Parish Priests*
Windele, John, *Cork – Historic and Descriptive notices of the City of Cork*, Guy and Co Ltd (1910).

Index